# MY JOURNEY AT THE
# NUCLEAR BRINK

# MY JOURNEY *at the* NUCLEAR BRINK

## WILLIAM J. PERRY

STANFORD SECURITY STUDIES

*An Imprint of Stanford University Press*

*Stanford, California*

Stanford University Press
Stanford, California

Library of Congress Cataloging-in-Publication Data

Perry, William James, author.
   My journey at the nuclear brink / William J. Perry.
      p.  cm.
   Includes bibliographical references and index.
   ISBN 978-0-8047-9681-1 (cloth : alk. paper)
   ISBN 978-0-8047-9712-2 (pbk. : alk. paper)
   1. Nuclear weapons—Government policy—United States—History.
2. Nuclear arms control—United States—History.  3. United States—
Military policy.  4. Perry, William James, 1927–.  I. Title.
UA23.P4655  2015
355.02'17092—dc23

                                                              2015020251

   ISBN 978-0-8047-9714-6 (digital)

Printed in the United States of America on acid-free, archival-quality paper. Typeset at Stanford University Press in 10/14 Minion.

*To my loving wife of sixty-eight years,*
*LEONILLA GREEN PERRY,*
*and to our children, grandchildren, and*
*great-grandchild who have given me*
*the best of all reasons to continue*
*my work to ensure that nuclear weapons*
*are never used again*

# Contents

Contents

# Foreword by George P. Shultz

Throughout his life and work, William Perry has distinguished himself as a man of high intelligence, absolute integrity, rare vision, remarkable accomplishment, and an unwavering sense of humanity. Evidence of these attributes is vividly apparent in the gripping stories contained in this memoir chronicling Bill's extraordinary efforts, over the course of his illustrious career, to reduce the nuclear threat.

Bill's engagement in the issue of nuclear security began in the mid-1940s when, as a soldier in the US Army of Occupation in Japan, he witnessed the massive devastation in the aftermath of World War II. Following his service in Japan, he became a high-level national security adviser to the US government and participated in the development of reconnaissance technology that could detect Cold War nuclear threats. During the Carter administration, Bill served as undersecretary of defense for research and engineering. He worked to shore up deterrence of the Soviet Union by offsetting their numerical advantage in conventional forces through the development of stealth and other force-multiplying high-technology systems still in effective use today by our military (his "offset strategy").

As secretary of defense under President Clinton, and in his subsequent Track 2 diplomacy work, Bill developed a successful negotiating style that combined incisive analysis, an ability to balance diverse security concerns, and effective persuasiveness. Bill used these diplomatic skills to establish military alliances with former adversaries in the post–Cold War era; an example is the Partnership for Peace in Europe. He succeeded in facilitating the Nunn-Lugar program to remove holdover nuclear arsenals from new republics after the Soviet Union broke apart. Bill also brought about international arms control initiatives and security arrangements for nuclear materials, vital steps on the road toward achieving nuclear security.

*Foreword by George P. Shultz*

I have had the pleasure of working closely with Bill and being inspired by him in our shared effort to achieve better control over nuclear weapons and fissile material. In the past decade, together with Sid Drell, Henry Kissinger, and Sam Nunn, we have convened a number of important conferences and have written numerous opinion pieces that have received worldwide attention. Phil Taubman described our efforts in his book *The Partnership: Five Cold Warriors and Their Quest to Ban the Bomb* (2012). We have emphasized the importance of the steps that must be taken on the road toward our ultimate goal of nuclear security. Sam Nunn's image of a mountain captures our idea. At the mountain's peak is a world free of nuclear weapons. At its base is a world where many countries possess nuclear weapons and where the fissile material to make bombs is often loosely guarded. In this world, there is a high probability that a nuclear weapon will be detonated at some time, wreaking unimaginable consequences. We have tried to put ourselves on a path to reach the mountaintop and, until recently, progress was being made.

The end of the Cold War produced an atmosphere that led to massive reductions in weapons, so today the world's nuclear weapons stockpile is less than one-third of the number in existence at the time of the 1986 Reykjavik meeting between President Ronald Reagan and General Secretary Mikhail Gorbachev. But now instability has returned, and we are threatened once again by the proliferation of nuclear weapons. Our joint efforts and Bill's personal commitment to counter this threat continue, with particular emphasis on educating young people on the dangers of nuclear weapons and ways to prevent their use. In addition to Bill's innovative nuclear security program for students at Stanford University, he has instituted an online course in order to spread the message to a vast audience of youth around the globe.

Bill's journey, so vibrantly recorded in this book, goes on as he works aggressively to stem the tide of nuclear weapons and guide the world onto a constructive path once again. Ever at his side in this quest is his wife, Lee. The wisdom that behind every great man there is a great woman is exemplified in the loving, productive partnership that Bill and Lee share. Lee has steadfastly supported Bill on his journey, at the same time accomplishing significant goals of her own. The military services awarded her a medal for her efforts to improve the quality of life for US military families, and—recognizing her tireless work to improve standards in an Albanian military hospital—the president of Albania conferred upon Lee the Mother Teresa Medal.

At every stage of his career, Bill has demonstrated his dedication to the wel-

George P. Shultz. Light at 11B: Joseph Garappolo and
Christian Pease, with permission.

fare of members of the US armed forces. He began his military service as an
enlisted man, so his concern for the well-being of every soldier—and every
soldier's family—is personal. He acknowledges the iron logic between military
capability and quality of life and agrees wholeheartedly with Sergeant Major
Richard Kidd's counsel to "Take care of your troops and they will take care of
you." Anyone who has served in the military, as I have in the Marine Corps,
knows that the troops must come first.

Bill's deep-seated commitment to improving the quality of life for military
families is illustrated by the actions he took after observing that the level of
military housing, particularly for families, was in dire need of improvement. As
Bill set about assessing the issue of military housing, he was fortunate to have

an additional pair of eyes and ears; while he was visiting the troops, his wife, Lee, was talking to servicemen's spouses. The result of their work was an ingenious and novel public-private partnership, authorized by Congress in 1996, that dramatically upgraded, and continues to maintain, the quality of military housing.

Such breakthroughs were surely on President Clinton's mind when, in the January 1997 Farewell ceremony for Bill, he awarded him the Presidential Medal of Freedom and said, "Bill Perry may well be recorded as the most productive, effective secretary of defense the United States ever had."

General John Shalikashvili, chairman of the joint chiefs of staff, offered this assessment of this extraordinary public servant:

> Yes, he is a man of vast talent. Yes, he is a man of enormous energy and infectious enthusiasm. Yes, he is a man of great caring for those who wear our nation's uniform for their families. But he is first and foremost a man of unshakable character. He is a man who will do what is right, no matter what the price.

Americans owe a debt of gratitude to Bill Perry, who has dedicated his life's journey to national security. It is a journey that he continues to pursue with expertise, energy, and unquenchable enthusiasm.

*George P. Shultz*

# Preface

The gravest security threat of our time is the danger of a nuclear weapon being detonated in one of our cities. That is my nuclear nightmare, born of long and deep experience, and it could unfold as follows . . .

A small, secret group operating in a covert section of a commercial power centrifuge facility enriches 30 kg of uranium to a level sufficient for a nuclear bomb.

The group transports this enriched uranium to a nearby covert facility. Over the next two months, the technical team there uses the enriched uranium to assemble a crude nuclear bomb, installs it in a large packing crate marked agricultural equipment, and transports the packing crate to a nearby airfield.

A transport airplane with markings of a civilian airline flies the crate to an international airport and shipping hub, where the crate is transferred to a freight aircraft headed for Washington, DC.

The freight aircraft lands at Washington's Dulles International Airport and the crate is delivered to a warehouse in the southeast part of the District.

The bomb is removed from the crate and loaded onto a delivery truck.

A suicide bomber drives the truck to a location on Pennsylvania Avenue midway between the Capitol (where Congress is in session) and the White House and at 11:00 a.m. triggers the detonator.

The bomb explodes with a power of 15 kilotons. The White House, the Capitol, and all buildings in between are destroyed. There are 80,000 instant deaths, including the president, the vice president, the speaker of the House, and the 320 members of Congress present when the detonation occurs. There are more than 100,000 seriously wounded and virtually no medical facilities available to treat them. Telecommunication facilities in Washington, including most cell phone relay towers, are inoperative. CNN, which shows videos of the devastation in Washington, reports that they have received a message claiming that five more bombs are hidden in five different US cities, and one will be set off each week for the next five weeks unless all American troops based overseas are ordered to return immediately to the United States. Within ten minutes the stock market drops precipitously and all trading is halted. The nation is hurled into panic as people begin to stream out of major cities. Manufacturing nationwide comes to a halt.

The nation is further faced with a constitutional crisis. The presidency has devolved to the Senate's president pro tem, who, when the detonation occurs, is being treated at the Mayo Clinic for pancreatic cancer and is not able to return to Washington, which is now under martial law. The secretary of defense and the chairman of the Joint Chiefs of Staff, both of whom were testifying to the House Armed Services Committee on their recent budget request, are also killed in the blast . . . .

We can hardly bear to imagine the catastrophic outcome of this hypothetical scenario—and yet we must. This example is only illustrative; the same end would result if a terror group bought or stole a nuclear bomb from North Korea or Pakistan, or stole fissile material from a poorly guarded reactor in one of the countries that still have highly enriched uranium or plutonium in insufficiently guarded facilities.

The danger of a nuclear bomb being detonated in one of our cities is all too real. And yet, while this catastrophe would result in a hundred times the casualties of 9-11, it is only dimly perceived by the public and not well understood. As a result, our present actions are incommensurate with the tragic consequences that would result from even a small-scale nuclear attack.

This book is one effort to inform the public of the grave dangers we face, and to encourage actions that could greatly reduce those dangers. I tell the story of my own conversion to a life with a compelling, overriding objective— to ensure that nuclear weapons are never used again.

My special experience has kept me acutely aware of nuclear dangers and contemplating the almost unthinkable consequence of a nuclear war. A lifetime in which I had firsthand experience and special access to top-secret knowledge of strategic nuclear options has given me what may be a unique, and chilling, vantage point from which to conclude that nuclear weapons no longer provide for our security—they now endanger it. I believe it is imperative to share what I, as an insider, know and understand about these dangers, and what I think must be done to keep future generations safe from nuclear dangers that are growing greater every year.

All through the years of the Cold War and the massive buildup of nuclear arsenals, the world faced the prospect of a nuclear holocaust either through miscalculation or accident. These dangers were never theoretical to me. My work as an analyst in the Cuban Missile Crisis and later my experiences in three high-level positions in the Defense Department kept me in close contact with those fearsome possibilities every day.

Although nuclear dangers receded when the Cold War ended, they have now returned in a new and alarming guise. Since the turn of the century, the relationship between the United States and Russia has become increasingly tense. Russia, whose conventional forces are considerably weaker than those of the United States and NATO countries, depends on nuclear forces for its security. Feeling threatened by the expansion of NATO to its borders and by the deployment of an American missile defense system in Eastern Europe, Russia has resorted to increasingly hostile rhetoric. And it is backing up this rhetoric by embarking on a major upgrade of its nuclear forces—a new generation of missiles, bombers, and submarines, as well as a new generation of nuclear bombs for those delivery systems. Most ominously, it has renounced its "no first use" policy and proclaimed that it is prepared to use nuclear weapons against any threat that it perceives, whether or not it is nuclear. It is increasingly worrisome that Russia, through a serious miscalculation, could confront a contingency where it believed that its security depended on initiating the use of nuclear weapons.

Beyond that growing danger, we face two new nuclear dangers largely absent from the Cold War era: a regional nuclear war, between India and Pakistan, for example; and a nuclear terror attack, as was illustrated in the preceding nightmare scenario.

The reality of a nuclear terror threat was brought home to me by an experience in 1996, during my last year as secretary of defense. A truck bomb was detonated near one of our airmen's dormitories (Khobar Towers) in Saudi Arabia. Nineteen airmen were killed in the blast, but hundreds would have been killed if the attacker had been able to get his truck closer to the dormitory (as happened in a 1983 attack in Lebanon that killed 220 Marines). The United States did not know who had perpetrated this attack, but we understood that its purpose was to force us to move our troops out of the country, as the US had done earlier in response to the Lebanon bombing.

I believed that our mission in Saudi Arabia was important and that it would be a serious mistake to pull out under that kind of pressure. So with cooperation and support from Saudi Arabia's King Fahd, we moved the US airbase to a remote location where we could achieve our mission but still ensure the safety of our troops. I released a public statement announcing the move, declaring that our new base would be heavily defended and that no terror group would keep us from accomplishing our mission in Saudi Arabia.

A response to my press release was posted on the Internet by a shadowy figure named Osama Bin Laden, who called for a jihad against American troops stationed in Saudi Arabia and directed a bizarre and threatening poem to me:

> Oh William, tomorrow you will be informed
> As to which young man will face your swaggering brother
> A youngster enters the midst of battle, smiling, and
> Retreats with his spearhead stained with blood.[1]

Five years later, on 11 September 2001, the world learned much more about Bin Laden, and I came to understand the full significance of his message to me. As analysts intensified their studies of Al Qaeda, Bin Laden's terror group, they learned that part of their declared mission was to kill not just thousands of Americans (as they did on 9-11) but millions, and that they had made serious efforts to acquire a nuclear weapon. I do not doubt that if Al Qaeda had succeeded in acquiring a nuclear weapon, they would have used it against Americans.

A nuclear nightmare such as I have dramatized could become a tragic reality if we do not take the necessary preventive actions now. These actions are well understood, but they will not be taken until the public engages in these issues. *My Journey at the Nuclear Brink* explains these dangers and describes the actions that could greatly mitigate them.

I remain hopeful that we can change the increasingly dangerous course we are on and offer my best counsel on how to do so. The public's will to act on such recommendations can only come from a deeper understanding of just how real and imminent the danger is.

*William J. Perry*

# Acknowledgments

The events I relate in this book form a "selective memoir" about coming of age in the nuclear era, my role in trying to shape and contain it, and how my thinking changed about the threat these weapons pose today. In this decades-long journey I have had the remarkable good fortune to have enjoyed the lifelong love and support of my wife, Lee, and to have worked alongside many extraordinary men and women who have shared my commitment to make the world a safer place. I am indebted to all of them, and especially to those who have helped me realize my goal of publishing this book.

To support the publication of this memoir and educational materials deriving from it, I formed the William J. Perry Project, under the sponsorship of the Nuclear Threat Initiative (NTI). Their top leadership team—Sam Nunn, Joan Rohlfing, and Deborah Rosenblum—have supported my vision for the Project from the start, providing encouragement, fiscal stewardship, and access to their knowledgeable and highly competent staff. The Project would never have seen the light of day without significant private support from the founding co-sponsors, including Douglas C. Grissom, Elizabeth Holmes, Ta-lin and Joyce Hsu, Fred Iseman, Pitch and Cathie Johnson, Joseph Kampf, Jeong and Cindi Kim, Marshall Medoff, and Mark L. Perry and Melanie Peña. I am very grateful for their generosity.

Another primary Project partner is Stanford University's Center for International Security and Cooperation (CISAC) and the Freeman Spogli Institute (FSI). They have provided office space, daily access to distinguished security experts, and an atmosphere of collegiality and shared purpose. My special thanks to Tino Cuellar, Michael McFaul, Amy Zegart, David Relman, and Lynn Eden.

Stanford further aided the Project's educational goals by supporting the pilot of a new course based on the lessons in this book so that we could develop online education materials. Stanford professors and scholars participating included Martha Crenshaw, James Goodby, Sig Hecker, David Holloway, Ravi Patel, Scott Sagan, George Shultz, and Phil Taubman. Guest lecturers from outside Stanford included Ash Carter, Joe Cirincione, Andre Kokoshin, and Joe Martz.

I wrote this book from memory. Even after forty, fifty, and sixty years, certain stories remain as vivid as if they had just happened. But I know better than to rely solely on my memory and am immensely grateful to those who supported this memoir with their time, expertise, recollections, fact checking, editing, and literary counsel.

The following people, all of whom played significant roles in my career and all of whom I call friends, agreed to be interviewed, providing perspective and corroboration on details in key events described in the book. They include Ash Carter, Sid Drell, Lew Franklin, Joshua Gotbaum, Paul Kaminski, Paul Kern, Michael Lippitz, Sam Nunn, George Shultz, Larry K Smith, Jeffrey Starr, and the late Albert "Bud" Wheelon. I am fortunate to have been able to collaborate with such wise and dedicated people.

I am grateful to Mark Langerman, chief of the Pentagon's Office of Security Review, for his guidance and help in shepherding my manuscript expeditiously through security review.

Four superb young military officers each contributed substantially to fact checking and source citation while earning their graduate degrees at Stanford: 2nd Lt. Robert Kaye, Ens. Taylor Newman, Ens. Joshua David Wagner, and Ens. Thomas Dowd. Judging from the fine work these top academy graduates did at Stanford, our military is in good hands.

Early in the Project, we convened an undergraduate student advisory board to research messaging about the dangers of nuclear weapons and to make recommendations about how to engage their generation in these issues. They inspired the development of our online education program. My thanks to each of them for their passion and commitment to our initiative: Claire Colberg, Isabella Gabrosky, Jared Greenspan, Taylor Grossman, Daniel Khalessi, Hayden Padgett, Camille Pease, Raquel Saxe, Sahil Shah, and Pia Ulrich.

I am especially grateful to the Project staff for their winning combination of skill, hard work, creativity, and commitment to educating and engaging the public on the dangers of nuclear weapons: Deborah C. Gordon, Christian G. Pease, David C. Perry, and Robin L. Perry. Special thanks go to Robin, who served as director as well as editor of this book. I never could have come this far without her patience, wisdom, and editorial skills.

Cindi King and Mark L. Perry offered critical legal guidance. Amy Rennert, Phil Taubman, Lynn Eden, and David Holloway provided invaluable publishing and editorial advice. I am grateful to Geoffrey Burn at Stanford University Press for believing in the value of this book, to John Feneron for expertly managing it through production, and to Martin Hanft for his incisive copyediting.

Finally, my deep thanks to Al Clarkson, a former colleague at ESL and long-time friend, who as it happens is also a novelist and skilled in all things literary. Al has been at my side from the first fledgling draft, quietly providing feedback to Robin and me, and gently steering us to a better book through his commentary, sense of narrative, and substantive editing. Between Al and Robin, I couldn't have asked for a better editorial team to shepherd the book through its many iterations.

*W.J.P.*

# Abbreviations

| | |
|---|---|
| ABM | Anti-Ballistic Missile |
| ACDA | Arms Control and Disarmament Agency |
| ALCM | Air-launched Cruise Missiles |
| AWOL | Absent without Official Leave |
| BMD | Ballistic Missile Defense |
| CIA | Central Intelligence Agency |
| CISAC | Center for International Security and Arms Control/Cooperation |
| CPA | Certified Public Accountant |
| CPD | Committee on the Present Danger |
| CTBT | Comprehensive Test Ban Treaty |
| CTR | Cooperative Threat Reduction |
| DARPA | Defense Advanced Research Projects Agency |
| DDR&E | Director of Defense Research and Engineering |
| DMZ | Demilitarized Zone |
| DoD | Department of Defense |
| DPRK | Democratic People's Republic of Korea |
| DRC | Defense Reform Caucus |
| ERTS | Earth Resources Technology Satellite |
| ESL | Electromagnetic Systems Laboratory |
| FSI | Freeman Spogli Institute |
| GMAIC | Guided Missile and Astronautics Intelligence Committee |
| GPS | Global Positioning System |
| GTE | General Telephone and Electronics |
| H&Q | Hambrecht & Quist |
| HLG | High Level Group |
| HP | Hewlett Packard |
| IAEA | International Atomic Energy Agency |

| | |
|---|---|
| IBM | International Business Machines |
| IC | Integrated Circuit |
| ICBM | Intercontinental Ballistic Missile |
| Joint STARS | Joint Surveillance Target Attack Radar System |
| LANL | Los Alamos National Laboratory |
| LMSC | Lockheed Missiles and Space Company |
| LWR | Light Water Reactor |
| MAD | Mutually Assured Destruction |
| MAED | Mutually Assured Economic Destruction |
| MIRV | Multiple Independently Targetable Re-entry Vehicle |
| NASA | National Aeronautics and Space Administration |
| NATO | North Atlantic Treaty Organization |
| NCO | Non-commissioned Officer |
| NORAD | North American Aerospace Defense Command |
| NPIC | National Photographic Interpretation Center |
| NPT | Non-Proliferation Treaty |
| NSA | National Security Agency |
| NSC | National Security Council |
| OMB | Office of Management and Budget |
| PFP | Partnership for Peace |
| RPV | Remotely Piloted Vehicle |
| SALT I & II | Strategic Arms Limitation Talks/Treaties I & II |
| SDI | Strategic Defense Initiative |
| SLBM | Submarine Launched Ballistic Missile |
| START I & II | Strategic Arms Reduction Treaty I & II |
| TEBAC | Telemetry and Beacon Analysis Committee |
| TERCOM | Terrain Contour Matching |
| UN | United Nations |
| UNPROFOR | United Nations Protection Force |
| US | United States of America |
| USSR | Union of Soviet Socialist Republics |

# 1      The Cuban Missile Crisis: A Nuclear Nightmare

*It shall be the policy of this Nation to regard any nuclear missile launched from Cuba against any nation in the Western Hemisphere as an attack by the Soviet Union on the United States, requiring a full retaliatory response upon the Soviet Union.*
—President John F. Kennedy, nationwide broadcast, 22 October 1962[1]

My phone rang on a beautiful fall day in 1962, just a week after I had celebrated my thirty-fifth birthday. I was the director of Sylvania's Electronic Defense Laboratories, which pioneered in sophisticated electronic reconnaissance systems directed at Soviet nuclear weapons systems. I was living with my wife, Lee, and our five children in a beautiful home in Palo Alto, California, near the picturesque San Francisco Bay. Life was good. But it was about to be turned upside-down.

The phone call was from Albert "Bud" Wheelon, my colleague on high-level government panels to assess Soviet nuclear capabilities. Wheelon, also in his thirties, was the youngest-ever head of the CIA's Office of Scientific Intelligence, as well as chairman of the Guided Missile and Astronautics Intelligence Committee (GMAIC), an expert group reviewing all intelligence on the Soviet missile and space programs. He asked me to fly to Washington to consult with him, and I told him that I would rearrange my schedule and fly back the following week. "No," he said, "I need to see you right away." His sense of urgency alarmed me. Our country was deep in a spiraling nuclear arms race with the Soviet Union, which just the previous year had broken the nuclear test ban to detonate their "monster" 50-megaton bomb. I took the night flight to Washington, DC, and met him the next morning.

Without a word of explanation he showed me photos of what I quickly recognized as Soviet missiles in Cuba. My instant reaction was dread. It was all too clear that this deployment could be the catalyst to trigger a nuclear exchange between the United States and the USSR. My study of nuclear effects told me that such an exchange could bring about the end of civilization.

For the next eight days I worked intensively with a small team analyzing data collected each day to make a report delivered by the director of the CIA to President John F. Kennedy. Every morning US tactical reconnaissance aircraft conducted low-level flights over Cuba and took high-resolution pictures of known and suspected missile and weapons sites. After the aircraft returned to Florida, the film was flown by military transport to Eastman Kodak in upstate New York, for rapid processing. By late afternoon the processed film was flown to our analysis center, located deep within the National Photographic Interpretation Center (NPIC), where analysts pored over it.

I was on one of two analysis teams, each made up of two technical analysts and three photo interpreters. The teams worked independently for about six hours, after which each reported its findings to the other team for critique. We were trying to determine critical information about the Soviet missiles being deployed: How many and what type were they? How soon would they be operational? When would the nuclear warheads be mated to the missiles?

By midnight, we began preparing our joint written report for Wheelon, who was often with us for the last few hours to participate in the critiques. Early the next morning, Wheelon presented his report, based on our photo analysis and other data, such as communications intelligence, to President Kennedy and his executive team for Cuba. Wheelon left the meeting after the presentation, but CIA director John McCone would remain for a discussion on how to respond to the latest developments.

We quickly determined the types of missiles and their range and payload, by correlating what we were seeing in Cuba with what we had seen on the missile test ranges in the Soviet Union. So we knew that the missiles were nuclear-capable with ranges that allowed them to target much of the United States. Within a few days our teams had concluded that some of the missiles were only a few weeks from being operational.

When I was not in the back room analyzing intelligence data, I was watching the political drama unfold on television, with President Kennedy ordering our navy to stop Soviet ships from crossing a designated line and the Soviet ships continuing to steam toward it.[2] What was at stake was spelled out in unambiguous terms by the president in his speech to the American people, with its stark warning that a nuclear missile launched from Cuba against any nation in the Western Hemisphere would be met with "a full retaliatory response upon the Soviet Union."

I understood exactly what a "full retaliatory response" meant. In the de-

US citizens watching President Kennedy's speech about the Cuban Missile Crisis, October 1962. Photo by Ralph Crane, copyright Getty Images, with permission.

cade before the Cuban Missile Crisis, I had been studying nuclear scenarios and their consequences. Indeed, every day that I went to the analysis center I thought would be my last day on earth.

I was a participant in this unfolding drama at the nuclear brink, but a bit player without firsthand knowledge of the discussions taking place at the president's daily team meetings. Defense Secretary Robert McNamara and others have written extensively about them, and it is particularly sobering to know that the president was being advised by his military leaders to conduct an attack on Cuba. We can only speculate what their advice would have been had they known that many of the nuclear warheads to be carried by the 162 missiles we had identified in Cuba were already on the island, contrary to our assessments.

Although the Cuban Missile Crisis ended without war, I believed then, and still believe, that the world avoided a nuclear holocaust as much by good luck as by good management.

All I have learned since has reinforced that belief. Looking back with the knowledge we now have of the actual conditions, I can see even more clearly the great danger that events would spin out of control and engulf the world in a catastrophic nuclear war. For example, we now know that the Soviet ships approaching our blockade of Cuba had submarine escorts, and that the Soviet submarines were armed with nuclear torpedoes. Because of the difficulties in communicating with a submarine, the commanders had been given the authority to fire nuclear torpedoes without authorization from Moscow. Only years after the crisis did we learn that one of the Soviet commanders had seriously considered firing one of his nuclear torpedoes at an American destroyer that was trying to force him to surface. He was dissuaded from doing so only by the other officers on the submarine.

Equally sobering was the realization that there were incidents not directly related to the showdown in Cuba that could have led to an immediate escalation to war. At the height of the crisis, an American reconnaissance plane, flying a long-scheduled mission, wandered off course and flew into the Soviet Union. Soviet air defense misread this as an American bomber and immediately scrambled attack aircraft. An American airbase in Alaska, in turn, scrambled fighter aircraft armed with nuclear-tipped missiles to protect the American reconnaissance plane.

Fortunately, the American aircraft commander, having blundered into Soviet airspace, discovered his error and flew out before any intercepts occurred. At about the same time, an American ICBM was launched from Vandenberg Air Base. This was a routine test launch that nobody thought to reschedule, but it could easily have been misinterpreted by the Soviets.

For the decade preceding the Cuban Missile Crisis I had been working to assess the threat from Soviet nuclear weapons and sensed a pervasive tension mounting in the last two years. What if a direct and immediate military confrontation between the United States and the Soviet Union should arise? In the nuclear era, a military confrontation would be an unrivaled nightmare, a moment for which there was no previous experience to provide guidance for a resolution that could prevent a nuclear catastrophe. At stake was civilization itself.

During those eight days in October, I lived just such a nightmare.

After the crisis abated, many American news reports trumpeted US "triumphalism," crowing that Khrushchev had "blinked."[3] This popular and insular thinking was specious, not only because Khrushchev's decision to back down spared the world from an unprecedented catastrophe, but because of the unintended consequence of the crisis: although it took a while to become apparent, the Cuban Missile Crisis accelerated the nuclear arms race already underway between the United States and the USSR.

In 1964, possibly because he had been forced to back down in Cuba, Khrushchev was replaced with Leonid Brezhnev and (initially) Alexei Kosygin. Brezhnev vowed that the Soviet Union would never again be at a nuclear disadvantage and accelerated the secretive Soviet ICBM and nuclear programs.

American defense officials, at first self-satisfied at the "victory," soon had to raise the already high priority on technical intelligence gathering because of the rapidly increasing scope and sophistication of the Soviet missile and space program. While defense laboratories like mine prospered, their positive business growth was directly tied to the increased danger to our country and the world, a dichotomy that would come to haunt those of us in the industry.

When we look back it is clear that the Cuban Missile Crisis was a signature event in the history of the nuclear era. Its most unforgettable and shattering aspect is the historic enormity of what was at stake: the Cuban Missile Crisis arguably took us to the brink of a nuclear holocaust. Often in that incomparably dangerous crisis, US decision-makers' knowledge was imperfect, and sometimes just wrong.

There is a surreal quality to some of the thinking during and after the Cuban Missile Crisis, old modes of thinking clearly at odds with the new realities of the nuclear weapons era: many advisors on both sides wanting to rush us into war; the representation of the crisis in the media as a drama of "winning" and "losing"; political approval of the leaders on both sides seemingly based on their willingness to start a war; and in the aftermath, the decision not to cooperate in reducing arms and tension—which would have been rational after such a close call—but rather to reinvigorate the arms race.

For the moment, the world had avoided a nuclear holocaust. But in the longer run—at least as seemed evident in the breathing room after that narrow escape—the Cuban Missile Crisis signaled a heightening risk. And after my almost unimaginable eight days in the fall of 1962, no other path seemed to beckon to me but one that led into the heart of the challenge to reduce the danger of nuclear weapons.

For me the Cuban Missile Crisis was a summoning that would eventually lead me from industry and the invention of modern high-tech spying on the Soviet nuclear arsenal; to leadership in the Pentagon in modernizing US conventional and strategic forces to shore up and maintain nuclear deterrence; to the later pursuit of cooperative international programs to reduce nuclear weapons through legislation, global diplomacy, and advocacy.

# 2                                        A Fire in the Sky

*The unleashed power of the atom has changed everything save our modes*
*of thinking and we thus drift toward unparalleled catastrophe.*[1]
— Albert Einstein; 23 May 1946

How is it that I was summoned to Washington to analyze intelligence data during the Cuban Missile Crisis? My journey at the nuclear brink actually began well before the crisis, on an infamous Sunday in 1941, four years before the first atomic bomb was dropped. These were the first stirrings that would lead me to a life encompassing military service, development of Cold War reconnaissance systems, government service, university teaching, and diplomacy—much of it focused on the goal of reducing the nuclear threat. I could not, of course, foresee this path on that distant Sunday. I could not know that I would be coming of age at the pivotal point when mankind created a weapon whose power radically altered the human condition. I could not know that meeting the challenge from that unprecedented threat to civilization itself would become my abiding concern.

That historic Sunday came just after I turned fourteen. I was visiting a friend in his Butler, Pennsylvania, home when his brother rushed in, shouting, "We are at war with Japan! They just bombed Pearl Harbor!" War with Japan had been brewing for more than a year, and many radio commentators had predicted its imminence. My fourteen-year-old response was immediate: I wanted to serve in the war as a pilot in the Army Air Corps, but I feared that the war would be over before I was old enough—and that is just what happened.

On my seventeenth birthday in October 1944, I drove to Pittsburgh, passed the exams for the Army Air Cadet program, and was sworn in. I was sent home to await an opening, which the army thought would occur in about six months. In anticipation, I left high school early so I could complete a few semesters of college before being called up. In May 1945, just as I was finishing my first semester at Carnegie Tech (now Carnegie Mellon), the army discontinued the Air Cadet program and I was given an honorable discharge, despite never having served a day of active duty. I finished two more semesters, after which, now eighteen, I enlisted in the Army Engineers. The army trained me in map-making and assigned me to the Army of Occupation of Japan, where I was sent to a base outside Tokyo for training.

Nothing I had read about the war prepared me for the massive devastation I would see in Tokyo. This once great city was decimated—virtually every building made of wood was destroyed by firebomb attacks. Survivors were living in vast wastes of fused rubble, existing on meager rations provided by the Occupation Forces.

After two months of training, our company boarded an LST landing ship bound for Okinawa to make high-precision topographic maps of the island. Okinawa was the site of the last great battle of World War II, and the fighting had been unimaginably bloody. Almost 200,000 Japanese soldiers and civilians died. The American casualties, far fewer, were still terrible, many of them the result of kamikaze (suicide) attacks.

I will never forget what I saw on our arrival at the port of Naha, the capital of Okinawa. Not a building was standing in what had been a thriving city. The survivors were living in tents or the rubble of buildings, and "the lush tropical

War devastation in Naha after Battle of Okinawa. Photo by Arthur Hager, US Marine Corps (in public domain).

landscape was turned into a vast field of mud, lead, decay, and maggots."[2] A memorial to the dead, the Cornerstone of Peace, erected at the site of the final battle in Mabuni, lists the more than 240,000 names of the known dead from that fierce and awful battle.

In Tokyo, and later in Naha, I saw through my young eyes the unprecedented devastation of modern war. I was witness to a wartime violence of historic proportions, and it was a transformational experience. This devastation had been rendered by thousands of bombers in hundreds of raids; a comparable devastation had been inflicted on Hiroshima and then on Nagasaki by *just one bomb*. I understood in a profound and visceral way that our new and unimaginable capacity to inflict horror and ruin had changed everything.

Bearing witness to this destructive power irrevocably shaped my life. It impressed on me that our world faced an enormous, never-before-seen danger in the nuclear age: not only the ruin of cities, as happened many times in World War II, but the end of our civilization. I came to understand what Einstein meant when he said, "The unleashed power of the atom has changed everything," and was haunted by his concluding words: "save our modes of thinking." But my thinking was already beginning to change.

I completed my tour in the army in June 1947. Although the images of destruction stayed with me, I was ready to put the war years behind me. I looked to the postwar promise of a peaceful and thriving new world and was eager to resume building my young adult life. I returned to school and rekindled my relationship with Lee Green, my high school sweetheart, and on 29 December 1947 we took our marriage vows in the living room of Lee's family home. Though deeply in love, I had no way of knowing then the profound influence this lifelong union would have on my life. We have shared an enduring love and a strong partnership that has sustained each of us through many challenges.

Lee and I finished the school year in our respective programs, but we would not stay on the East Coast for long. I wanted to go to Stanford University to finish my degree. When I returned from my deployment in Japan, San Francisco had been my port of debarkation—I was struck by the beauty of the Bay Area and the feeling that here everything was new and anything was possible. So I applied for a transfer to Stanford, and with my GI Bill in hand, Lee and I drove across the country in the summer of 1948 to start our new lives in California, where I earned my B.S. and M.S. in mathematics at Stanford University.

I was both awed by the purity and beauty of mathematics and inspired by the scholars at Stanford. But my G.I. Bill ran out when I finished my master's

Bill and Lee Perry while at
Stanford, 1949

degree, and with a growing family to support and no independent source of
income, I could not afford to continue at Stanford. I took a position as math
instructor at the University of Idaho for a year while exploring ways to pursue a
Ph.D. One of those explorations paid off with an attractive offer to teach math
at Penn State while pursuing my degree.

Beyond my doctoral studies at Penn State and teaching three classes every
semester, I also began working half-time for a local defense company, Haller,
Raymond & Brown (HRB). Although I took the defense job out of financial
necessity, I quickly discovered that I enjoyed applying my mathematical skills
to thorny problems in defense, and did it well.

I had started my graduate program with the intention of becoming a math
professor. But the march of perilous world events continued, an unsettling
backdrop to that decision. Just two weeks after I had completed my master's
program, North Korea invaded South Korea, and the Cold War, with its huge
buildup in nuclear weapons, started in earnest.

I could relate in a very personal way to the Korean War, having witnessed
in Okinawa the results of battles comparable to those now unfolding in Korea.
Moreover, I fully expected to be called to serve in this war because while at

Stanford I had taken the advanced ROTC program for veterans and had been commissioned as a 2nd Lt. in the US Army Reserves. However I was never called, so was able to continue my graduate studies.

During my years at Penn State, I grew more and more concerned about the burgeoning danger facing our nation as we confronted a belligerent and aggressive Soviet Union. They detonated their first atomic bomb in 1949; then, in 1953, they announced that they had successfully detonated a hydrogen bomb. I saw how profound a change this was. The atomic bomb, whose horrors we had first seen in Hiroshima, was 1,000 times as destructive as the largest conventional bomb. The new hydrogen bombs we were testing had the destructive power of 1,000 times the Hiroshima bomb. So, in a brief ten years mankind had increased its destructive power by 1,000 times 1,000—by 1 million times—a magnitude of destruction nearly impossible to comprehend.

Now the Soviet Union, which was assisting North Korea in a war in which thousands of Americans were dying, also had this destructive capability. To me, the future loomed more dangerously with each new development, causing me to rethink my career choice. I decided on my chosen path in mid-1953, when a new defense laboratory opened in Mountain View, California, only a few miles from Stanford. It was established by the army to devise defenses against the nuclear-armed missiles being developed in the Soviet Union. After arranging to complete my Ph.D. thesis in absentia, I applied for work at the new lab and was offered a position as a senior scientist. In February 1954, Lee and I loaded our kids into our "woodie" station wagon and once again made the cross-country drive to California, returning to the Stanford area where I reported for work at Sylvania's Electronic Defense Laboratories. There I became deeply involved in the top-secret reconnaissance programs that shaped my career in defense, led to my involvement in the Cuban Missile Crisis, and began the evolution in my thinking about the deadly legacy of nuclear weapons.

Today it is difficult to grasp the spirit of those early secretive Cold War years. Ignorance in understanding key details of the Soviet nuclear threat had given rise to a grave insecurity. It was feared that the Soviets were seeking to achieve a "first-strike" capability, and it became imperative to learn more about Soviet nuclear forces—their numbers, deployments, and performance capabilities. To avoid a tragic military miscalculation and to better manage spending on arms, a powerful new reconnaissance ability—based on new technologies not then fully in hand—was urgently needed.

I was to tackle this seminal challenge in the years ahead.

# 3    The Rise of the Soviet Missile Threat and the Race for Data to Understand It

> *[It] wasn't free-floating fear of nuclear weapons that made war too scary to contemplate; it was the hard-won, detailed knowledge, held by both sides, of what nuclear weapons could do, how many there were, what they were pointed at, and the certainty that they would penetrate any defense.*
>
> —Thomas Powers, *Intelligence Wars*[1]

Early chapters of my journey to reduce the nuclear danger were devoted to obtaining "the hard-won, detailed knowledge . . . of what nuclear weapons could do." The international situation, forged by the historic violence of World War II and the unresolved and growing postwar enmity between the largest allies in that conflict, the United States and the USSR, was more dangerous than ever. An arms race between the two superpowers to build and amass ever more destructive nuclear weapons was ramping up with no end in sight. The secretive and hostile spirit constrained any immediate chance of an enlightened mutual initiative to reverse the growing "overkill" in runaway nuclear arsenals. To prevent a nuclear Armageddon, there was only the grim pragmatism of the doctrine of MAD (mutual assured destruction), a shared terror that presupposed always-rational and always-well-informed actors on both sides—together with indefinite good luck.

The United States knew so little about the Soviet missile and space program, dispersed as it was across the eleven time zones of that huge country, that a national debate ensued during the 1960s about whether we suffered a "missile gap" versus the Soviets. We needed to know much more not only about the force size and deployment of Soviet nuclear weapons but also about their performance abilities—range, accuracy, the size they could deliver, and other crucial characteristics. It would take a revolution in reconnaissance technology to achieve this.

The reasons for a new and sophisticated reconnaissance were complex, but an essential strategic consideration was whether the targeting accuracy of Soviet ICBMs and the size/yield of their nuclear warheads were capable of destroying our land-based retaliatory nuclear weapons in a first strike, those weapons usually "hardened" (protected) and more difficult to destroy than "soft" targets such as cities. In theory, if the Soviets could threaten US land-based nuclear weapons in a first strike, then the already perilous equilibrium of mutual assured destruction would be undermined as a reliable deterrent because the extent of damage from US retaliation would be greatly lessened, encouraging the Soviets and putting the United States at catastrophic risk. Similarly, were the Soviets to develop and field effective defenses against a nuclear attack, some in the Pentagon feared that deterrence would be weakened because an effective defense could lessen the threat from a US retaliation.

The US Cold War reconnaissance triumph—the vital knowledge it gained us—although it offered no guarantee of safety, was a fundamental means in those times of mitigating the threat of a nuclear catastrophe—of shoring up mutual assured destruction—by making war "too scary to contemplate."

And it was a way forward. Better knowledge of the nuclear threat constrained "worst case" threat assessments and their likely effect of increasing the scope and pace of the arms race. And better knowledge might lead to greater cooperation in the future as the enormous expense of an arms race, especially a "blind" one, would curtail both nuclear powers. Necessity was truly the mother of invention in the case of US Cold War reconnaissance technology and led to remarkable ingenuity and intelligence successes.

⌐

This phase of my journey began in 1954 at age twenty-six, when I took a job as a senior scientist at Sylvania's Electronic Defense Laboratories in Mountain View, California. One of my first projects was to evaluate a proposed electronic countermeasure system to interfere with ("jam") the guidance signal of an attacking Soviet intercontinental ballistic missile (ICBM). We knew that the Soviets were already developing a nuclear ICBM and that it used radio guidance to make it accurate against US targets. Before building the jammer, we had to resolve two major issues: the characteristics of the guidance signal; and the extent of the damage reduction we could effect by misdirecting Soviet missiles.

Because of the immense destructive power of nuclear weapons, it was far from obvious that misdirecting an ICBM would significantly reduce damage. What if the jammer redirected the missile from Boston to New York or from

Pittsburgh to Cleveland? Nevertheless, I analyzed the statistical likelihood of damage reduction using jamming for a large variety of attack scenarios. Ironically, I used the "Monte Carlo" statistical technique developed by Stan Ulam and John von Neumann for calculations needed to design the H-bomb.[2]

From one aspect, the results of my analysis were positive. They showed beyond reasonable doubt that effective jamming could reduce the expected fatalities from a medium-size nuclear attack by about two-thirds. It was clear that if the jamming were successful, the United States would suffer "only" 25 million immediate fatalities instead of 75 million. As grim as was that result, it was a significant underestimate of the full consequence of the attack: it did not include the long-term deaths from radiation fallout and "nuclear winter," or take into account that there would be no way to treat the tens of millions of wounded; nor did it address the total disruption of our economic, political, and social systems. Put in the starkest terms, there is no measure by which we can adequately quantify the devastation a mass nuclear attack would have on our civilization.

My calculations, which were meant to establish the plausibility of a defensive system against a nuclear attack, instead taught me that there is no acceptable defense against the destructive power of a mass nuclear attack. The only meaningful defense is to prevent the attack from happening.

I concluded that our priority should not be on pouring resources into a futile defense from a nuclear attack, but on preventing that attack. This fundamental realization has served as a guiding principle throughout my long career in defense.

C. P. Snow, in *Science and Government*, made the pertinent comment about scientists calculating the millions of deaths potentially "saved" by Ballistic Missile Defense (BMD) systems defending against a nuclear attack.

> What will people of the future think of us? Will they say . . . that we were wolves with the minds of men? Will they think that we resigned our humanity? They will have the right.[3]

While I was determining the potential effectiveness of jamming the Soviet ICBMs, I was also considering how to determine the characteristics of their guidance system. Our laboratory developed systems designed to intercept radio guidance signals during Soviet ICBM test flights—the army deployed several of these monitoring systems at ground stations around the perimeter of the Soviet Union. Because an ICBM reaches altitudes of several hundred miles in flight, the signals of interest would rise above the radio horizons of our sites, typically at ranges in excess of 1,000 miles from the intercept locations.

After the Soviets—and the United States—switched to inertial guidance (based on high-precision accelerometers) for their ICBMs and there were no longer radio guidance signals to intercept, the US collection sites intercepted even more important signals: telemetry signals used during missile test flights to measure the performance of the missiles in flight, together with beacon signals by which stations on Soviet test ranges tracked the test missiles. Intercepting and analyzing these signals were engrossing challenges. The Soviets used these signals to determine whether the missiles had achieved their design parameters; by working backward, we used them to determine what those design parameters were.

We had considerable success both in the intercept and the analysis of these signals. Our ground stations were successful in intercepting telemetry and beacon signals on virtually every test flight of Soviet ICBMs (and space vehicles). The challenge of interpreting these signals to determine the characteristics of the missiles persisted for many years during the Cold War, a period in which the United States steadily refined its understanding of the performance abilities of Soviet missile systems. Although the subtleties of interpretation (as well as collection of data and its processing) are beyond the scope of this book, the important consideration in the present context is that we robustly continued our creative interpretive work in support of improving the US understanding of the range, accuracy, deployment, and numbers of Soviet missiles.

Because of the importance and difficulty of this problem, the government needed to bring together the US officials and government contractors who were working on it. Thus was born the Telemetry and Beacon Analysis Committee (TEBAC), established by the CIA and National Security Agency (NSA) so that the various information collectors and analysts could share information and accelerate the assessment of Soviet ICBMs. This elite and highly classified activity was crucial in preventing US miscalculations in the Cold War. TEBAC gave our senior decision-makers accurate information about the capabilities of Soviet nuclear weapons; and, of course, the Soviets themselves embarked on determined monitoring of US capabilities. Otherwise, both sides would have made a worst-case assessment of the other, leading to an open-ended, ever-increasing buildup of nuclear weapons at greater cost and posing more danger to the already perilous weapons equilibrium. TEBAC was responsible for a definitive and generally accurate description of the most dangerous Soviet missiles.

Perry receives Army Outstanding Civilian Service medal from General Alva Pitch, February 1962, for determining the frequencies, intended recipients, and optimum way of intercepting signals of Soviet antennas. Perry's award led to subsequent appointments to government scientific and defense panels. From the archives of General Dynamics C4 Systems Inc.

As vital as TEBAC was, it did not yield the number of Soviet nuclear weapons, numbers especially hard to obtain through the Iron Curtain. The most successful early attempts resulted from imagery collected by U-2 reconnaissance planes flying high over the huge USSR. The U-2s collected images from key areas and facilities of the Soviet missile and space program. For several years beginning in 1956,[4] the United States flew these missions to take high-resolution pictures of vital areas: ICBMs, anti-ballistic missiles (ABMs), and nuclear test ranges. Flown every few months, these flights gave us an intelligence treasure.

After the U-2 photos arrived in Washington, they were taken to the National Photographic Interpretation Center (NPIC) for analysis. When the photography included coverage of missile and nuclear weapon sites, a special technical group was assembled to work with the photo interpreters. The group varied from session to session, but participating in nearly all were Albert "Bud" Whee-lon (Space Technology Lab), Eberhardt (Eb) Rechtin (Jet Propulsion Lab), Carl Duckett and Randy Clinton (Army Missile Command), Bob Fossum (my col-league from Sylvania), and myself. Our group would meet for three twelve-hour days (called "jam sessions") analyzing the new data and writing a report describing and assessing the Soviet weapons covered by the photography. That report was generally regarded by the intelligence community as the definitive report on the weapons analyzed.

On 1 May 1960 the Russians shot down an American U-2 and captured its pilot, Francis Gary Powers. The jam sessions were over.

But the CIA was painfully aware of the vulnerability of the U-2, and it had been developing a satellite-based photo reconnaissance system. Fortunately, that system, code-named "Corona," became operational the same year the U-2 was shot down. Corona had a capability that the U-2 would never have: broad area coverage. Corona could cover the entire landmass of the Soviet Union, all eleven time zones, in one operational run of several weeks, provided that Coro-na's cameras were not blocked from seeing the ground by clouds. But Corona lacked an important capability of U-2 reconnaissance—cameras able to take high-resolution imagery, a deficiency corrected in later photo satellites. (The amazing story of the creation of Corona is told brilliantly in *Secret Empire,* by Philip Taubman.)[5]

As we were working to understand the true nature of the Soviet missile threat, there was a strident claim made that the Soviets were far ahead of us—that there was a "missile gap." In that politically charged atmosphere the direc-tor of the CIA, Allen Dulles, convened a special panel in August 1959—named the Hyland Panel after its chair, Pat Hyland, president of Hughes Aircraft—to assess the claim. The members of the panel, besides Hyland, included the heads of the Army Missile Command, the Navy Submarine Missile Force, the Air Force Missile Command, and the Jet Propulsion Laboratory. Besides these venerable defense "graybeards," Hyland invited Wheelon and me, both "young pups" in our early thirties. This brought to the Hyland Panel expertise from our jam sessions and put Wheelon and me in the unusual position of advising our "seniors."

For nearly a week we reviewed all of the available data; listened to briefings of intelligence analysts from the CIA, NSA, and all three services; and talked among ourselves extensively. We came to a unanimous conclusion: the Soviet ICBM program was not a crash program, and it had only a few missiles already deployed. The report, not made public until decades later, concluded that the Soviet Union had an effective ICBM program but had not yet deployed large numbers of missiles, stating: "The Panel believes that a Soviet IOC [initial operating capability] with a very few operational missiles (10) is at least imminent."[6]

Although the findings of the Hyland panel had dissipated the immediate fear of Soviet missile dominance among top military and government officials, those findings—declassified only recently—could not be used to assuage public concern at the time. Tensions between the two nuclear superpowers continued to mount, reaching a peak in October 1961 when the Soviets broke the nuclear test moratorium by detonating the "Tsar bomba" (called by Adlai Stevenson, US ambassador to the United Nations, their "monster bomb"). At 50 megatons, it was the largest bomb ever tested.[7] (We now know that "Tsar bomba" was actually a 100-megaton bomb, scaled down to avoid damaging the drop aircraft and to reduce fallout.)

This was the backdrop for the most dangerous nuclear crisis we have ever experienced—the Cuban Missile Crisis, discussed in the opening chapter. I described my involvement with that crisis and how both nations used the crisis, not as a rationale for moderating the nuclear arms race, but for accelerating it.

As a result, the Cuban Missile Crisis led to substantial new business for the US defense industry in general, and Sylvania's laboratory in particular. Technical intelligence gathering became an even higher government priority, and defense labs prospered.

A clear sign of the acceleration of the arms race was that the Soviets began testing not one but two new ICBMs, precipitating a heated debate in the US intelligence community about the characteristics of these missiles. Air Force intelligence argued that one of the new ICBMs (the SS-8) was designed specifically to carry the 100-megaton "monster bomb," so a very high priority was put on assessing its characteristics.

During testing the Soviet ICBM generally completed its powered flight below the radio horizon of our ground intercept stations, significantly limiting our analysts' ability to determine the rocket engines' characteristics and the missile's size. So the army decided to take their telemetry intercept systems airborne, and authorized us to build two systems—one to be deployed in Turkey and the other in Pakistan.

In the fall of 1963, I flew to Pakistan to review the operation of that newly fielded system. I arrived at the airbase in Peshawar just hours before the alert-

Perry and his Sylvania colleagues join General J. J. Davis at Moffett Field to inspect the airborne telemetry intercept system deployed in Turkey and Pakistan, 1962. From the archives of General Dynamics C4 Systems Inc.

ing system there predicted an imminent test launch in the USSR of the suspect ICBM, and I persuaded the pilot to let me fly along on the monitoring mission. What a thrill it was, flying at 40,000 feet, high above the Hindu Kush Mountains, and looking deep into the Soviet Union. Tempering that thrill was the certain knowledge that we were flying to determine the characteristics of an ICBM that, if ever used, would kill millions of Americans.

Our airborne platforms did in fact obtain a few powered-flight intercepts from the SS-8, but it was not until the Soviets paraded the missile in their 1964 October Revolution Parade that we were able to obtain high-definition photographs of it. The Soviets held these parades partly to bolster the morale of their own people and partly to intimidate our European allies, but we used them to bolster our intelligence database. These photographs, together with TEBAC's telemetry analysis, revealed conclusively that the SS-8 was designed to carry a relatively light bomb. The scare about a monster bomb died down, as did the push in the United States to build our own monster bomb.

For me, the period after the Cuban Missile Crisis turned out to be one of heightened intensity in another sense. By 1963 I found myself re-evaluating my nearly ten-year tenure at Sylvania. I had been director of Sylvania's Electronic Defense Laboratories for the prior three years and had found the job challenging and exciting. I was proud of our many achievements. Our work was fulfilling, our reputation was strong, our team was motivated, and our business was expanding. We had doubled in size while I was director, and more growth was in sight. Most important, we were leaders in helping the US intelligence community carry out its mission of understanding the Soviet missile and space systems. And the tenor of the times made it clear that our mission was of the highest importance.

But I also had a growing concern that our lab was falling behind in key technologies. Our parent company, Sylvania Electric Products, a world leader in manufacturing vacuum tubes, was finding it very difficult to embrace the new solid-state technology, which promised to make obsolete their most profitable product line. This syndrome, which I call "the liability of leadership," appears every time a disruptive new technology is introduced.

Our lab excelled in analog technology, but a disruptive new digital technology was emerging based on Intel's new solid-state devices, together with new small, high-speed computers on the drawing boards of companies like Hewlett Packard (HP). The introduction of integrated circuits by Intel brought into the market new products much superior to earlier ones. I wanted to be on the leading edge of applying the new digital technology and the new compact computers, and I knew that they could play a critical role in meeting our growing reconnaissance challenges. But I could see that our laboratory, tied to analog technology, could not continue its leadership position. I was also becoming increasingly frustrated with our parent company's bureaucracy and began to think that instead of fighting the negative influence of the big company, I should form a new, more flexible company designed to promote mission fulfillment, team building, and technology leadership.

My 1963 Christmas holiday was fully occupied with those thoughts, and by the end of the holidays I had made my decision. Early in January I turned in my resignation and, joined by four of my top managers, left to form a new company, which we named ESL, Inc.[8]

# 4 An Original Silicon Valley Entrepreneur and the Advance of Spy Technology

*It's too risky to invest in ESL if you can't describe your products or tell us who your customers are.*
— Franklin P. Johnson, Draper and Johnson,[1]
to Perry (paraphrased), April 1964

Nearly all my friends and relatives thought me foolhardy to leave a good position with Sylvania—I was now director of their Electronic Defense Laboratories—for what seemed a highly risky venture in the heart of what is now Silicon Valley. The year was 1964, before Silicon Valley became known as an incubator for young, high-tech entrepreneurs with audacious ideas—indeed, before it came to be called Silicon Valley. But the Digital Age was awakening, and I was confident that I had the right idea, believing I could improve the conditions of success we'd had at Sylvania by leaving behind the smothering influence of a parent company steeped in bureaucracy and burdened with an aging technology.

The cornerstone of our new company, ESL, would be a dedication to the Cold War intelligence mission. As president and CEO, my full attention was on making sure that as we grew in size and capability, ESL would make an indispensable contribution to that quest. And in step with my work at ESL, I planned to continue serving the intelligence community as an unpaid consultant, just as I had during the Cuban Missile Crisis and before.

Two challenges were foremost in my mind: How could we obtain more complete telemetry data from performance tests of all Soviet ICBMs? And how could we intercept key signals needed to learn the true capabilities of the Soviet BMD system then in early development? These would be difficult challenges, and to meet them, I would need all of the technologies that were then emerging in Silicon Valley.

I believed that digital technology would eventually change our world in profound ways, and so we put all of our resources into developing technologies based exclusively in the digital domain, helping secure ESL's place as a leader in these pioneering new technologies. I also planned to focus on satellite reconnaissance systems, since I knew that they would be needed to overcome the limitations of ground and air intelligence collection systems.

My experience gained in founding and managing ESL was to prove indispensable to all my later work in reducing the threat from nuclear weapons. It was the paradigm. At ESL I went to school on many different aspects of the nuclear crisis, and the lessons I learned made all the difference then and later in my quest. I learned that wrestling with the challenge of the nuclear crisis demanded organizational innovation and independence. We were undertaking a business; but more deeply, we were embarked on a mission, and that mission was the over-riding factor. The nuclear crisis was an unprecedented problem, a turning point in the long march of history, for which the stakes could not be higher, and for which traditionally successful corporate arrangements must be augmented with features we often had to invent as we went along.

There was the need to fashion a suitable environment in which creative minds were free to pursue the often difficult and challenging sleuthing involved in bringing the Soviet threat into focus; here the essential rule was that organizational politics give way to a transcendent spirit of cooperation, an acknowledgment of the common good, promoting collaborative analysis and the encouragement of daring analytic approaches. Failure did not bring about stigma—indeed, if you never failed, you were not reaching far enough. There was the constant need to streamline bureaucratic procedure to facilitate the experimentation that was key to finding solutions and answers, especially given the constant time-urgency of the work. And there was the fact that the latest high technology proved central in all phases of the Cold War intelligence mission—sensors, collection, processing, analysis, and presentation of results.

The lessons I learned at ESL were an essential foundation. Not the least important was a practice I adapted that others have called "management by walking around." I visited project teams often and informally. I found it essential for me to get to know the problem-solvers, their triumphs and quandaries, their lines of attack in thinking about puzzling and recalcitrant problems. I learned a common dialogue, with a shared frame of reference, for working with the project teams. I spoke the language and understood the core ideas.

From the beginning, ESL, dedicated to dealing with the nuclear crisis, required its own way of operating. For example, the company was launched with no outside investments. The reason? The pioneering Silicon Valley venture capital firm Draper and Johnson strongly considered funding us, but since we could not disclose our products or customers, they reluctantly (and understandably) declined.

Hence ESL was entirely employee owned. Each of the founders and the first few hundred technical staff bought ESL's capital stock; the stock was offered to no one else. None of us were independently wealthy, but most of us had worked for nearly ten years in the electronic defense industry and had built up retirement funds dispersed to us when we resigned. So each family's nest egg became the capital on which ESL was built. Given the stakes of our vital challenge, this fundamental commitment seemed appropriate.

ESL's five founders each invested about $25,000, and subsequent employees from $5,000 to $10,000—a lot of money in 1964 for young engineers. The motivation of each employee to protect and build that nest egg was powerful. We started ESL with capital of just over $100,000; the total capital by the end of the first year was more than $500,000, all raised from founders and staff.

As our business grew, we became the first company to move into Moffett Park in Sunnyvale, California, an area that eventually housed more than a hundred Silicon Valley companies, including Atari, Yahoo, and the iconic deal-making restaurant Lion and Compass. In the beginning, however, our first building, a graceful, tan, two-story structure, stood quietly alone at the edge of Moffett Park overlooking acres of tomato fields, framed by the backdrop of California's Pacific Coast Range. In a few short years, however, ESL became a complex of multiple buildings housing a considerable array of dynamic and highly original reconnaissance-related projects oriented toward monitoring vast stretches of the world.

In the early days of ESL, one of our most urgent new programs was an effort to determine whether the Soviets could field an effective BMD against our ICBMs. American defense planners sounded alarms about the Soviet BMD system our imaging satellites had been observing under development. Intense debates arose over its capabilities and how much its deployment could weaken our deterrence. (Ironically, more than fifty years later, the Russians developed the same fears about an American BMD system deployed in Europe.) During the mid to late 1960s, some US strategic thinkers argued that we needed to build and deploy a comparable defense system, and that we should considerably increase our ICBM force to compensate for those missiles presumably destroyed by the Soviet BMD system in a nuclear exchange. We were thus poised for another major acceleration of the nuclear arms race. Accordingly, the intelligence community was under immense pressure to understand the capabilities of the Soviet BMD system, and ESL continued to incubate new ideas, some of which yielded rich results.

In this period, we had proposed and won several contracts for small satellite-based systems employing digital components that had just been released by Intel, systems that proved to be quite successful. At about that time, the government requested proposals on a large-scale satellite intelligence collection and processing system. Although ESL was still a young and small company, we audaciously put together a first-class design team and proposed to build the receiving subsystem, which would have resulted in a contract an order of magnitude larger than any of our previous contracts.

Since we had the best design (so we thought), we became overly confident that ESL would win the contract. Based on that confidence, we foolishly did not have a "Plan B," so we were caught with too large a staff and too small a contract base when we lost the bid. Typically that would trigger a company to lay off some of its staff, but we took an unusual, riskier path, believing that our talented team was too good to be easily replaced. We knew that firing talented staff would send the wrong message and permanently change the kind of company we had become, so we quickly improvised a workaround. We went to key companies in the area and offered to "loan" them our surplus staff for six to twelve months: the companies would pay the employees only their direct salary, and ESL would keep them on its books and cover all of their indirect expenses such as benefits. All of our loaned employees were back at ESL within a year, and they—and all their colleagues at ESL—understood that loyalty was a two-way street. The next year our business resumed its high growth rate, and we were very glad that we had those employees back to work on our new programs.

We also continued to build ground-based systems. One example in particular typifies the complexity of the new reconnaissance challenges of that era and the remarkable responses they often inspired. Lew Franklin, one of ESL's most creative engineers, was inspired by "a moon bounce communication program" being conducted by Jim Trexler of the Naval Research Laboratories. Trexler had observed that when Soviet radars were turned on, they would be reflected by the moon back to the earth whenever the moon was in the right position. Lew calculated that the moon was so large it would reflect the Soviet BMD radar signal to earth strongly enough for that signal to be received by a large antenna on the ground in the United States, and that quite possibly this would allow the determination of its signal characteristics. Located only a few miles from us at Stanford University, in the pastoral foothills above the main Stanford campus, was one of the largest antennas yet built—an impressive "dish" 150 feet in diameter and a landmark seen from miles away. The Stanford dish was being used to map the moon by illuminating it with powerful transmitters connected to the dish. But the manager of that program used the dish only part time and gave us permission to use it at other times. We connected an ultrasensitive receiver and recorder to it at the time the moon was in the right position to serve as a reflector. Operating late at night, the ESL team did, just as predicted by Lew, receive the Soviet signal and was able to make a high-quality recording of it.

Lew and his team spent the next day extensively analyzing the signal, and that evening I flew to Washington, DC, to present the results to the CIA's Bud Wheelon and Defense Department officials. With this high-quality signal recording, we were able to make a definitive assessment. The Soviet radar, while it could perform detailed surveillance of our missiles and satellites-in-orbit, did not have sufficient precision to direct missile fire at our ICBM deterrent force.

But the pressure to build an American BMD system was only slowed. Several years later, President Nixon announced the installation of a BMD system called Safeguard, its stated mission to protect some of our deployed ICBMs. Less than a year after becoming operational, Safeguard was quietly dismantled with no apparent loss to US security.

While ESL was operating its BMD radar receiver with the large Stanford dish, we observed an unexpected interference problem. By a curious coincidence, all the taxis in the Palo Alto area, locale of the Stanford dish, operated their dispatch radios at the same frequency as the Soviet BMD radar. We had to design digital equipment to filter out those unwanted taxi signals originating about 10 miles from us so that we could read the Soviet radar signals that traveled almost 500,000 miles from earth to the moon and back to reach our receiving site!

Another case of innovation was the solution of a most difficult problem in airborne intelligence-collection systems. A precision direction-finding subsystem could play a vital role in locating the signal, but accurate airborne direction-finding for intercepted signals had been impossible at very high frequencies. The problem was that the aircraft frame reflected the radio signals along multiple paths (multipaths), leading to erroneous readings of the signal's direction. Ray Franks, a typically innovative ESL engineer, had an epiphany—

modeling those multipath signals for a given aircraft and storing that model in an onboard digital computer that could correct for the multipath errors "on the fly." His ingenious idea worked amazingly well. Its success depended on the availability of high-speed digital computers small and rugged enough to be carried on the aircraft: Hewlett Packard had just brought to the market a suitable model, the HP 2000, and ESL became one of Hewlett Packard's best customers for that product.

We found other powerful applications of digital technology. Members of our technical staff soon realized that our digital-processing systems were applicable to data other than "signals." Two of our brightest scientists, Bob Fossum and Jim Burke, applied the new systems to digital images. NASA had just launched Earth Resources Technology Satellite (ERTS, later known as Landsat), which relayed low-resolution digital images back to earth, and the CIA had launched a new photo-reconnaissance satellite that relayed back to earth high-resolution digital images. The digital age had reached photography.

As a result, ESL received contracts to design digital-processing systems for the huge quantities of digital imagery now streaming to earth. Originally the work focused on receiving the digital stream of data and converting it to pictures. But it was soon evident that much more could be done. The data could be manipulated to improve the images in various ways—remove noise, correct for spatial distortions, and improve image quality. Given the early state of digital technology, these tasks were extremely demanding. We rented space on the largest-capacity IBM computers then commercially available (IBM 360), and the software we developed entailed many dozens of man- and woman-years. We were, in a sense, anticipating Photoshop, but it would be years before consumers could buy digital cameras or personal computers that could process digital imagery.

The ultimate gain beyond receiving and processing signals was interpreting them. Traditionally, intelligence interpretation had been reserved for government agencies, but when ESL was founded the most important intelligence targets had become highly technical: ICBMs, nuclear bombs, ballistic missile defense systems, supersonic aircraft, and drones. Collecting definitive data on these Soviet weapons required technical reconnaissance systems at least as complex. The government began to contract with companies possessing that expertise, and ESL was in the vanguard. We had long-term contracts for analyzing telemetry, beacon, and radar data. And we had contracts for assessing the performance characteristics of ICBMs, satellites, BMD systems, and military radars. We were at the heart of the national imperative to obtain "hard-won, detailed knowledge" of the Soviet nuclear threat.

A corollary thread of our intelligence analysis work was our involvement with the Arms Control and Disarmament Agency (ACDA). My first exposure to ACDA came shortly after President Kennedy created it in 1961, and both Sylvania and ESL received analysis contracts from ACDA. Through my work for ACDA, I met and became a long-term colleague of Wolfgang Panofsky[2] and Sid Drell,[3] two intellectual giants in the field of nuclear arms control. With them, I believed that arms control and the reduction of nuclear weapons must become a key factor in mitigating the danger of a nuclear catastrophe, halting and reversing the runaway "balance of terror."

In thirteen years we built ESL from a fledgling startup to a company making significant technical contributions to our country's intelligence assessment of nuclear weapon threats to the United States. By 1977 we employed one thousand employees (and I knew all of them), achieved strong financial success, and had earned a national reputation.

I had no inkling at the time, but soon I was to find that the same management principles would serve me well in the very different environment of the Defense Department. I was about to take a new turn in my journey, one that would carry me further along the nuclear brink and place me in a new role. Both the digital technology and the management approaches I had used in developing reconnaissance systems were to prove invaluable as I became responsible for the creation of new weapons designed to prevent the use of nuclear weapons—a classic paradox of the nuclear era. My role would change, the resources would differ, but my fundamental mission would remain the same.

# 5    A Call to Serve

*For a technical person, this is the most interesting job in the world. It will
expand your mind in ways you cannot now imagine.*[1]

—Gene Fubini to Perry (paraphrased); March 1977

Just as ESL verged on a major increase in sales and stock price, my life took
a dramatic turn. In January 1977 Harold Brown,[2] the secretary of defense in
the new Carter administration, asked me to be his undersecretary of defense
for research and engineering. I had never considered entering government. I
felt a strong commitment to stay with the company I had founded, my family,
and my home—all in California. I discussed the offer with Lee, who strongly
supported my inclinations, but the calls continued until I agreed to come to
Washington to discuss what the job would entail.

I soon understood more fully than ever that at that moment in the nuclear
era, a serious crisis in nuclear deterrence was emerging, one that lay beyond the
mandate for reconnaissance. It appeared that a dangerous imbalance was developing in military forces between the United States and the USSR, a grim dynamic in a time when all depended on preventing the use of nuclear weapons.

I had immense regard for Harold Brown, for whom I had done some consulting when he was the director of defense research and engineering (DDR&E)
during the Kennedy administration. He was one of the smartest people I had
ever worked with, so I listened very carefully to his reasons for wanting me in
this job. He said that the nation was facing a real security danger—the Soviets
had caught up with us in nuclear weapons, which, combined with their long-
time three-to-one advantage in conventional weapons, made our deterrence
posture insecure. He wanted me to incorporate the new digital technology
being pioneered at ESL into our conventional military systems, believing that
could *offset* the Soviet numerical advantage. And because the job entailed managing very large sums of money, he wanted someone who had "met a payroll."

I then talked at length with his colleague and advisor, Gene Fubini.[3] Brilliant and volatile, Fubini had been Brown's principal deputy while Brown was
DDR&E. Fubini argued persuasively about the exciting technical challenges of

transforming the nation's military systems with new technology, presciently concluding, "For a technical person, this is the most interesting job in the world. It will expand your mind in ways you cannot now imagine."

I also met with Charles Duncan, the new deputy secretary of defense, who told me that he had put his stock in a blind trust, and that he thought that I would be able to do the same with my ESL founder's stock, which was the great preponderance of my net worth.

I did have initial reservations, however, as to whether my management style, which worked well in industry, would also work well in government. I had never taken a course in business management—I had learned how to manage on the job. But I concluded that it would be sufficient to learn the specifics of this new and challenging job, and that I would not have to learn a whole new way of managing people. On balance, then, I started to believe that I could succeed in this hugely challenging and critically important job.

Added to these reflections was my sense that I understood the essential role of digital technology in offsetting the Soviet quantitative advantage in conventional battlefield forces, and that our technology would give us an abiding economic advantage in the costly Cold War arms race.

With Lee, who agreed to put her career on hold, I bought a house in Washington and said a bittersweet farewell to the company I had founded and the family and good friends we left behind.

There were no views of the Santa Cruz Mountains or the Pacific Coast Range from the windows of my new office in Washington, but from my experience in the defense business and on government advisory groups, I was no stranger to the long, echoing, and busy halls of the massive Pentagon, one of the remarkable buildings in the world and an architectural testament to the strength and breadth of our military.

It took me several months to get on top of the complex job of undersecretary of defense. It was a world apart from my corporate years in reconnaissance, but it was immediately clear that this new position could be highly relevant to prevention of a nuclear disaster.

Fortunately, I had much expert help. Fubini would stop by my Pentagon office every Saturday morning to offer support and advice. My new principal deputy, Gerry Dinneen, an outstanding engineer who had been director of the MIT Lincoln Laboratory, arrived to take on his responsibilities about the time I did. George Heilmeier, talented director of the Defense Advanced Research Projects Agency (DARPA), agreed to stay on for another six months, until he could be replaced by Bob Fossum, who had managed the Systems Laboratory at ESL. And I was able to recruit a superb military assistant in my first month. Fubini advised me that an able military assistant was indispensable, and that the best and brightest young military officer he knew of was Air Force Lt. Col. Paul Kaminski,[4] who had just completed a year of study at the National Defense University. However, when I requested his services, the Air Force chief of staff, David Jones, said that Kaminski had already been assigned to another job. Fubini, with characteristic flare, told me to call Jones back and tell him to cancel Kaminski's other assignment and send him to work for me. I did, and he did—this was my first taste of the leverage I would have in my new position.

I was now responsible for the production and testing of all the weapons of the military services and of the defense agencies, as well as overseeing all military research and engineering, and each of the military services understood that my support was necessary for the success of their programs. My starting title was DDR&E, a position earlier created in reaction to the Soviet launch of Sputnik. Harold Brown, the second to hold that job and now secretary of defense, believed it was too limiting because it entailed only engineering responsibilities. He broadened my authority to include the production as well as development of defense systems and also to include communication and intelligence systems. Since I was now taking on substantially more responsibility, Brown asked Congress for authority to change my title to undersecretary of defense for research and engineering, which would also include the responsibilities of the Defense Department's acquisition executive. Congress approved that change later in 1977, and I was sworn in a second time.

My first Senate confirmation hearing was also my first introduction to the Senate Armed Services Committee. My defense industry background had made me familiar with most of the issues that concerned the Senators, so the hearing went smoothly. Most memorable was my introduction to Senator Sam Nunn of Georgia.[5] Although one of the committee's youngest members, Nunn was clearly the most knowledgeable on defense issues, and had already distinguished himself by being critical of NATO's stewardship of tactical nuclear weapons. At the hearing he asked the toughest, most insightful questions and put me through a regular "wire brushing" to test my ideas on offsetting the Soviet's numerical advantage. It made a strong impression on me, and though I did not understand it at the time, this introduction marked the beginning of a long and fruitful collaboration on issues of nuclear security, out of which has grown a significant friendship.

But there was a surprising price to pay for my new job. In the hearing prior to my first swearing in, Senator John Stennis, chair of the Senate Armed Services Committee, refused to approve the blind trust that I had established for my ESL stock, even though a similar trust had been approved for Charles Duncan and, several years earlier, for David Packard. Senator Stennis held that my position as defense acquisition executive was too sensitive to allow any connections to industry, even those shielded by a blind trust. Having already left ESL and moved to Washington, I didn't think it feasible to reverse those moves, so I complied by selling all of my ESL founder's stock. Some months later, ESL's board decided to sell the company to TRW at a significant multiple of the market price at which I had divested my shares. A week after the sale of ESL, I was interviewed by a reporter who seemed intent on exposing the cost to taxpayers of the Secretary's Mess at the Pentagon, one of the perks of defense officials. He asked what it cost me to eat in the Secretary's Mess. Without hesitation, I replied, "About a million dollars."

The next year salt was rubbed into that wound: the IRS audited my 1977 tax return. We had taken as allowable business expenses the charges for moving our furniture from California to Washington, but the IRS disallowed them because the IRS "knew" that we would have been reimbursed by the government. However, during that period the government did not reimburse moving expenses for presidential appointees. When Lee, a CPA specializing in tax accounting, explained this to the disbelieving auditor, he made a hurried check, determined she was right, and said he would close the case. At that point Lee was unwilling to close the case. She had since found evidence of other allowable expenses we had not claimed, and, given that the auditor had reopened our file, she claimed them. After tense discussions the auditor was forced to admit that Lee was right, and he authorized a payment for her claims. That action yielded only a small financial return, but a sizable psychic one. Although I felt that we had been treated unfairly on both financial issues, both Lee and I still believe that accepting the position of undersecretary, even given the financial bath, was the right decision. We never looked back.

Becoming undersecretary would turn out to be one of the most profound moves of my life, changing everything that came after. As it turned out, Gene Fubini's prediction was exactly right. This job expanded not only my mind but also my comprehension of how military policy is shaped in Washington. My access to those at the forefront of crafting and implementing our national defense would prove crucial to all of my subsequent work in nuclear security;

moreover, I got my first exposure to international diplomacy, which was to be decisively important later in my career.

Most sobering was the dawning responsibility of my challenge to mitigate the nuclear threat. I was to find myself facing the most immediate and growing problem for the United States in maintaining deterrence—truly a moment of truth in the Cold War, and with no margin for error. Our fashioning of revolutionary battlefield improvements would entail state-of-the-art technology and considerable design improvisation—and we had to get it right the first time.

If I had campaigned for key responsibilities in my journey, I could not have obtained any more pressing and demanding ones than those with which I was now entrusted.

# 6  Implementing the Offset Strategy and the Emergence of Stealth Technology

*Dear President Carter,*

*I am deeply concerned that the Soviet Union could make a surprise missile attack on the United States that would destroy our country, and so I have designed a moon bomb that could save us. I propose that we build a very large rocket, whose payload would be a very long strand of steel cable, one end of which would be firmly attached to the earth. We would then launch the rocket at the moon, playing out the cable behind it as it rose. When the rocket landed on the moon, a robot would attach the other end of the cable to the moon. The timing would be determined so that as the earth rotated, it would pull the moon towards it, causing it to smash into the Soviet Union.*

—A concerned citizen (paraphrased from letter), March 1977

My first priority as undersecretary was to create, and then to implement, as soon as feasible, the "offset strategy." This is what we called the overall project that was designed to compensate for the Soviet size advantage in conventional forces and thus re-establish general military parity and shore up deterrence.

My first sense of the conceptual challenge came early, when President Carter sent me the "moon bomb" letter to answer. My executive brought me that letter along with a proposed answer prepared by a Defense Department physicist, who had calculated the needed weight of the cable and size of the rocket, and, of course concluded that the idea was infeasible. I signed the reply letter and, in an inspired moment, penned an added note: "Even if the moon bomb were feasible, it will not be the policy of this administration to destroy an entire hemisphere." That was the first decision I made that inextricably combined technology with policy!

Although paraphrased for simplicity, the moon bomb letter was real. The author's off-the-wall technology and policy ideas capture the all-too-real, often hysterical fears during the darkest days of the Cold War. The Committee on the Present Danger (CPD), a group of well-known defense thinkers and military professionals, was alleging that the United States faced a "window of vulnerability" because of Soviet arms developments. Many serious observers thought that our security situation had grown desperate. Schoolchildren were being taught to "duck and cover" under their desks in the event of a nuclear attack.

How had we arrived at this fearful position?

As World War II ended, President Truman ordered a major demobilization of our armed forces—a reduction of our army from about 8 million men to half a million—together with the demobilization of our massive defense industry. Stalin, however, kept his Red Army at about 3 million men, established modern air defenses, and elevated the status of the air force. Most significantly, he ordered a buildup and modernization of his defense industry. Stalin was deeply impressed by the performance of America as the "arsenal of democracy" in World War II, calling it "the war of machines" and vowing that the Soviet Union would be prepared to win the next war of machines.

President Truman, knowing that the United States then had a monopoly on nuclear weapons, did not respond to the Soviet arms buildup. But the advent of the Korean War immediately taught Truman—despite General MacArthur's contrary urging—that nuclear weapons were not really usable. Truman elected to fight a conventional war of attrition, for which the United States was ill prepared. Scrambling to counter the North Korean army, and later the Chinese army, Truman did remobilize the US defense industry; but he chose to meet the army's manpower needs not by making a significant increase in the army's authorized strength but by calling up reserve forces. (As I've noted, I was a member of the army reserves, but my unit was not ordered to report.)

In 1952, Eisenhower was elected and in six months negotiated an armistice and wound down the war, returning the reserve units to their civilian status. By that time it was clear that the United States was facing a long, protracted struggle with the Soviet Union, and Eisenhower understood that the numerical advantage of the Red Army would be a serious concern. But he reasoned that our overwhelming nuclear advantage would offset the Red Army's numerical advantage in conventional forces. This was Eisenhower's offset strategy, based on his conviction that sustaining a large standing army would, in time, cripple America's economy (a policy that eventually did just that to the Soviet economy).

From Eisenhower's presidency until Carter's, we had offset the large Red Army with our nuclear weapons, both strategic and tactical. We believed that the Soviets had an invasion plan (Nazi Germany's Operation Barbarossa[1] in the opposite direction) in which they would send the Red Army from the western border of East Germany to the English Channel.

The US strategy to stop that advance was to use tactical nuclear weapons against Red Army troops inside West Germany; in other words, to attack with nuclear weapons on the territory of our allies. Our strategists reasoned that the Soviets would not dare use their strategic nuclear weapons in response because of our great advantage in those weapons and their delivery means. Accordingly, we employed truly remarkable technology to develop a family of nuclear weapons for our army in the field. Incredibly, the army, in perhaps a long-conditioned reflex, treated tactical nuclear weapons essentially as big bombs, to be used like any other bombs, just not requiring use in nearly the numbers of conventional bombs. Thus the army fielded these weapons as though they were simply organic evolutions of prenuclear arms: nuclear charges for artillery pieces, nuclear charges for large bazookas (Davy Crockett), and nuclear charges for demolition mines. Predictably, the Soviet Union developed its own tactical nuclear weapons, and, in the event of war, planned to use them to destroy Western Europe's communication and political centers.

As I look back at this strategy and the weaponry, I think that we showed an almost primordial behavior that in our perilous new times was extraordinarily reckless. Although today the United States still has theater nuclear bombs that can be deployed on tactical as well as strategic bombers, we no longer have a strategy of using nuclear weapons on the battlefield. The Russians, on the other hand, still have a significant arsenal of tactical nuclear weapons about which we have only sketchy information, since to date they have been unwilling to discuss them in arms agreement talks.

In 1977, then, the United States was confronted with two serious security challenges in nuclear weapons. First, the deterrence of a Red Army attack on Western Europe depended on our superiority in strategic nuclear weapons, yet the Soviets had reached strategic parity by that year, with some American analysts claiming that the Soviets were pulling ahead. Second, the strategy of using battlefield nuclear weapons in West Germany was a dangerous and reckless idea, even if we had superiority in strategic nuclear weapons.

In a world dangerous as never before, we needed a new offset strategy—one that was compatible with the realities we were facing. At the heart of our new strategy was a plan to develop not tactical nuclear weapons but innovative conventional weapons that would enable revolutionary, decisive battlefield prowess even against considerably larger forces. Executing that strategy was my greatest priority as undersecretary. That mission, involving many initiatives and an abiding faith in new technology as an affordable and winning battlefield force multiplier, was a considerable conceptual challenge, a significant implementation challenge, and perhaps most of all, a management challenge.

Secretary Brown and I agreed to base the new offset strategy on the emerging digital technology with which I already had significant experience. Early in my tenure I visited the Defense Advanced Research Projects Agency (DARPA), which like my office had been created two decades earlier in response to Sputnik. I requested detailed briefings on advanced sensors and smart weapons, which were to be the foundation of the new offset strategy. George Heilmeier, the DARPA director, spotlighted an audacious research project in an early phase at Lockheed Aircraft. This project was exploring an entirely new way to configure military aircraft that would make them immune from attack by radar and/or infrared-guided antiaircraft missiles so predominant in military arsenals around the world, notably the Soviet military. I saw immediately that this so-called stealth technology, if successful, would give our air force a sudden and overwhelming advantage in tactical close air support, even when engaging a numerically superior opposing force: the foe's antiaircraft defenses could be rendered ineffective, which in turn could enormously multiply the effectiveness of all our ground and naval operations. I told Heilmeier that he would have all the resources he needed to prove out the concept as quickly as feasible.

Within six months the energized Lockheed stealth project team, under the inspired direction of Ben Rich, conducted a successful flight test of a prototype aircraft in a convincing proof of principle. Flying down a radar test range, the experimental plane demonstrated that an attacking military aircraft could be configured with a radar signature that would be roughly equal to that of a small bird. On the strength of this remarkable demonstration, I placed the stealth program in deep security and brought in the air force to work jointly with DARPA to define, develop, and build a stealthy fighter-bomber that would become the F-117, with the goal of achieving a successful test of an operational aircraft in just four years.

The time required to bring a new military aircraft to operation is typically much longer than four years, with ten to twelve years not uncommon. Given the urgency of the offset strategy, however, I knew we needed a customized management process for the F-117, and as well for the other stealth programs and the new cruise missile program that would form the core of the new strategy. I established and chaired a small review team for which my military assistant, Paul Kaminski, was executive secretary; the relevant service civilian and military acquisition executives constituted the rest of the team. We met monthly to review each program, with the program manager demonstrating the progress over the previous month and detailing any barriers that could prevent his meeting the demanding schedule. We adjourned no meeting until the service officials specified what actions they would take to overcome the barriers identified. I then concluded the meeting by directing the service acquisition executives to find all funds needed to carry out those actions, redirecting money from other programs if necessary—effective immediately. At some of the earlier meetings, the acquisition executives who disagreed with my directives protested to their service secretaries, who would in turn appeal to Secretary Brown. In each such case, Brown supported my decision. After the first few such rulings, the objections subsided and the pace of our progress accelerated. Under the expedited acquisition process, the F-117 program met its cost target as well as a demanding schedule, demonstrating the principle that time over-runs are a major cause of cost over-runs.

The legislative process also worked to our advantage. All the stealth programs were highly classified, and we briefed only a few selected members of Congress, including the chairs of the Armed Services Committees whose responsibility it would be to shepherd the needed appropriations through Congress without detailed and time-consuming general presentations. Absolutely essential was the full-hearted support of Senator Nunn. Respected by fellow senators for his fairness and deep knowledge of defense, he fully understood the vital importance to US national security of meeting the performance goals of the offset strategy.

I knew this special management process must be used sparingly, so I limited it to the stealth programs and the cruise missile program, which I thought the highest priorities in the offset strategy. I would have liked to reform the entire defense acquisition system to improve efficiency and efficacy throughout the Pentagon, but I never had the time or energy as undersecretary to undertake that most formidable task. (As will be explained later, I did return to the task as an advisor to the Defense Department after I left office and, then again, when I became the deputy secretary of defense.)

As one of the most talented young officers in the air force, my military assistant Paul Kaminski was indispensable to the management of the stealth programs. After I left office, he became program manager of all air force stealth programs. The remarkable success of these programs depended on the dedication and talent of many people, but foremost were Kaminski and Lockheed's Ben Rich. Major Joe Ralston, who later became vice chairman of the Joint Chiefs of Staff, also played a key role. Beyond that, I probably could not have succeeded in moving these vital programs through the Congress without Senator Nunn, to whom other senators turned for reassurance that these programs, about which they knew little, were truly in the national interest.

To chart the remarkable achievement of fielding the F-117: the full-scale development of that fighter-bomber began in November 1977; the first successful flight of a production F-117 took place in October 1982; the F-117 became operational in 1983. Initially regarded by US military with some skepticism, the F-117 proved itself beyond question some years later in Desert Storm.

Although the F-117 stealth bomber is best known to the public, we developed an entire family of other stealthy weapons systems as well: a large bomber (which became the B-2); short- and long-range cruise missiles; reconnaissance aircraft; and even warships. The original offset strategy force-multiplier systems themselves proved to be multipliers of new offsetting military capabilities. A notable example is Sea Shadow, an experimental stealth warship developed by Lockheed, builder of the F-117. Sea Shadow successfully demonstrated not only a very low radar cross-section but also very low susceptibility to sonar detection. Though it never became operational, Sea Shadow validated the high-leverage design principles that have since been applied to the latest class of US destroyers and cruisers now under construction. The offset breakthroughs have proven durable, prevalent, and highly versatile.

To grasp the broad and sweeping new battlefield advantages suddenly brought by the radically novel and highly technological offset strategy, advantages proven in the years since, it is essential to see that the full strategy comprised features additional to the crucial stealth technology. Success ultimately depended on three interrelated components: a new family of intelligence sensors that could identify and locate in real time all enemy forces in the battle area; a new family of munitions that could strike those targets with great precision—that is, "smart weapons"; and a new way of designing attacking aircraft and ships to allow them to evade enemy sensors—that is, stealth systems, the F-117 being the first.

When I became undersecretary, the development of smart weapons was well underway. I greatly increased the emphasis on them and substantially accelerated their fielding into service. They ranged from smart artillery shells (the

Copperhead[2]), to smart short-range missiles (the Maverick[3] and Hellfire[4]), to long-range cruise missiles (the ALCM[5] and the Tomahawk[6]). Many of these smart weapons remain central today to our military's firepower.

If conceiving the offset strategy took a large leap of faith, building it required ingenuity, hard work, and the patience to withstand setbacks. About halfway through my time as undersecretary, I took the Pentagon press corps on a tour of military test sites for demonstrations of the smart weapons. The demonstration at White Sands, New Mexico, was an unqualified success. Tested against an obsolete tank, a Copperhead artillery shell made a direct hit that totally destroyed the target. The air-launched munitions all made direct hits on their targets. Confident after these dramatic successes, I took the press corps to Point Mugu, California, to witness the testing of the submarine-launched Tomahawk missile. Secretary Brown accompanied us. We all stood on a hill overlooking the bay in which the target submarine was submerged. Precisely as planned, the Tomahawk was launched. Unfortunately, as it breached the surface, it spun out of control and made a watery crash a few hundred yards from the submerged submarine. My heart sank. However, I turned to Secretary Brown and said, "Not to worry. We have another Tomahawk ready to launch." Minutes later it was launched, but with the same dismal outcome. Secretary Brown, obviously irritated, looked at me and said, "So what should I tell the press?" The best I could manage was, "You'll think of something!" And he did. He pointed out to the press that the purpose of testing was to reveal design deficiencies, that this test obviously had done so, and that very shortly we would discover and correct the deficiency. Within a few weeks we did just that. The Tomahawk has since proven one of our most reliable weapons, having been launched with great effect hundreds of times during the two Iraq wars.

Also key were smart sensors, an indispensible component of the offset strategy. When I came to office, I intended to adapt the remarkable US technology in reconnaissance satellites with which I was very familiar to our conventional military forces. The hugely successful Cold War satellite systems incorporated state-of-the-art digital technology, and that technology, in addition to enabling superb satellite-borne reconnaissance, pointed the way to successful ground and airborne surveillance systems that directly supported our battlefield commanders.

One such system, the Airborne Warning and Control System (AWACS), was already well into its development when I took office.[7] AWACS was a sophisticated flying radar giving US battlefield commanders the location and direction of every aircraft in the battle area, in real time. Clearly AWACS stood capable of revolutionizing air warfare, and it did so.

Why not also revolutionize ground warfare, giving the ground commander the location and direction of every ground vehicle in real time? The system to meet that challenge, Joint STARS,[8] was just beginning its development when I left office. By the time of Desert Storm, Joint STARS was in its final test stage. The late General Norman Schwarzkopf, US commander in Desert Storm, ordered that Joint STARS be used on the battlefield even prior to completing its full operational tests. It turned out to be remarkably successful in the field, and now no ground commander would want to go into battle without it.

Another smart airborne sensor was Guard Rail, a system we had developed at ESL.[9] Originally applied to peacetime reconnaissance, it turned out to be applicable to locating high-value targets in the battle area.

A revolutionary component of the offset strategy was the Global Positioning Satellite (GPS) system.[10] It began as an experimental program a few years before I took office, and by 1979 four US GPS satellites were in orbit. Twenty-four satellites were planned, but funds had not been budgeted. During the planning for the Fiscal Year 1980 budget and with the concurrence of Secretary Brown and the Office of Management and Budget (OMB) in the White House, the GPS program, assessed as interesting but not essential, was to be terminated as a cost savings.

Alarmed, I asked Secretary Brown to postpone this decision for a week while I visited the GPS test site at Holloman Air Force Base for an on-the-spot evaluation. I believed GPS indispensable to the offset strategy, but I had to be certain it would work as described. I planned the trip to arrive at Holloman when all four existing GPS satellites were in orbit over the base. (Four satellites could provide full accuracy, but for limited times at any given location.) The GPS program manager, Lt. Col. Brad Parkinson, had been described to me as an enormously gifted engineer, and I was about to discover that for myself. After briefing me on the program, Parkinson ushered me into a helicopter sitting inside a 10-meter circle painted on the runway. The pilot lifted off with the helicopter windows blacked out. We flew blind for a half hour, using only GPS signals to locate ourselves. We then returned to the base, and the pilot landed the helicopter blindly but precisely within the 10-meter circle.

I was convinced. I returned to the Pentagon prepared to take all necessary actions to save the GPS program. Fortunately, Secretary Brown agreed with me and the program's funding was restored. I made one compromise: to drop the satellite constellation from twenty-four to sixteen, a decrease that limited the coverage of GPS at northern latitudes. However, I was confident that when the GPS became operational, its evident value would restore the funding to field the other eight satellites, and that is what happened.

The GPS technology proved even more important to military applications than I had first imagined; it has since become ubiquitous in the civil sector, which I had not imagined. I am proud of my role in keeping GPS technology alive at a critical time in our history. Secretary Brown, however, played the key role in convincing the president to overturn the OMB cancellation directive, and Brad Parkinson brought GPS to a stage where it was too valuable to be canceled. Parkinson now is a Stanford professor pioneering in making ultraprecision time measurements with satellites to verify gravitational constants. Great credit for much of the original scientific work on GPS goes to Jim Spilker, an entrepreneur and visionary also at Stanford today. (The latest building in the new Engineering Quad at Stanford is the Jim and Anna Marie Spilker building.) People such as Harold Brown, Ben Rich, Paul Kaminski, Joe Ralston, Brad Parkinson, and Jim Spilker, together with other technology Merlins of the sophisticated reconnaissance revolution in the Cold War, continue to support my faith that human beings can and do respond to grave problems in our era.

The new "system of systems"—stealth, smart sensors, and smart weapons—was developed under the highest priority during the late 1970s, produced in the early 1980s, and fielded in the late 1980s, just in time for Desert Storm, an unplanned proving ground for these remarkable military technologies developed during the Cold War.

Desert Storm commanders had near perfect intelligence; in contrast, Iraqi commanders could not even detect F-117 fighter-bombers as they dismembered Iraqi military units, since the stealthy design made them undetectable by Iraqi radars. The F-117 flew about a thousand missions in Iraq, dropped about two thousand precision-guided munitions, of which about 80 percent hit their targets, a precision and reliability previously unimaginable. Not a single aircraft was lost during the nightly runs over Baghdad, which was defended by hundreds of modern Soviet-designed air defense systems.

The weapons of the offset strategy, which led to the remarkable military success in Desert Storm, remain important to the continuing dominance of the US military as well as to shoring up deterrence. I am gratified that we were able to realize the ambitious vision of the offset strategy, proud of my role in it, and admiring of the leadership Harold Brown and Paul Kaminski brought to it.

Others were also vital to the success of the initiative. The offset strategy would not have received the timely finding needed without the full support of Senator Nunn. The systems had to be produced in quantity and fielded widely, and that happened during the Reagan administration under the leadership of Dick De-Lauer, the undersecretary of defense for research and engineering for much of that administration. Even after the weapons were fielded, the military needed to develop—and succeeded in developing—tactics and training appropriate for the revolutionary new systems. When Desert Storm began, I was surprised and pleased to see how General Charles Horner exploited the unique capabilities of the F-117, using it for night operations (since its stealthy properties gave it full "invisibility" only during those hours), and using it over the most highly defended area, Baghdad, as well as to take out Iraqi air defense units to give nonstealthy aircraft a "free ride."

Not everyone was on board with the offset strategy. During its development, a group called the Defense Reform Caucus (DRC) mounted vigorous opposition. The DRC originally had focused its concerns on the high cost and complexity of fighter aircraft, especially the F-15 and the F-18, and there they made a compelling case because of the cost and schedule over-runs attendant to those programs (problems apparently endemic to fighter aircraft based on the present over-runs on the F-22 and F-35 programs). From that reasonable position, they evolved into what I believe was an unreasonable position—that new technology would inevitably lead to higher costs and delayed schedules in any military system. Basically they argued that the new technology might work well in the lab but would be ineffective during the "fog of war" and too complex for our troops to operate. They contended that the new integrated circuit (IC) technology would be insufficiently rugged and reliable. As was apparent to anyone who had used both an electromechanical calculator and an IC-based Hewlett-Packard calculator, the reverse was true. The DRC was assuming that the new IC technology would increase complexity and cost, when in fact, the introduction of integrated circuits, whether in military or civilian applications, has led to dramatic decreases in cost and increases in reliability. Not understanding that, the DRC argued that we should meet Soviet numerical superiority in conventional forces by matching it with more troops, more tanks, and more aircraft.

The best case for the thinking advanced by the DRC was made by James Fallows in his book *National Defense*, published 1981.[11] At the time of its publication, I was out of office and working at Hambrecht & Quist (H&Q),

a high-technology investment banking firm, but I was also spending part of my time at Stanford on security studies. I rebutted him in an article, "Fallows' Fallacies," which appeared in the Spring 1982 edition of *International Security* (MIT Press).[12] There I made the technical arguments as to why ICs should not be equated with complexity; that in fact they would decrease cost and increase reliability. I also pointed out fundamental flaws in the troop-matching strategy of the DRC: first, the substantial increase in the defense budget necessary to match the Soviet military numerically; and, second, the ensuing requirement to restart conscription to reach the required manpower, both of which I believed were politically infeasible ideas.

The opposition by the DRC slowed down some of our programs but stopped none of them. I did, however, worry that our troops might not be able to adapt to the new technologies. After the Vietnam War, our troop morale, training, and capability were low, and those were the troops that would operate the systems of the offset strategy as they were fielded. The army was acutely aware of the problem (with or without the offset strategy) and, with the ending of the draft, thought they had a solution underway. With the longer term in service of soldiers in an all-volunteer army, the army leadership believed that an intensive training program would pay off, and they had established a truly impressive one. I was reassured by their determination to rebuild the army and especially by their commitment to training. I became confident that when our systems were ready for operation, our soldiers would be ready to operate them. And that proved to be the case.

After Desert Storm, Congressman Les Aspin,[13] then chair of the House Armed Services Committee, held a hearing on lessons learned from that conflict about smart weapons. Now out of government, I was called as a witness; the committee also called Pierre Sprey, a leader of the DRC. My testimony was that the weapons of the offset strategy operated just as expected; that the air force had evolved near-optimum strategies for using them; and that they had played a fundamental role in the lopsided victory and remarkably low losses of American forces. Sprey stuck with the long-standing assessment of the DRC that the new smart weapons would not work well in the "fog of war." After his testimony, Chairman Aspin wryly noted to Mr. Sprey that based on his testimony, he would conclude that we should have lost in Desert Storm.

Reflecting on the engrossing and heady days of its implementation, I believe that the revolutionary offset strategy, a ground-breaking technological and human feat, continues to be one of the crucial US accomplishments in this age of nuclear weapons. As much as any major national project, it has dramatized new ways of thinking for hazardous times. As a sobering but pragmatic measure to help prevent a nuclear tragedy, it dispelled any Soviet confidence that they had gained a decisive military superiority, and it did so with remarkable economy and breathtaking speed. And if economics was inevitably to contain and slow the nuclear arms race, the advantageous cost-effectiveness of the offset strategy was surely central here.

But perhaps there is an even more basic lesson: today's technology imperative. If revolutionary technology has brought nuclear weapons and their danger into the world, revolutionary technology is essential to creating progressively better regimes of safety, regimes ranging from the hostile mode of mutual deterrence via matching weaponry; through verification of compliance with large-scale arms reduction agreements in more moderate times; through highly reliable security systems to protect nuclear materials in still safer times of global cooperation. Just as with the US reconnaissance revolution of the Cold War, the offset strategy and its revolution in battlefield performance was a triumph of humans and technology, pointing our way forward. Certainly it was an episode that played a key role in my journey.

But even as we pursued the offset strategy to maintain our deterrence by modernizing our conventional forces, we were also modernizing our nuclear forces. So I will next bring you into the intense debates behind another crucial imperative I faced on day one at the Pentagon, the buildup of the US strategic nuclear forces as another mandated project in shoring up deterrence.

# 7        Buildup of the US Nuclear Force

*We've degenerated into a discussion on what mode was the best, the land mode or the sea mode or the air mode and I'd like to suggest a fourth mode—I call it the com-mode.*

                —Cecil Garland, Utah rancher, CBS Broadcast, 1 May 1980[1]

By the mid-1970s the Soviets were at parity with the United States in nuclear weapons and their delivery means. We no longer had what President Eisenhower had seen as a nuclear offset to the long-standing three-to-one numerical advantage of the Red Army. When I became undersecretary, a serious debate was underway about whether we could now deter the Soviet Union from military attacks.

Paul Nitze,[2] a former deputy defense secretary, was the most articulate voice for a bipartisan citizens group called the Committee on the Present Danger (CPD), which asserted that for the first time the United States faced a "window of vulnerability" to a Soviet surprise nuclear attack. President Carter's strategy was to increase the capability of our conventional forces through technology enhancements, an idea that led to the offset strategy, whose basic development took priority during the next few years. But partly in response to the pressure from the CPD, President Carter decided that we must maintain nuclear *parity* with the Soviets to ensure an unambiguous deterrence. In a sense, the political pressure to maintain nuclear parity was at least as strong an influence on our programs as the imperative of maintaining nuclear deterrence.

But keeping the size of our nuclear force on pace with that of the surging Soviet program was not the only issue. In order for our deterrent to be credible, we had to be certain that our nuclear forces would survive an attack and then penetrate to their targets in the Soviet Union.

Thus I undertook major actions to upgrade our nuclear forces at the same time I was implementing the offset strategy for our conventional forces. The obvious irony was that upgrades to our conventional forces were driven by "new thinking" (using our superior technology to offset the Soviet's numerical advantage), but that upgrades to our nuclear forces were driven by "old thinking" (that the Soviets were actually planning a disarming first strike).

Discussions of the adequacy of our defensive forces are typically based on their ability to deter. Indeed, that is a fundamental requirement. But I was soon to learn that it was not the only requirement, and not necessarily the primary driver of force size. Our deterrent forces were also weighed on a political scale: do they give us parity with the forces of the Soviet Union? I did not regard that as the key issue, but I can testify that during the Cold War, no US president was willing to accept nuclear forces smaller than those of the Soviet Union. And I believe that this perceived imperative did more to drive the nuclear arms race than did the need for deterrence. Similarly, the discussions of the need for a Triad are typically based on the need for deterrence. But I am convinced that we could have confidence in our deterrence even if we had only submarine-based missiles. Thus, once we were satisfied that we had adequate deterrence, the reality was that the size and composition of the deterrent force was determined primarily by a political imperative: that our force was at parity with the forces of the Soviet Union. (This same imperative seems still to apply. We do not need thousands of nuclear weapons to deter Russia today, but for political reasons we are unwilling to reduce our deployed weapons below the equal numbers—1,550 deployed strategic nuclear weapons—agreed to in the New START arms agreement.)

Historically, our strategic nuclear forces and their security-in-deterrence had been based on the strategy of a Triad: *airborne*—B-52s, which could deliver gravity bombs over targets in the Soviet Union; *seaborne*—Polaris missiles (submarine-launched ballistic missiles—SLBMs), which would be launched below the waves from submarines patrolling around the periphery of the Soviet Union; and *land-based*—ICBMs, primarily Minuteman missiles, each carrying multiple warheads, which were deployed in hardened underground silos in the United States. The Triad had arisen through a complicated history, but it had become well entrenched, even sacred, and was quite resistant to challenge. While each of our nuclear systems is expensive, they take up a relatively small part of the defense budget (less than 10 percent when I was secretary). This is because they do not require large numbers of personnel, which are the most expensive part of our defense budget.

I judged that our SLBMs were so invulnerable to attack that a US nuclear force composed solely of SLBMs would give us adequate and reliable deterrence. However, our very capable and secure Polaris system in the field was aging, and the Trident replacement program was already underway to bring major improvements (more warheads per missile, greater accuracy, and better "quieting" to degrade surveillance, tracking, and location by enemy sonar detection systems). But the Trident program was beset by technical problems serious enough that my first priority in strengthening our deterrent force was to get Trident back on track. I visited the Lockheed Missiles and Space Company (LMSC), the Trident primary contractor, and met with Bob Fuhrman, the president of LMSC. He shared my concern and had appointed his best manager, Dan Tellep, to be the Trident program manager. After I met with Tellep, I was satisfied that he understood the program development shortfalls and was taking robust corrective actions. In time, the Trident became one of our most successful and reliable weapons systems; Tellep went on to become president of LMSC, then CEO of Lockheed, and eventually chairman of Lockheed Martin.

I also undertook a fundamental rebuilding of the air leg of the Triad, the aging B-52 force. As the Soviet Union increased its already extensive air defense deployments, the concern grew that many B-52s would be shot down before reaching their targets. The previous administration had moved to replace the B-52s with the B-1, which was nearly ready for production. My first action was to cancel the production plans for the B-1, a technologically marvelous anachronism, because it did not significantly improve our ability to penetrate the massive Soviet air defense network. (I wanted to cancel the program entirely, but to keep the support of some strong B-1 proponents in Congress, I agreed to maintain a small B-1 research and development program.) My second action was to authorize and closely oversee the development of the Air-Launched Cruise Missile (ALCM) program. The B-52s would carry the cruise missiles and launch them several hundred miles from the Soviet Union, where the bombers could not be reached by the Soviet surface-to-air missiles deployed densely around targets in the USSR. Further, we developed rotary launchers for the ALCMs, each of which could carry eight ALCMs; each B-52 could carry one rotary launcher. The capacity of the B-52 could be expanded to a total of twenty nuclear bombs by adding two external pylons, each of which could carry another six missiles.

It became clear that the ALCM, a relatively inexpensive modification that extended the lifetime of the B-52s by several decades, was truly cost effective. Because of their low altitude of flight (200 feet) and low radar signature, the ALCMs could readily penetrate the huge Soviet air defense network and allowed the B-52s to become "stand-off" delivery vehicles, thereby greatly enhancing their survivability (and the survivability of their crews). A key ALCM component was a new, highly accurate guidance system that used terrain matching to achieve very high delivery accuracies of better than 100 feet. This so-called TERCOM (Terrain Comparison or Terrain Contour Mapping/ Matching) system was a technological wonder designed around an IC-based on-board computer that stored and used extensive imagery of the Soviet Union obtained by our reconnaissance satellites. An added critical ALCM component was a small, lightweight, highly efficient turbofan jet engine developed by a true genius and yet another technology Merlin, Sam Williams, the founder and president of Williams International, a small, innovative company unknown to most people. The joint ALCM/Tomahawk program was run with great effectiveness by one of DoD's best program managers, Admiral Walter Locke.

After the F-117 stealth fighter-bomber program had been successfully launched, I authorized the development of the B-2, a long-range, high-payload stealth bomber. The B-2 did not need to operate in a "stand-off" mode, since its exceptionally small radar signature allowed it to fly directly over adversary air defense systems. The contract for the B-2 was awarded to Northrup Grumman during my last year in office.

I believed (and still do) that these two programs, the ALCM and B-2, alone gave the United States an unambiguously strong deterrent force. They typify how we used our technology to respond effectively and economically to the Soviet challenge, instead of using "moon bombs" or tripling the size of our conventional armed forces, the first a bizarre piece of fantasy and the second an old, familiar mode of thinking.

The ICBM leg of the US nuclear Triad consisted of Minuteman and Titan missiles. The Titans were aging, but the Minuteman III force was relatively modern and each missile carried three highly accurate warheads. The CPD postulated that a Soviet surprise nuclear attack—a "bolt-out-of-the-blue"— could destroy the Minuteman missiles in their silos, a concern I thought was greatly exaggerated. To begin with, our silos would protect the missiles from any attack except a direct or near-direct hit. Based on our intelligence, we did not believe Soviet ICBMs were accurate enough to give Soviet leaders confidence that their attack would destroy our missiles in their silos. Moreover, even if the Soviets were to attain such a high-precision guidance system, they would have to be concerned that we would launch our missiles before their ICBMs arrived (known as "launch on warning"). Our warning system was (and is) good enough to provide a ten- to fifteen-minute warning, and our Minuteman missiles can be launched in less than a minute. (I have substantial concerns that we continue to sustain a "launch on warning" capability now that the Cold War has ended—an issue I take up later when I argue that we should not risk the danger of a "false alarm" in the post–Cold War period.) But CPD argued that the president, even if he had enough warning time, would hesitate to give the launch order—that he would be worried (with some reason, as I would soon learn from personal experience) about the alert being a false alarm.

When I became undersecretary, I inherited the MX ICBM, a ten-warhead missile and follow-on to the Minuteman, that was already under development. In theory, concentrating ten warheads on a single missile makes it an especially inviting target for a preemptive attack. Under that assumption, the remedy was to find a way of basing those ICBMs that made them relatively invulnerable to, and able to "ride out," a Soviet surprise first strike. As it turned out, all solutions seemed worse than the putative problem!

Without doubt, trying to resolve this issue became the most quixotic and frustrating quest I had as undersecretary. From the beginning, we were inundated with proposals: basing the MX on airplanes; basing it on trains; basing it on trucks; basing it submerged on the Continental Shelf. Each such proposal was soon revealed to be very complex and expensive, and each had its own set of vulnerabilities. Although it invoked the gravest national danger, this scenario of putative ICBM vulnerability and the proffered solutions to it might strike people today as something of a farcical comedy, one set up by overwrought thinking.

Nevertheless, after much debate, we settled on a unique silo-based system. We would build two hundred MX missiles (each with ten warheads), but base them in forty-six hundred silos in the Great Basin spanning much of Nevada and Utah. We would conduct the basing such that the Soviets could never be certain which silos contained the missiles; hence the Soviets would have to target forty-six hundred silos, a losing attack strategy, thus reducing the likelihood of a preemptive attack. Not surprisingly, the citizens of Nevada and Utah objected to the plan.

Before the president gave final approval for the new MX basing system, he decided that the Defense Department would participate in a nationally televised public forum in Salt Lake City on the merits of the program. I was to represent the Defense Department. When I arrived in Salt Lake City, almost immediately I saw a poster depicting the state of Utah, the presumed location of the MX silos, inside a big bull's-eye with a mushroom cloud above it. I began to wonder whether I should have called in sick that day, but my excellent adventure continued. When I arrived at the convention hall, it was already filled, largely with Utahans hostile to the MX. The highlight (or lowlight, if you will) of the forum occurred when a Utah rancher who was representative of a citizens' group addressed me as follows: "We've degenerated into a discussion on what mode was the best, the land mode or the sea mode or the air mode and I'd like to suggest a fourth mode—I call it the com-mode."

At that moment I knew that the proposed MX basing was a lost cause. Deep down, I was relieved.

The next administration, not surprisingly, was highly critical of our feckless efforts to devise a secure MX basing mode, and, in their first year, they proposed a new mode: basing the silos so close together that the attacking Soviet warheads would suffer from "fratricide." Like the others, that approach was demonstrated to have serious flaws, so the proponents dropped it, finally concluding: "What the hell. Let's just base them in regular silos." This they did, giving up on attempts to reduce the vulnerability of the ICBMs to attack. That is probably what should have been done in the first place. The overall US deterrent force was (and is) so secure in its totality that the secure basing mode for the MX was an unnecessary "belt and suspenders" approach. I have always regretted that I let myself be stampeded by the prophets of doom into that unnecessary exercise. A postscript: after the first Bush administration negotiated a treaty limiting the number of warheads that could be deployed, the first thing to go was the MX, which is no longer deployed, even though it was our newest ICBM.

After a truly dismal experience at the infamous MX debate, I went to sleep that night in a Salt Lake City hotel, where I was awakened at a late hour by a call informing me of the disastrously failed hostage rescue attempt in an Iranian desert. I had not been party to the mission to rescue the American embassy hostages (or even briefed on it), but I was overwhelmed with sadness for the special ops forces lost, for the hostages not freed, and for my colleagues at the Pentagon who would take responsibility for the disaster. All in all, that day was without a doubt the worst day in my term as undersecretary.

In spite of the unhappy memories of that day in Salt Lake City, I continue to believe in the importance of the measures we took in those years to maintain the strength of our strategic Triad against the determined Soviet program to make their own nuclear forces more sophisticated and lethal. They played a key role in the continuing deterrence of a nuclear tragedy, even if they could never guarantee safety in the rancorous, often uncooperative spirit of those times.

But key American strategic themes in the imperative to prevent nuclear war were maturing. One was appreciation of the value of technology—for example, the triumphant elegance, pragmatism, and economy of employing the highly advanced ALCM to rejuvenate the aging B-52, an enlightened solution that suddenly devalued massive and costly Soviet investments in their own strategic forces. This deployment underscored the increasingly prohibitive expense to their side of the nuclear arms race, doubtless one more signal of the wisdom of moving ahead to balanced arms reduction. Another theme was the appearance of people who measured up to the enormous scope of the implementation miracles required to maintain deterrence, such as Ben Rich, who spearheaded the F-117 program, and Dan Tellep, who rescued the crucial Trident program, allowing it to take its place as the new and indispensable SLBM component of the Triad. And even if it has an ironic value, perhaps the almost obsessive doctrinal hair-splitting in the vulnerability scenarios of the MX debate marked a reduction of the authority of such thinking. Definitely a shift in strategic out-looks could be sensed in those days.

# 8      Nuclear Alerts, Arms Control, and Missed Opportunities in Nonproliferation

*My warning computer is showing 200 ICBMs in flight from the Soviet Union to the United States.*

—Watch officer in a phone call to Perry (paraphrased),
North American Aerospace and Defense Command, 9 November 1979

During my third year as undersecretary, I was awakened in the middle of the night by a phone call from the watch officer at NORAD. The general got right to the point: his warning computer was showing two hundred ICBM missiles in flight from the Soviet Union to targets in the United States. For one heart-stopping second I thought my worst nuclear nightmare had come true. But the general quickly explained that he had concluded this was a false alarm—he was calling to see if I could help him determine what had gone wrong with his computer. He would have to report the incident to the president the next morning, and he wanted as clear an understanding as possible about what had happened and how that error could be prevented from ever occurring again. It took us several days to ascertain that an operator had mistakenly installed a training tape in the computer. It was human error. A catastrophic nuclear war could have started by accident, a frightening lesson that I have never forgotten.

How great was the danger that this error could have led to a nuclear war, rather than be relegated to a footnote in the history of nuclear weapons? What led the watch officer to come to the correct conclusion? We can never know with certainty what was going on in his mind during those fearsome minutes. I have tried to put myself in his place and imagine what would have gone through my mind, assuming I was still rational after a shock of that magnitude.

I would have been immediately skeptical that any leader in the Soviet Union would believe that such an attack could succeed in disarming the United States;

even if the attack succeeded in destroying many of our ICBMs and bombers, US submarines would respond with thousands of nuclear warheads that would annihilate the Soviet Union—Soviet leaders understood that.

Moreover, I would have noted that the indicated attack was a singular event—that is, there were no other events going on in the world consistent with a Soviet leader being willing to take such a terrible risk. That line of reasoning would have led me to conclude that this was a false alarm.

These two conclusions provide an alarmingly scant basis for a decision of this nature, a decision made under the most extreme stress imaginable.

And while I was prepared to be skeptical of the putative warning, what if the watch officer had not been? What if this human error had occurred during the Cuban Missile Crisis, or a Mideast war? Had the watch officer come to a different conclusion, the alert would have gone all the way to the president, waking him, and giving him perhaps ten minutes to make a decision about the fate of the world with little context or background to inform that choice.

That is why I regard as seriously flawed the nuclear alert decision process— it expects the president to make this fearsome decision in minutes and with very little context. But that was how our decision process worked then, and essentially, still works today.

With such a decision process, a huge premium must be given to the context that informs the decisions made—by the watch officer, by the commander of NORAD, and by the president—and by their counterparts in the Soviet Union. Achieving context is one of the critical reasons (largely overlooked) for pursuing arms control agreements. Yes, a successful arms control agreement in 1977 could have put a brake on the arms race then underway, decreasing the cost of our weapons and the threat we posed to each other. But even more important, it would have engaged us in a dialogue with our deadly foe, given both sides a degree of transparency, and, most critically, given us context—a better understanding of our opponent—to inform the awesome decisions we were expected to make in a heartbeat. In my judgment, the context gained was far more important than the numerical arms reductions achieved. As long as the quantitative terms of a treaty "do no harm," the treaty serves a larger purpose in giving us essential context.

Thus, even as the Carter administration was strengthening American strategic nuclear forces, it initiated negotiations that would set bilateral limits on those forces. As exemplified in the 1971 Strategic Arms Limitation Treaty (SALT I) with the Soviets, arms control and disarmament activities had been cautiously progressing for a while. On both sides, the unsustainable psychology and economics of the growing nuclear arsenals were signaling practical limits. These realities were beginning to trump the Cold War spirit of suspicion and enmity between the superpowers. Accordingly, President Carter moved to reach agreement with the Soviets on a follow-on nuclear arms limitation agreement to SALT I, which had been in force since 1972.[1]

The intended new treaty, SALT II, would redress a major shortcoming of SALT I, which limited missiles but not warheads, a limitation that gave an incentive to the parties to deploy multiple warheads on each missile. While the ABM limitations in SALT I were a positive value, the ICBM limitations perhaps violated the "do no harm" principle in allowing this loophole. The Soviets had exploited the loophole and developed an ICBM (which we called the SS-18) able to carry ten independently targeted nuclear warheads (or in the strategic parlance, MIRVs), and the United States was responding with the MX missile, also able to carry ten warheads. So SALT I perversely provided an incentive for a signatory nation to increase the number of warheads in its nuclear arsenal. This outcome was leading to a potentially dangerous instability: if the Soviets could target a US MX silo with sufficient accuracy, then one of their warheads alone could destroy ten of ours, a scenario that arguably provided an incentive for the Soviets to launch a surprise strike against the United States.

After a long and sometimes contentious negotiation, SALT II was signed. It would need Senate ratification, likely a tough battle, particularly since the Committee on the Present Danger (CPD) had immediately argued that the treaty limits would make us more vulnerable to a Soviet surprise attack. My reservations about SALT II were just the opposite: while SALT II closed the MIRV loophole in SALT I by limiting warheads as well as missiles, the SALT II limits on MIRV systems were, in my view, far too modest, allowing each side to have 1,320 MIRV systems. Even so, SALT II represented a step in the right direction.

For the ratification battle, President Carter asked Vice President Walter Mondale to lead the effort. Mondale, in turn, chose Admiral Bobby Inman, the director of the National Security Agency (NSA) and me as his team to work with the Senate. Inman and I scheduled one-on-one meetings with every senator to begin in late November 1979. Senator Robert Byrd organized the meetings and participated in the most important ones.

Along with these meetings, a national debate on treaty ratification was scheduled on network television in December 1979. Admiral Noel Gayler, the former director of NSA, and I were selected to represent the administration; Senator John Culver of Iowa represented the Senate. Paul Nitze led the three opponents of ratification from the CPD. Senator Culver opened the debate with a stirring, well-reasoned argument for the treaty. Paul Nitze followed, and I was shocked when in his opening statement he flatly accused Senator Culver of lying. Not surprisingly, the "debate" then faltered and became anything but a thoughtful and deliberative airing of pros and cons.

As it turned out, SALT II never reached a Senate vote. In late December 1979, the Soviets invaded Afghanistan and President Carter took punitive actions. Cancellation of American participation in the Moscow Olympics was the best known, but perhaps the most significant was Carter's quiet withdrawal of his request for ratification of SALT II. (SALT II never went into force, but the goal of limiting MIRVs was addressed later by the first Bush administration in START II, discussed in a later chapter.)

In spite of the hopeful appearance of bilateral arms control and reduction talks between the United States and the USSR at this point in the Cold War, when I look back on those years, I see a historically all-too-familiar irrational, impassioned thinking, a thinking that has led to wars throughout human history, and a thinking in the nuclear age more dangerous than ever. This thinking drove the frenzied debates on nuclear strategy, drove the huge additions in destructiveness we made to our nuclear forces, and brought us to the brink of blundering into a nuclear war. It was a colossal failure of imagination not to see where this was leading. Even before the nuclear arms buildups of the 1970s and 1980s, our nuclear forces were more than enough to blow up the world. Our deterrent forces were fearsome enough to deter any rational leader. Yet we obsessively claimed inadequacies in our nuclear forces. We fantasized about a "window of vulnerability." Both governments—ours and that of the Soviet Union—spread fear among our peoples. We acted as if the world had not changed with the emergence of the nuclear age, the age in which the world had changed as never before.

But even so, the early arms control and reduction initiatives, while not always successful, did indicate the beginnings of a fresh way of thinking. This new thinking, thought by many to be naive, was instead quite realistic, given the context of the Cold War, a war in which nuclear weapons were being amassed in "overkill" numbers in a surreal arms race.

But another challenge in putting nuclear weapons in perspective was arising with the issue of their proliferation elsewhere in the world. Besides trying to limit nuclear arms by treaties, the United States was working to prevent the proliferation of nuclear weapons to other countries. The US made efforts to stop covert nuclear programs we knew of in the Republic of Korea, Taiwan, Iran, Iraq, Pakistan, India, Israel, and South Africa. This effort was fully successful only in the Republic of Korea and Taiwan. Preventing proliferation was not my responsibility, but conceivably I could have had some influence on our government's efforts if I had made it a priority. Focused primarily on the threat from Soviet nuclear weapons, I paid but nominal attention to the fledgling proliferation programs of other nations. Today we face a regrettable legacy of failed efforts to prevent nuclear proliferation; that spread is now much harder to stop than it would have been during the infancy of those programs.

There is much more to say about nuclear decision processes, arms control, and proliferation later in my journey, for like other facets of the effort to reduce the danger from nuclear weapons, they remain priorities. Such endeavors entail considerable diplomacy, and I needed to gain experience in that art. During my undersecretary years in which I took on the responsibilities of the offset strategy, the buildup of US strategic nuclear forces, and other military needs of the time, I found opportunities to accumulate that experience and skill, which would be of deep importance later in my journey. I took advantage of these opportunities through visits to key nations where I learned to deal with other people at the center of the nuclear challenge. It is important to recount some of these indispensable experiences and the diplomatic strategies that grew out of them.

# 9    The Undersecretary as a Diplomat

*On 1 January 1980, President Carter unilaterally revoked the 1955 Mutual Defense Treaty with the Republic of China—Carter had decided to play the "China Card" against the Soviet Union.*[1]

Since my job as undersecretary of defense for research and engineering did not involve me directly in political decisions, I tried to keep my work nonpartisan. I trusted that when the members of Congress understood that, they would more likely accept my testimony on its merits. Nor did my job, with three important exceptions, typically require diplomatic contacts. The three exceptions involved China, NATO, and the Camp David Accords.

Although its particulars varied among presidential administrations, the grand strategy of the United States in the Cold War was containment of the Soviets: the West must check Soviet expansion by enlightened and affordable policies short of war while patiently awaiting the eventual failure of the Soviet system from its internal contradictions. An additional strain on the Soviets ensued from their unrealistic assumption that they could indefinitely impose their stifling will on "satellite" countries as well as induce highly nationalistic communist states such as China and Yugoslavia to accept the leadership of the Soviet Union in "revolutionizing" the world. A primary strategic intent of containment was to limit Soviet adventures of geographic expansion and curtail military confrontations with the West, thereby serving the goal of preventing nuclear conflict. President Carter's semiformal alliance between the United States and China thus seemed highly appropriate to me; I was eager to help him implement it, and I soon got my chance.

I was sent to China by President Carter as part of his agreement to help that nation modernize its conventional military forces. I was to be shown their military equipment and manufacturing capability, after which I would recommend a program to accomplish that objective. I assembled an impressive team, including high-ranking military officers from each of the services and experts from the most relevant technologies. We were received by a comparable Chinese team, which accompanied us for an eight-day tour of China's key installa-

Perry arrives in China as undersecretary to advise on
modernization of conventional military forces, October 1980.
From the archives of General Dynamics C4 Systems Inc.

tions, from the tank factory in Inner Mongolia to the missile test range in the
Gobi desert.

On nearly every visit, the lab director or plant manager would begin with an
emotional apology for the backward state of his facility as caused by the Cultural Revolution. I would respond by asking him what he was doing during the
Cultural Revolution. Always the answer was a variation on: "I was sent to a pig
farm to be re-educated through physical labor." A few broke down in tears. Toward the end of our trip, I asked the same question to the young Chinese major
who had been my interpreter. He hesitated a few moments, and then told me
that he had been a Red Guard at the beginning of the Cultural Revolution but
had left when his ailing father was sent to a pig farm and, fearing his father
would die, he went himself to that pig farm to care for his father. What a heartening story of Confucian values trumping communist values. (Fourteen years
later, when I arrived at Beijing as secretary of defense, this same major, by then

a brigadier general, was waiting to greet me at the bottom of the deplaning stairs—it was a happy, emotional reunion.)

Shortly after my China trip, I saw the remarkable documentary *From Mao to Mozart,*[2] which depicted violinist Isaac Stern's visit to Shanghai at about the same time as my visit. An especially poignant scene is an interview with the director of the Shanghai Music Conservatory, who tells of being locked in a closet during the Cultural Revolution because the Red Guard thought Western music a corrupting influence. That interview parallels the stories of oppression told to me by plant managers all over China. It is almost impossible for Americans to relate to the incredibly self-destructive actions of the Red Guard during the Cultural Revolution.

My previous work in reconnaissance systems made our visit to the missile test range in the Gobi Desert particularly memorable. Over the years I had studied closely the development of this range through the excellent satellite photography taken by the United States. When we arrived at the range, it all looked familiar to me. When we were shown the ICBM test pad on which a test ICBM stood poised to be launched in a few days, I walked confidently up to the launch gantry and, based on my long study, gave our American group a tutorial on China's ICBM program. A week later, when I returned to my office in the Pentagon, I found on my desk a satellite picture of the same launch pad with a group of people standing in front of the ICBM, but one figure stood apart from the others. Some clever photo interpreter had circled the lone person and labeled the figure "Dr. Perry"!

My deputy Gerald Dinneen accompanied me on the trip, and he and I developed cordial relations with our two Chinese counterparts, as did our wives with their two counterparts. The four women became constant companions, and the other Chinese began calling them "The Gang of Four."[3] The Cultural Revolution was but a few years back, and at first it surprised me that the Chinese could joke about those bad times; but I soon learned that the Chinese sense of humor is irrepressible.

Our final assessment was that Chinese labs and factories were too far behind those of the United States for a useful transfer of technology. We recommended that China first build up its civilian technology capability, especially in electronics, so that in a decade we would be better able to work together effectively. They did so with a skill and determination the world has come to identify with China; but after the massacre of Chinese civilians in Tiananmen

Square in 1989, the US was no longer willing to share military technology with China.

My exposure to diplomacy in NATO was a considerably different experience from that in China. As the US defense acquisition executive, I had substantial dealings with the acquisition executives of other NATO nations, dealings both political and diplomatic. We met twice a year in Brussels to deal with acquisition issues affecting the nations in the NATO alliance in their countering presence to the Warsaw Pact military forces led by the Soviets. At bottom, the goal was enhancement and maintenance of NATO military readiness.

NATO's deterrence posture, a crucial part of overall deterrence in the Cold War, depended importantly on showing an effective ability of NATO forces to operate jointly in the field. Hence the major acquisition-related issue for NATO military operations was to ensure interoperability among the multinational forces, most obviously in communication systems and ammunition stores. But even though we needed to communicate readily with one another in battle, each NATO nation had designed its own military communication system, one that might not operate at the same frequency or modulation as those of other NATO nations. It was all too familiar old-fashioned thinking that needed to change. Convincing each nation to make the necessary compromises for effective intercommunications became a high priority. And the same need for interoperability also applied to common stores, such as fuel and ammunition. The problem of military force interoperability has been constant in history. An historic example: the Duke of Wellington came close to losing the Battle of Waterloo because his allies were unable to use each other's ammunition.

Efficient defense acquisitions were also vital in NATO. Were each nation to design its own fighter aircraft or air-to-air missiles, R&D expenditures would grow much more costly as a result of the substantial redundancy, and no nation would enjoy the cost benefits of large production runs. The United States typically took the position that all NATO nations should buy US military systems to obtain the lowest unit cost for everybody, owing to our large production base. Not surprisingly, other NATO nations did not embrace this approach, and a lively competition ensued that created high unit costs for every alliance member. In my role as the US acquisition executive, I tried a new approach, proposing that we agree on what I called a "family of weapons." For example, the United States would build the long-range air-to-air missiles to be used by all NATO nations; in turn, the European nations would form a team to design and build the short-range air-to-air missiles to be used throughout the alliance, including by the US. After prolonged discussion, the idea took hold, and by the end of my third year as undersecretary, NATO nations were moving forward on that plan. But a year after I left office, the plan, having lost its champion, gradually faded as the old, inefficient ways of acquisition again became the norm. It was, however, a crucial learning experience, introducing me to the art of diplomacy with other nations, singly and in large groups. And it dramatically reinforced to me the need for cooperation among nations in dealing with the existential demands of the nuclear era. After all, NATO interoperability is vital to a successful deterrent in Europe, not only an economic benefit. Cooperation at many levels and in many forms must become a byword, a principle of policy, in keeping nuclear weapons from being used.

I also participated in an instance of more traditional diplomacy, and I learned from it yet again the heartening ability of humans to cooperate and rebuild, even in the face of great destruction and conflict. Here I was a close witness to, and closely involved in the follow-up to, the Camp David Accords, the landmark diplomacy of the Carter administration. I well remember the somber air when I visited the Oval Office during President Carter's negotiations with Egyptian president Sadat and Israeli prime minister Begin (my visit to advise the president on one aspect of the negotiation). President Carter later confided to me that he had never met a more stubborn negotiator than Prime Minister Begin. But I can remember even more vividly the thrill I felt when I went out to Andrews Air Base late one evening to greet the president when he returned from the Middle East, having made a breakthrough in the discussions with Egypt and Israel. This was the only real peace treaty ever achieved in the Middle East, and I have always believed that it never would have been achieved without Carter's tenacious and creative diplomacy. Certainly he should have received a Nobel Prize for his successful diplomacy there.

A few days after his return, President Carter held a reception in the White House for Egyptian and Israeli leaders; prior to that reception, Secretary Brown held one for the defense ministers of Egypt and Israel. I was at Brown's reception, talking with Ezer Weizman, the Israeli minister of defense, when General Kamal Ali, the Egyptian minister of defense, walked into the room. Weizman went over and greeted him, brought him back, and said to me, "I'd like you to meet General Ali. He's a tough old buzzard. We shot him down three times, but he kept coming back!" Weizman and Ali formed a strong bond at that time that lasted the rest of their lives. These two men, more than any others, made the peace agreement work in practice. At that reception I discovered one reason

Weizman was so dedicated to keeping the peace. His son, also there, who had suffered a severe head wound in the Yom Kippur War, had a metal plate in his head and experienced some cognitive disabilities. So I understood the authenticity of Weizman's words to Ali, when he said, "We've had three wars that have inflicted terrible costs on our people, especially our young people, and we must not have another one."

The peace treaty called for supporting both Israel and Egypt with US military equipment, and I was directed to visit both countries and work out the details. I went to Egypt first and worked intensively with General Mohammed Hussein Tantawi, who was the minister of defense production. (When I visited Egypt in 1995 as defense secretary, Tantawi was the minister of defense, and in 2012, after the Arab Spring uprisings, he was acting head of state prior to the election of a new president.) The meetings were businesslike and productive, and the Egyptian military was grateful to have access to the superior technology enjoyed by the US military. I then went to Israel and easily worked out the details for cooperation. But all the Israelis really wanted to talk about was what it was like in Egypt! They were all eager to visit Cairo, an unthinkable trip for them before now. I was deeply impressed with how quickly people can change from accepting lifelong enmity to seizing the opportunity for friendship.

These three missions allowed me to broaden my own knowledge and skills in important ways. In my ongoing journey to reduce the danger from nuclear weapons, I had been working in different ways to support the abiding imperative of risk reduction: I had been a witness in Japan to the radical new destructiveness; I had been an entrepreneur/spy developing technological reconnaissance essential to monitoring and sizing the secretive growing Soviet nuclear arsenal; and I had been a strategist and "weaponeer" in revamping our battlefield prowess to block Soviet attempts to hold superiority in conflicts. It was becoming clearer that as the superpowers pragmatically intensified their bilateral dialogue to cope with the specter of the costly and dangerous nuclear arms race, there would be increasing communication and cooperation—in short, a call for diplomacy—to mark the changing geopolitical relationship between Moscow and Washington. Diplomatic experience would be vital.

As I will explain later, the diplomatic skills that I began to develop on these three missions, and that I developed further during the 1980s, would be invaluable when I became the secretary of defense and continually put in demanding and complex new situations presenting intense challenges in diplomacy.

But now I was to enter a phase of my journey in which the essential quality seemed to be irony. President Carter was denied a second term, and I returned to life outside the government and beyond its power to make and implement policy. The irony lay in what turned out to be a rich and many-sided civilian experience, which now seems indispensable in sustaining my mission to diminish the danger from nuclear weapons. I stood aside and reflected on what I had learned in the whirl of the Pentagon. I entered the public debates on the great nuclear weapons questions of the day such as the Strategic Defense Initiative; I returned to academic life and encountered students and learned much from them that is crucial if that day is to come when the world is no longer threatened by nuclear weapons; I pursued informal but important nuclear diplomacy in many parts of the world, meeting government officials and influential experts who would be of invaluable help in later years in the continuing quest to mitigate the nuclear danger when I returned to the Pentagon as defense secretary; I met like-minded experts who would join me in the quest for reducing the nuclear peril; and I experienced tangibly the changing episodes of my journey as the Soviet Union passed into history and the Cold War ended, bringing in a new period with its own powerful dynamics—both opportunities and dangers—in the nuclear crisis.

# 10 Back in Civilian Life: The Cold War Ends, but the Nuclear Journey Continues

*I call upon the scientific community in our country, those who gave us nuclear weapons . . . to give us the means of rendering these nuclear weapons impotent and obsolete.*[1]

—President Reagan, 23 March 1983

After President Carter's decisive defeat for re-election, Lee and I once again made the drive across the country to California, the place we had come to call home. If I had any doubts that I would continue my journey at the nuclear brink, they were quickly dispelled.

First, a proposal (the Strategic Defense Initiative) was made to devise a new "defense" against a nuclear attack, a proposal I quickly gave a bad review. Second, I began a concentrated and wide-ranging unofficial diplomacy on the nuclear threat with prominent Soviets and others around the world, an emerging diplomatic environment that seemed one harbinger of the beginnings of a new spirit and way of thinking to reduce the danger. Third, I now had welcome time to think and teach about the changing dynamics of the nuclear crisis. And fourth, I lost no opportunity to stay abreast of new and salient technology.

After we had returned to California, Lee rejoined her former CPA firm, and just in time to help with 1980 tax returns. ESL, the company I had founded, was now owned by TRW, and since I had just been in charge of defense acquisition, I did not want to go to work for a major defense company whose success could depend on defense programs that I had started. Instead I joined an investment-banking firm, Hambrecht & Quist, in San Francisco. A small high-tech investment banker, H&Q had taken ESL public many years before, and George Quist had been on the ESL board of directors until its sale to TRW. I believed that my experience at the Pentagon assessing and applying high technology would benefit H&Q's small but influential venture capital business focused on innovative technology (even though very few of their investments were in the defense field).

I was also approached by Professor John Lewis, the codirector of the Center for International Security and Arms Control (CISAC, now called the Center for International Security and Cooperation) at Stanford, and I agreed to become a part-time senior fellow at the center. Two of my degrees were from Stanford, one of the great universities in the world, and I was excited by the idea of joining CISAC, where I could continue to refine my thinking about national security and the nuclear weapons issue. At Stanford I created a new course called "The Role of Technology in National Security." Throughout history technology has been crucial in national security, but of course never before had it changed at the dizzying pace I had witnessed from my late teens, as a soldier in Okinawa, to my early fifties, when I was responsible for accelerating that pace. Influenced in my graduate years at Stanford by the brilliant mathematician Professor George Pólya and by my own experiences as a university lecturer, I had once thought of a teaching career in theoretical mathematics; but now, among a small elite who had confronted the looming nuclear danger, I saw the importance of bringing a perspective into the classroom about that real-world challenge, especially among the young who would soon confront it.

I also became active in an important and growing form of diplomacy called Track 2, a nongovernmental international diplomacy complementing Track 1 diplomacy pursued by government officials. During the 1980s and the first three years of the 1990s, I journeyed to Russia nearly every year with a Stanford delegation to meet with Russian scientists and academicians. The purpose of Track 2 meetings was to branch out beyond official positions in hope of finding new paths government officials might later follow, a goal sometimes more readily achieved through a mix of informal and formal diplomacy. Such groundwork is not only important to the effectiveness of overall diplomacy, but in the context of the suspicious atmosphere of the Cold War, one of the few meaningful dialogues going on. But before I characterize the highlights of the Track 2 diplomacy, it helps to have a sense of the flow of those days by describing the sudden appearance of an old and familiar thinking out of place in the nuclear era and that intruded on my new endeavors. It would not be the first of these intrusions.

This new instance of old thinking—superficially resembling new thinking—emerged from the high levels of government and captured headlines in the early eighties. On 23 March 1983, President Reagan stunned the world by calling on America's scientists and engineers to develop a defense system that would make nuclear weapons ineffective. He said:

> I call upon the scientific community in our country, those who gave us nuclear weapons . . . to give us the means of rendering these nuclear weapons impotent and obsolete.

His speech was inspired by a new concept of missile defense based on powerful modern technology: a vision of Soviet ICBMs being destroyed in flight by beam weapons deployed in a constellation of American satellites. The project created to turn this vision into reality was called the Strategic Defense Initiative (SDI), almost immediately dubbed "Star Wars." The concept—the advanced technologies and their merging into a system—might have seemed dazzlingly new, but I knew that the ultimate goal of this enterprise, just as with the earlier ideas of jamming Soviet ICBM guidance systems and of perfecting a ballistic missile defense capability, remained out of reach.

Shortly after President Reagan's speech that inspired the Strategic Defense Initiative, I was invited by the *Washington Post* to write an op-ed debating the merits of SDI in which I criticized his proposal, pointing out that "If we spend two decades developing, testing, and then deploying a system to defeat the Soviet ICBM and SLBM forces, they certainly have ample time to consider, develop, and deploy a variety of countermeasures."[2] In a later scientific journal article I argued that in SDI, what is feasible is not desirable and what is desirable is not feasible.[3] My skepticism about the technical feasibility of the SDI carried a special weight because I had spent much of my career successfully applying advanced technology to revolutionary ends. I also pointed out a perverse danger from the SDI—namely, that a missile defense system, even if ineffective, could stimulate anew the nuclear arms race.

I knew that developing the high-powered beam weapons and the needed rockets and constellation of satellites would undoubtedly be extraordinarily difficult and enormously expensive, but my arguments about the infeasibility of the SDI were more fundamental. After all, its success would depend on a nonresponsive target. The SDI would be vulnerable to what chess players call "the fallacy of the last move." It would necessarily be built and deployed over a long period, more or less in full view of the Soviet military. They would form a relatively good idea of what we were building and adjust their offensive systems accordingly. Moreover, such adjustments would be relatively inexpensive compared with the SDI system, which promised to be very costly.

The Soviet Union had given us an historical example of this in the 1960s, when they built a very expensive, nationwide system of air defense. As we watched it being deployed, we adjusted our plans for B-52 bomber attacks by redirecting the bombers to fly over the Soviet Union at altitudes of a few hundred feet, thereby avoiding most of the detection radars of the Soviet air defense systems, which had been designed on the assumption of high-altitude B-52 strikes. Over a period of about ten years, the Soviets, aware of our change in bomber tactics, modified their air defense systems to try to defeat our new tactic. As I discussed earlier, the United States then developed air-launched cruise missiles (ALCMs) to be carried by the B-52s and to be launched while the bombers were still hundreds of miles from the Soviet Union and invulnerable to Soviet air defenses. The air-launched missiles would not only fly over the Soviet Union at an altitude of 200 feet, but they would present very low radar signatures (unlike the large and nonstealthy B-52s that were built in an earlier period), which would defeat the detection and target-acquisition capabilities of Soviet radars. These relatively inexpensive modifications to our B-52 strike tactics and weapon delivery modes almost entirely nullified any effectiveness of the massive and costly Soviet air defense system. Thus we were able to extend the lifetime of the aging B-52 force until it could be replaced by a bomber capable of defeating the Soviet air defense system (which was to be the B-2).

As I have recounted, my thinking about offense versus defense in the nuclear era had already changed years before, when I had both observed and personally determined through my own calculations the sobering limits to "damage-reduction" through defensive systems. Offensive systems, and most disastrously in the nuclear era, have a fundamental advantage, especially when the offensive system is designed to be used only once. When the US World War II bomber force had to fly repeated missions over the same German targets, the Germans had time to adapt their air defense systems to changes in our offensive strategies, and the Germans exacted heavy losses on our bomber forces. But even then, the attrition rates obtained by a good air defense system were in the range of 4 to 8 percent. Since our bombers had to make repeated flights over their targets, this loss rate was devastating for the pilots and crews: few would survive to reach the service quota of flying twenty-five missions. But in a nuclear war with an ICBM attack of one or two sorties, an air defense system that shoots down only 10 percent of the attackers is catastrophically inadequate. To be effective against an ICBM attack, a defensive system must exact attrition rates well in excess of 90 percent—the first time! No historical data supports contentions that such attrition rates could be achieved by any defensive system in real combat situations.

I explained in my op-ed that if the United States began the SDI, the Soviets would certainly mount programs to counter it. And their most predictable strategy would be to try to overwhelm the SDI with numbers. The Soviets could deploy thousands of decoys with their warheads, thereby multiplying the number of targets the SDI must deal with, a huge problem of target-discrimination. And the Soviets could build more missiles and warheads, at a much lower cost than the SDI. So even if we never deployed the SDI system, simply starting it could precipitate a new and more dangerous phase of the nuclear arms race.

As it turned out, we never did build the SDI system. Yet the offense-defense dialectic goes on in the post Cold War in a different form, with the deployment of American ground-based BMD systems, stimulating Russia and China to build decoys and more ICBMs.

When I think of the persistent history of the forlorn idea of defense against a nuclear attack, I am tempted to think that the notion especially typifies Einstein's grim and painfully realistic observation that "the unleashed power of the atom has changed everything save our modes of thinking." It has certainly been normal in history to think of fashioning defenses against evolving military threats. But nuclear weapons, unleashed in a large-scale attack, bring a sure destruction, one so massive as to rule out any successful defense. Defense-in-conflict, a traditional mode of thinking, is here no longer plausible. In a nuclear war, the long-standing "norm" of reliance on defense has become a self-deception, a most human and understandable one, and one that is rooted in an aversion to the new reality.

⤳

Although events stimulated me to continue my thinking and teaching about the imperatives of the nuclear era, and my new life outside government gave me a good environment in which to reflect, I found that an essential experience that taught me much about future strategy was my diplomacy in the Track 2 interactions. During my yearly meetings with Russians through the 1980s and the early 1990s, there were many boring discussions during which the Russian delegates expressed the all-too-familiar party line, blunting the whole point of Track 2 meetings, which is to branch out beyond official positions in hope of finding new paths government officials might later follow. But I met some very impressive Russians and, most important, formed an intellectual bond with a few of them that served me well at the time and even more valuably when I became defense secretary.

I had already learned directly and indirectly about the possibility, and the great importance, of such relationships. I had learned this in my exchanges with Chinese political and military officials and technologists; in my dealings with NATO heads of state and prominent ministers and officials; and in working with former battlefield enemies among Israeli and Egyptian military officers. In the atmosphere of the nuclear weapons crisis, it *was* possible to overturn long-standing suspicion and hostility.

One impressive Russian with whom I became friends was Andrei Kokoshin.[4] At our first meeting I commented favorably on a paper he had written on radar technology. He was pleased to have had his paper receive careful attention, and we had a lengthy discussion. In later meetings we discussed many different technical issues, during which he explored ideas well beyond the party line. After the breakup of the Soviet Union, I arranged for a Russian delegation to visit Stanford, and Lee and I hosted the visitors at our house. I invited Andrei, whose English is excellent, to speak to my class—his lecture was a highlight for my students that year. I was always surprised at how easy it was to make real friends with the Russians I met. Each of them had been taught to be suspicious of Americans, and I had to assume that they would be especially suspicious of a former official of the hated Pentagon. Yet it didn't work that way. Once they understood that I would listen to their arguments and offer rational rebuttals, they got over their suspicion and engaged me on the merits of the issues.

During my subsequent years as deputy secretary of defense and then secretary of defense, I met Andrei on my every trip to Russia. He had become the deputy minister of defense and hence was one of my key interlocutors. Our long-standing friendship during our Track 2 period greatly facilitated the business we later conducted as government officials. As I will describe, the trust Andrei and I developed during the 1980s let us move very quickly on the urgent implementation of the Nunn-Lugar program for dismantling nuclear weapons left behind in republics of the former Soviet Union.

Although Track 2 discussions with most of the Russians were sterile throughout the greater portion of the 1980s, I noticed a distinct and crucial change in the spirit of the times around 1988, just a few years after Mikhail Gorbachev had taken office and proclaimed a new condition of "glasnost," or open discussion. Most of us doubted that the glasnost policy was authentic, but

I was surprised at the 1988 Track 2 meeting in Moscow by the vigorous, open debate. Most of the disagreements were not between Russians and Americans, but between various members of the Russian delegation!

By our next meeting, which was held in Tallinn, Estonia, the political atmosphere stimulated by glasnost had become intense. Ashton B. Carter[5]—a Track 2 colleague and Rhodes scholar who would go on to a distinguished academic and defense career and would become a close friend—and I both attended this meeting and sensed immediately that big changes were brewing. The Estonians we talked with were clearly contemptuous of our Russian colleagues, and spoke openly about their strong belief that Russians were "occupiers" of Estonia and that Estonia should regain its independence (which it had enjoyed in the brief interval between World War I and World War II). They exhibited this yearning for independence in dramatic ways during our visit. For example, we observed the first raising of the Estonian flag (which was strictly illegal). All of the conference participants were amazed when they saw the Estonian flag on display as we walked from our hotel to the conference hall. At every break we went out to see if Soviet authorities had taken it down; but they did not. Then that evening we attended a concert in which a visiting Finnish chorus ended their concert by singing Sibelius's *Finlandia Hymn* (which was on the program), followed by the Estonian national anthem (not on the program and in fact illegal to perform in public). The audience, many in tears, sang along with the chorus. There could be no doubt that glasnost was genuine and that deep changes, changes more profound than the Soviet government realized, were underway in the USSR.

I also visited China each year during the 1980s. The Stanford delegation was led by CISAC's John Lewis, a political science professor fluent in Chinese and then writing a book about how the Chinese developed their nuclear bomb. I was able to follow up on contacts I had made during my visit there as undersecretary in 1980, and I made new contacts that proved valuable when I returned to the Pentagon in 1993. One of the most important was Jiang Zemin, then minister of electronic industries. On one visit he hosted me for lunch and asked for advice on a program he was planning that entailed China's making a major investment in memory chips, a market then dominated by a few Japanese companies. I recommended against his initiative; he disliked that advice but followed it. (Subsequent developments in that market validated my advice.) At the luncheon he presented me with a poem he had written in Chinese extolling my supposed prowess in technology. Although the poem greatly exaggerated my abilities, it characterized the gracious hospitality of our Chinese hosts. When I was secretary of defense and Jiang Zemin the president of China, I was able to conduct official business more readily because of the camaraderie at the Track 2 meetings with him and other Chinese officials.

As beneficial as these exchanges were, our Track 2 meetings in China ended on 4 June 1989 with the massacre in Tiananmen Square, which not only stopped our Track 2 meetings but also ended high-level official meetings with the Chinese government for the next five years.

Besides the Track 2 meetings, I enjoyed teaching my new class, which had become very popular, on the role of technology in national security. My discussions with the bright, inquisitive students energized me, and I benefited as much from them as they from me. The most interesting part of the class for me was the students' reaction to my discussions of the Manhattan Project, Cold War false alarms, and the Cuban Missile Crisis. These events seemed to them like ancient history. But I had lived through the dangers of the Cold War and they were etched in my mind. I wanted to make those pivotal times vivid to my students, because that history—in many ways a radical and unexpected turning point from all before—could profoundly affect their lives. That teaching challenge was one of the many reminders of how much the problem of awareness lies at the center of changing the way we think in the nuclear age.

Besides engaging in Track 2 diplomacy during this period, I also served as a technology advisor to the government. I was a member of the President's Foreign Intelligence Advisory Board, through which I stayed current on significant intelligence issues. As a member of the President's Blue Ribbon Commission on Defense Management, chaired by Dave Packard, I was the principal author of its report on acquisition reform, "A Formula for Action." I was also a member of the President's Commission on Strategic Forces, chaired by Brent Scowcroft, and both Ash Carter and I were members of the Carnegie Commission on Defense Governance. This latter was one of several advisory groups on which Ash Carter was a colleague. We began collaborating both on our work with Russia and on acquisition reform. (That friendship led to our later working closely together on the Nunn-Lugar program when I became defense secretary and Ash led the Pentagon's nuclear threat reduction efforts. After we both left the Pentagon, Ash and I formed the Preventive Defense Project, a joint research program between Stanford and Ash's academic home, Harvard.)

These advisory roles, as well as my work serving on numerous high-tech company boards that kept me abreast of the latest in technology, were crucial in allowing me to "hit the deck running" when I returned to the Defense

Department in 1993, first as deputy secretary of defense and, one year later, as secretary of defense. The report I wrote for the Packard Commission became *my* formula for action after I returned to office.

Much has been written about the corrupting effects of the "revolving door" on the probity of government officials, but my experience in industry, in academia, and on government advisory boards was beneficial to the government when I returned to office. Another prominent example is Ash Carter, who has been in and out of Harvard, business, and government several times, to the clear benefit of the government.

When I was not teaching, engaged in Track 2 work, or consulting with the government, I was working with about a dozen emerging high-technology companies. The companies benefited from the lessons I had learned in founding my own company; I benefited from staying closely in touch with the latest in digital technology.

My prevailing realization from these activities was this: I saw more clearly that the over-riding purpose of my work was to lower the danger of a nuclear catastrophe, and so I placed a special focus on my Track 2 diplomatic meetings with Russians during the 1980s. I saw the historic changes sweeping the Soviet Union. The most remarkable evidence was the Reykjavik summit meeting. Over two days, 11–12 October 1986, in Reykjavik, Iceland, President Reagan and Secretary of State George Shultz sat across the table from President Gorbachev and Minister of Foreign Affairs Eduard Shevardnadze and, with no "talking points" prepared by their staffs, Reagan and Gorbachev discussed the possibility of both nations eliminating their nuclear weapons and delivery means. In one breathtaking afternoon that unbelievably bold move seemed possible.

In the end, the two leaders were not able to reach agreement—the major stumbling block being Reagan's unwillingness to accept Gorbachev's insistence that America's new SDI program be limited to "laboratory experiments." Even though the initiative failed, the two leaders did reach historic agreements on reducing nuclear arms, agreements well beyond earlier ones that had only limited the growth of those weapons. Most significant was the Intermediate-Range Nuclear Forces (INF) Treaty, signed in 1987, which abolished an entire class of ballistic missiles (those with ranges from 300 to 3,400 miles).[6] The INF Treaty was also significant because it allowed very intrusive inspections: for example, it permitted US inspectors to monitor all missiles produced in Votinsk, Russia, to verify that none were of a prohibited range.

President George H. W. Bush followed up on these arms control initiatives.

In 1991, he signed the Strategic Arms Reduction Treaty (START I),[7] which called for reducing the number of ICBMs and warheads on both sides; ICBMs were reduced to 1,600 and deployed nuclear warheads to 6,000. In January 1993, just before President Bush left office, he signed another Strategic Arms Reduction Treaty (START II),[8] of enormous significance for strategic stability because it banned MIRVs on ICBMs. Considering the well-known theory that a MIRV might "invite" a surprise attack because of the economy-of-destruction of one attacking Soviet warhead taking out a US missile (still in its silo) armed with ten warheads, the ban on MIRVs was seen as enhancing strategic stability by eroding any incentive for an "out-of-the-blue" attack. Hence this treaty solved the problem that all the MX mobile-basing modes of the past had eventually been judged incapable of solving. (Unfortunately, START II is no longer in effect. As I will discuss later, the Russians withdrew from the treaty and began building a new class of MIRVed ICBMs after the George W. Bush administration withdrew the United States from the ABM Treaty with the Russians.)

Mikhail Gorbachev had become the leader of the Soviet Union in 1985, and he initiated three major reforms: détente, glasnost (open discussion), and perestroika (economic reform). Détente was an outstanding success, as measured by the landmark nuclear arms agreements, and glasnost succeeded well beyond Gorbachev's actual intent. Perestroika, however, was a dismal failure. A few years after it had started, I attended a Moscow conference in which a prominent Russian economist compared the Russian implementation of perestroika with Great Britain deciding to switch over to driving on the right side of the road gradually: the first year for cars; the second year for trucks; and the third year for buses!

The failed economic reforms, combined with the Russians' heady embrace of glasnost, led to great unrest among conservative members of Gorbachev's cabinet. Those tumultuous days might well have led to civil war. I visited Moscow several times during that dangerous period and worried deeply that a bloodbath lay ahead. My most memorable meeting during that period was in Budapest in August 1991. David Hamburg, visionary leader of the Carnegie Corporation, had convened a meeting of experts on the Soviet Union, including Sam Nunn, Ash Carter, and myself, to assess the ongoing events in Russia and in the newly freed Eastern European states. He had invited two Russians: Andrei Kokoshin, my friend from earlier Track 2 meetings, who later became deputy defense minister; and Andrei Kosyrev, who later became foreign minister. On the eve of the meeting, a crisis broke out in Moscow. A group of high-level officials in Gorbachev's cabinet placed Gorbachev under house arrest at his Crimean retreat and seized control of the government. The "coup plotters," as they came to be called, then held a press conference announcing (falsely) that Gorbachev was ill, and that they were assuming his powers; they then declared a state of emergency. When they arrested Gorbachev, it is likely that the coup plotters also seized a primary symbol of his power: the "cheget" (what we call the "nuclear football")—the communication equipment needed for ordering a nuclear strike. If so, a potentially catastrophic power lay in their hands for several days.

Immediately after the coup plotters' announcement that they had seized power, huge crowds of Muscovites protested in the streets. Boris Yeltsin, around whom the opposition to the coup centered, barricaded himself in the Russian parliamentary building (called the White House) along with hundreds of supporters. Kokoshin and Kosyrev failed to show at our meeting, and we soon learned that they were among those who were barricaded in the White House. We feared for their lives. But fortunately key units of the Russianarmy refused orders from the coup plotters to storm the White House, and almost as quickly as it began, the crisis ended. Kokoshin and Kosyrev arrived at our meeting in Budapest before it had concluded and commanded the center of attention for the rest of the proceedings. It had been a sobering, frightening drama of political turmoil in a major nuclear-weapons power.

In December 1991, the heads of the fifteen USSR republics met in Minsk and agreed to dissolve the Soviet Union. On Christmas Day 1991, Gorbachev resigned and the Soviet Union was formally dissolved the next day. This historic dissolution was greeted with relief and enthusiasm by most of the citizens of the newly independent republics. But with independence soon came imposing economic and political problems for which the new governments were unprepared. On my visits to Russia and Ukraine in those days, I was appalled by the disorder and poverty evident everywhere. The elderly begged in the streets; middle-aged women hawked their furniture, clothing, and jewelry to buy food for their families; gangs of youths menaced pedestrians; speculators connived with corrupt officials to buy valuable state property for a penny on the dollar. Yeltsin, the new president of Russia, had no programs in place that could deal with these devastating problems. American economists were advising Yeltsin on how to create a viable market economy, but some of their advice was ill suited for the immediate Russian crisis, and in the turmoil much of the advice simply could not be implemented. Understandably and unfortunately, democracy was discredited in Russia during the 1990s, and many Russians still blame America for their problems during those days, even though the American advisors were trying to be helpful.

The breakup of the Soviet Union had a hugely important unintended consequence: "loose nukes"—one of the deepest ironies of our dangerous times. A Harvard team led by Ash Carter and funded by the Carnegie Corporation wrote the definitive report calling attention to this issue. They noted that the world was now "blessed" with three new nuclear nations: the Ukraine, Kazakhstan, and Belarus, inheritors of the nuclear weapons the Soviet Union had long based on their territory before the USSR was dissolved. Thousands of nuclear weapons now resided in three nations that had no confident way of securing them—nations that were embroiled in profound economic, political, and social upheaval.

This danger was immediately obvious to Senator Sam Nunn, who went to Moscow and met with Gorbachev shortly after the Russian leader had been released from house arrest. He came away believing that the danger to our nation, and indeed the world, was unacceptably high. When he returned to Washington he joined with Senator Dick Lugar to consider what they could do to contain the danger of loose nukes.

As Nunn and Lugar were planning their actions, David Hamburg invited Ash Carter, John Steinbruner of the Brookings Institution, and myself for a meeting in Nunn's office to discuss those actions. I had been leading studies at Stanford on how the United States could help Russia convert its giant military-industrial complex to commercial products to create an engine of recovery for the disastrous Russian economy. Ash's study at Harvard concluded that intense cooperation between the US and Russia was needed to deal with the loose nukes danger. The Stanford study likewise emphasized cooperation between the two nations as essential. It cannot be stressed enough that in those times both studies were counterintuitive in calling for immediate and deep cooperation between the two long-standing opponents.

Nunn, Lugar, and their staffs were in the early stages of developing a cooperative action plan, and, demonstrating bold adaptability to the changing dynamic of nuclear weapons, decided to seize this opportunity to resolve the loose nukes predicament. Ash stayed after the meeting to work with the staff to draft what came to be called the Nunn-Lugar legislation, designed to end the crisis. Two days later Nunn and Lugar convened a breakfast meeting with a bipartisan group of senators to get support for the new legislation. Ash briefed the senators on the new nuclear dangers. Nunn and Lugar explained their legislation to deal with those dangers, a boldly innovative procedure that authorized the Pentagon to assist the nuclear states of the former Soviet Union in containing the new nuclear dangers. Our military would provide funding and join in the leadership needed to end the danger from a large force of deployed nuclear weapons not adequately secured.

This meeting proved to be decisive. A week later the Nunn-Lugar amendment to the annual defense budget passed in the Senate 86 to 8. Shortly thereafter Congressman Les Aspin gathered the necessary support in the House, which passed the amendment by voice vote.

After passage, Nunn and Lugar set up a congressional fact-finding trip to Russia, Ukraine, and Belarus. They asked Ash and me to join them on the trip—as well as David Hamburg of the Carnegie Corporation, which had sponsored the Stanford and Harvard research on the effects of the turmoil in the former Soviet Union. That trip was deeply disturbing. We found that the loose nukes problem was potentially even more serious than we had believed. On the flight home, we all agreed that it would be profoundly in the interests of the United States to help those nations deal with the problem, and we discussed how to best implement the new legislation. Ash and I believed this preventive legislation enormously important in dealing with potentially the most serious problem America would face. Neither of us had the least idea that a year later we would have the responsibility for implementing it.

But the fates were arranging for my return to the Pentagon, this time as the second-ranking executive in the Defense Department. There were opportunities to reduce significant portions of deployed nuclear arsenals in the aftermath of the breakup of the Soviet Union, something not seriously imagined in the dark years of the Cold War. One of the most enlightened pieces of legislation ever to emerge from Capitol Hill, Nunn-Lugar, stood ready for implementation to remove the deployed weaponry in question, ominously referred to as loose nukes. The ensuing developments form a central portion of my journey, playing out in several episodes carrying from the early days of my return to Washington and on through an intense program to reform weapons acquisition and achieve the nimble military essential in the new nuclear era. After a year as deputy secretary, I was to become the secretary of defense and go on to lead the implementation of Nunn-Lugar, deal with a nuclear crisis with North Korea, the peacekeeping mission in Bosnia, and the coup in Haiti. It is a pivotal segment of my journey that follows.

# 11    A Return to Washington: The New Challenge of "Loose Nukes" and the Lurching Reform of Defense Acquisition

*Our first priority will be to remove all nuclear weapons from Ukraine, Kazakhstan, and Belarus during President Clinton's first term.*
—Personal goal set by Perry and Carter, February 1993

In January 1993, two months after Bill Clinton was elected president, I was speaking in Jamaica at a congressional retreat. During a pause between sessions, as I was discussing with David Hamburg and Sam Nunn the makeup of President Clinton's new cabinet, Les Aspin, just confirmed as secretary of defense, called me and asked me to be his deputy. I told him that I did not want to uproot my life again to return to government, but, after some discussion, I agreed to stop in Washington on my way home to meet with him. Lee shared my reluctance, but David Hamburg and Sam Nunn strongly advised acceptance, pointing out that I would be in a powerful position to deal with the loose nukes problem. They also suggested that the deputy could lead the defense acquisition reforms I had recommended in the Carnegie Commission and the Packard Commission reports.

These two challenges—loose nukes and defense acquisition reform—might seem unrelated, but I knew that both lay at the heart of the immensely complex mission of preventing the use of nuclear weapons. As knowledgeable insiders, Hamburg and Nunn clearly understood that both needed immediate attention. For senior leaders at the Pentagon, the two issues would simultaneously clamor for resolution in conflict with other issues important to them. Resolving that conflict would be neither orderly nor approachable in linear fashion.

In Washington, after a long Pentagon meeting with Aspin that left me unconvinced, I had dinner with his assistants, Larry Smith and Rudy deLeon, two of the ablest people ever to serve in government. When I was undersecretary of defense during the 1970s, I had worked closely with Larry, and had great respect for him. As the chief staff member on the Senate Strategic Arms Subcommittee, he had played a key role in keeping the nuclear arms race from spiraling out of control. Larry and Rudy re-emphasized, and strongly, the preventive imperative of dealing with the loose nukes problem, the grave new danger whose resolution admittedly was already foremost in my own thinking.

They too underscored the chance at last to reform defense acquisition, realizing that a nimble military acquisition capability is fundamental to the effective application of new technologies and innovative doctrines. Without a streamlined acquisition process, these other opportunities would be squandered.

Finally, they noted that Secretary Aspin had no management experience and needed a deputy who did. Smith and deLeon envisioned emulating the Pentagon leadership of Melvin Laird and David Packard, generally regarded as a highly successful defense management team. (Laird and Aspin had both been congressmen from Wisconsin; Packard and Perry, business executives from Silicon Valley.)

So Lee and I decided once more to pull up our roots in California and return to Washington for another four years. This separation was even more painful than the first. Again, we left behind family and dear friends; we sold the home we loved; I divested myself of all stock I had acquired over the previous twelve years; and, most costly, I surrendered the options I owned in several very promising companies on whose boards I served, an "opportunity cost" ultimately amounting to more than $5 million. Lee resigned again from her accounting firm, this time for good. I took a leave of absence from Stanford, planning to return there in four years.

As you might imagine, neither of my first two priorities as deputy secretary—implementing the Nunn-Lugar bill and carrying out the recommendations of the Packard Commission for acquisition reform—proved easy.

∽

The challenges I faced in enacting Nunn-Lugar were parochial economic interests and a widespread failure of imagination in realizing the danger in large numbers of loose nukes. Since the previous administration had authorized no money for implementation, I was starting from scratch. My first challenge was to find money in the previous year's budget already committed to lower-priority programs and request it be transferred to Nunn-Lugar. I was greeted with considerable pushback from the affected program managers and their congressional sponsors. But the secretary of defense has the power, if he chooses to use it, to face down such opposition. I was determined and I prevailed.

I had to organize a dedicated, determined staff that shared my vision of the importance of Nunn-Lugar. Ash Carter, nominated by Aspin as assistant secretary of defense for international security policy and the ideal leader for implementing Nunn-Lugar, left Harvard and came to Washington as a temporary consultant while his confirmation process dragged on. We both felt an overwhelming urgency about implementing Nunn-Lugar, and I allowed Ash considerable reach as a consultant. But there were ramifications. One of the civil servants in Ash's Pentagon department reported to a member of the Senate Armed Services Committee that Ash had "presumed the duties of the office," a cardinal sin to senators. I was notified that Senator Dirk Kempthorne was putting Ash's nomination on indefinite hold. Stunned, I was determined to fight back. I considered asking Senator Nunn to intercede but feared it might intensify Kempthorne's determination. Instead, I visited the senator with Jamie Gorelick, the DoD's gifted general counsel at my side. I began with a "mea culpa," acknowledging that Ash had indeed presumed his office but that it was my fault, not his. I explained that I had been trying very hard to get DoD moving on the immensely pressing loose nukes issue and had pushed Ash too hard for results—Ash was simply doing what I had urged him to do. I requested that Senator Kempthorne withdraw his hold on Ash's nomination and hold me responsible. Surprised, the senator accepted my apology and withdrew his hold; Ash, with key support from Senator Nunn, was confirmed later that week.

From this episode (and others similar to it) I understood yet again the need for raising the awareness of people about the danger of nuclear conflict and the over-riding need to prevent it. People's capacity to understand was there; the requirement was to galvanize them to think and act on it.

In the meantime, we had assembled a premier group of four deputy assistant secretaries who did not require confirmation and who could set forth expeditiously on the delayed Nunn-Lugar mission. All four members of Ash's Nunn-Lugar team were women: Elizabeth Sherwood, Gloria Duffy, Laura Holgate, and Susan Koch, all Russian experts and three of them conversant in that language (which Ash and I were not). During our first visit to Moscow attendant to implementing Nunn-Lugar, Ash and I and the four deputy assistant secretaries faced across the table the Russian minister of defense, General Pavel Grachev, and five other Russian generals. The Russians showed amazement at the composition of our party and radiated skepticism that women could

Perry meets with Elizabeth Sherwood, Ash Carter, and Russian defense minister Grachev in the Pentagon.

contribute meaningfully. When General Grachev asked me a complex question about one phase of the implementation, I said, "Dr. Sherwood will have full responsibility for carrying out that part of the implementation, so I will let her answer that question." She did—in Russian and in considerable detail. Jaws dropped on the Russian side of the table. The postscript: three years later, when we had successfully completed the last phase of the missile dismantlement and were having a small celebration with General Grachev, a Russian photographer came over to snap a picture of Grachev, Ash Carter, and me, but Grachev stopped the photographer and said, "Get Liz in this picture. She's the one who made all of this happen!" It was a gratifying moment for Liz—and for Ash and me. And in its own way, a parable of awareness and cooperation needed in the nuclear era.

⤳

Although my top priority was reducing the transcendental danger of loose nukes, I also had the responsibility for maintaining our conventional forces, an ongoing requirement fundamental to nuclear deterrence and that notably entailed a reform of defense acquisition. Here it is important to recall that as undersecretary in the 1970s, I had put my greatest energies into implementing our offset strategy, our goal then being to increase significantly the capability of our conventional forces to ensure the effectiveness of our nuclear deterrent in an era of nuclear parity. Now in the 1990s we needed to sustain the superiority of our conventional forces so that we could continue to maintain our security without the use, or the threat of use, of nuclear forces. We wanted to decrease the role of nuclear weapons (and their numbers), and we could only safely do so if our conventional forces were strong.

This principle of the interplay between conventional and nuclear forces is fundamental to deterrence in the nuclear era. The dangerous example today of the consequences of failure to maintain strong conventional forces is Russia. Given the decline in their conventional arms, the Russians are embarked on a major nuclear buildup and leaders have starkly stated that they plan to use those nuclear forces if faced with a security threat, even if that threat is not nuclear.

The biggest obstacle to maintaining modern equipment in our conventional forces was the high cost and long schedules entailed in developing new weapons systems. Our defense acquisition system was hopelessly inefficient. When I had been undersecretary during the Carter administration, I had the title of the defense acquisition executive, and I immediately faced a dilemma: our acquisition system was inefficient, and I had the authority to make improvements; but I judged (correctly, I remain convinced) that the intense campaign needed for top-to-bottom acquisition reform would erode the time, energy, and concentration demanded for the highest immediate priority—devising and implementing the offset strategy at the fastest possible rate to shore up a declining nuclear deterrence. Rather than giving my time and energy to reforming the entire acquisition system, I chose to work around it for the most urgent programs: the Stealth programs, the cruise missile programs, GPS, and several of the smart weapons programs.

It was an unhappy dilemma for me. I knew the traditional processes creating bureaucratic delay and how easy it is to overlook or downplay the importance of streamlining those processes. And I knew that we were entering a period of strategic uncertainty, which created a vital need for establishing a nimble, adaptive US military. The morale and dedication needed by the people designing and fielding the weapons systems, people we depend on and place great demands on, are well served by an efficient acquisition system. Even though this is a truism, nothing is more foundational to our ability to adapt militarily in an ever-changing, dangerous world.

Although I did not undertake acquisition reform when I was the undersecretary, I did learn from the success of the streamlined methods we used on the offset programs. I saw that there were proven steps that could greatly improve overall acquisition efficiently, and I looked forward to the time when I could implement those steps widely.

Between my two terms in office, I served on the Carnegie Commission and the Packard Commission, both of which made recommendations on how to reform defense acquisition. For the Packard Commission I was the principal author of a report entitled "Defense Acquisition Reform: A Formula for Action," in which we concluded: "Many have come to accept the 10- to 15-year acquisition cycle as normal or inevitable. We believe that it is possible to cut this cycle in half. This will require radical reform . . . and concerted action by the Executive Branch and Congress."[1] At the time I was appalled that Secretary Weinberger, who believed the system did not need fixing, ignored the report. Now it was my turn.

I soon discovered how much easier it is to make recommendations than to implement them. It certainly helped that my authority was greater than it had been as undersecretary and that I enjoyed very strong support from Vice President Al Gore, who was pushing hard to increase efficiency throughout government. But I needed the right team to carry out the mission in "A Formula for Action." I was joined by a very strong undersecretary of defense (the position I had previously held) in John Deutch (a position later held by Paul Kaminski). But I knew that most of the acquisitions were made in the services, so I set out to hire acquisition executives (assistant secretaries) for each of the three services—executives with extensive experience in defense acquisition and, in most cases, the components of our nuclear deterrent force.

I hand-picked a "dream team," worked hard to persuade them to accept (each took a significant salary cut), and then submitted them for confirmation. Immediately the White House personnel office complained that two of the three were registered Republicans. "Can't you find any Democrats?" I explained how few people possessed the essential technical and management skills, and that many of the most qualified were uninterested in taking a salary cut to move to Washington. Further, I argued, the jobs were technical, not political, and far too important to be reserved for patronage appointments. The personnel official I dealt with was unimpressed by those points, so I reluctantly told Al Gore that unless he intervened, the defense component of his efficiency initiative was imperiled. He did, and though the problem was resolved, we had already lost several months and we lost even more time in the agonizingly slow confirmation process.

Finally, by November we had the team on the job: Gil Decker (army), John Douglas (navy), and Clark Fiester (air force). Douglas was a retired air force brigadier general who had held senior positions in air force acquisition. Decker and Fiester had held jobs equivalent to mine when I managed ESL. All three had reputations as smart, honest, and outstanding managers; all lived up to their reputations. Three years later, when General Gordon R. Sullivan, the army chief of staff, retired, he told me he thought the best thing I ever did for the army was get Gil Decker as its acquisition executive. Clark Fiester, also an outstanding acquisition executive, died in a tragic air accident in 1995 while visiting an air force base. Art Money then became our third acquisition executive. Decker, Fiester, and Money had started their careers during the Cold War, as had I, participating in the reconnaissance-technology revolution that was a key component of deterrence.

The reform initiative reached far and wide. My last acquisition initiative as deputy involved the defense industry itself. With the Cold War behind us, the nation sought a "peace dividend" in the federal budget. At the beginning of President George H. W. Bush's term defense spending was $512 billion; at the end of President Bill Clinton's second term, defense spending was $412 billion—a "defense dividend" of $100 billion per year. (It is probably not a coincidence that during the last few years of that period the United States actually achieved a surplus in the federal budget.)

But I was determined that the spending decreases would not leave us with the "hollow army" that resulted from the sharp defense cuts after the Vietnam War, a most dangerous outcome in our times. Accordingly, we executed the military and defense civilian drawdown gradually (about 4 percent a year over nearly eight years, counting the earlier Bush drawdown implemented by Dick Cheney). And we maintained high levels of training throughout the military regardless of budgetary considerations.

I was, however, concerned that our procurements would become more costly if industry did not make comparable reductions, without which defense would pay high overhead costs because of excess capacity in the defense industry. I asked Secretary Aspin to host a dinner for the leading defense executives during which I would explain my vision of the defense procurement budget for the next five to ten years. I told the executives that they should not retain facilities and staff unsupportable by the budgets that I projected, since DoD would not support excess overhead. I was later told that at that dinner, Norman Augustine, president of Martin Marietta, whispered to his two seatmates: "Next year at this time, one of us is not going to be here!" Six months later, he helped fulfill that prophecy by negotiating a merger with Lockheed. Augustine is also reputed to be the one who dubbed this dinner meeting, "The Last Supper."

As deputy secretary of defense I had given top priority to addressing both the Nunn-Lugar program and defense acquisition reform, and was able to put in place many of the key people and processes to carry out the needed tasks entailed by both challenges. I was soon to become secretary of defense, and the vital early work to implement Nunn-Lugar and to streamline our ability to field innovative battlefield systems would serve well in the new, difficult, and important work ahead.

# 12          I Become Secretary of Defense

*I hope that you will not be overly apologetic about being soft-spoken.*
*Some of our illustrious predecessors on this planet were soft-spoken.*
*George Washington, Robert E. Lee, Omar Bradley, Abraham Lincoln,*
*Jesus. You stay just what you are.*

—Senator Robert Byrd, US Senate confirmation hearing, 2 February 1994[1]

On 15–16 December 1993, I was in Moscow with Al Gore, Strobe Talbott, later
deputy secretary of state, and Ash Carter, participating in the program known
as the Gore-Chernomyrdin Commission, which Vice President Gore had established with Russian prime minister Chernomyrdin to facilitate cooperation
between our two countries.[2] As the meeting came to an end, Strobe pulled me
aside to tell me that President Clinton had asked Les Aspin to step down as
secretary of defense. The president's decision had come to a head over the disastrous "Black Hawk Down" incident, in which eighteen American soldiers
had died after rebels shot down a Black Hawk helicopter during peacekeeping
operations in Mogadishu, Somalia.[3]

On our return flight from Moscow, Strobe, Ash, and I, together with Geor-
giy Mamedov, the Russian deputy foreign minister, stopped off at Kiev and
negotiated the Trilateral Statement with officials of the Ukrainian Foreign
Ministry.[4] In essence, the Ukrainians agreed to give up their nuclear weapons inherited in place after the breakup of the Soviet Union, the United States
agreed to help them in the complex and expensive task of dismantling the missiles and warheads, and Russia agreed to take the resulting fissile material and,
when appropriate, blend it down to fuel for America's nuclear reactors. (Today,
much of the electricity generated in America by our nuclear reactors comes
from blended-down fuel that had been used in nuclear weapons of the former
Soviet Union.)

The Ukraine weaponry was one of the most dangerous legacies of the Cold
War nuclear arms buildup. When the Soviet Union dissolved into fifteen independent republics, Ukraine inherited nearly two thousand nuclear warheads
that the Soviets had based there, most on ICBMs we called the SS-19 and SS-

24.[5] That made Ukraine the third largest nuclear power in the world, with more nuclear weapons than France, China, and the United Kingdom combined. The Ukrainians had no organization or experience in securing the weapons, and the country was going through social, economic, and political turmoil. We saw this as an exceptionally dangerous situation. Ash and I took as our highest priority the dismantling of those Ukrainian weapons, but there was substantial resistance in that fledgling republic to surrendering their nuclear force. Many Ukrainians feared that Russia might challenge their new freedom and that their nuclear weapons could protect them in such an event. The Ukraine authorities said their country would relinquish its nuclear weapons only if the United States gave it a security guarantee, which the US was unwilling to do.

The solution, conceived by Strobe Talbott, was the above Trilateral Statement with Russia and Ukraine. Crucially, and along with the provisions cited above, Russia and the United States formally agreed to recognize Ukraine's boundaries, which offered Ukraine some security. Ash and I assisted Strobe in working out the final wording of the Trilateral Statement with the Russian deputy foreign minister and the Ukrainian foreign minister in the early hours of the morning after we had flown in from Moscow. In January 1994 the three presidents signed the agreement, and we were ready to start the Nunn-Lugar program in earnest.[6]

Often radical change in history seems to occur with a surprising abruptness and sometimes as well with a quietness. After decades marked often by a stubborn impasse in a tense nuclear standoff between the United States and the Soviet Union and their "overkill" arsenals, suddenly we had negotiated a highly cooperative agreement among the Americans, the Russians, and a freed former Soviet Republic, to dismantle and convert a sizable force of nuclear weaponry. In its various aspects, the Trilateral Statement foreshadowed the changing nature in the post Cold War of the challenge to prevent a nuclear disaster and exemplified valuable principles to follow for success. First: the loose nukes problem was a portent of later global concerns with securing nuclear materials from being obtained by terror groups and other aggressive actors. Second: immediate, forward-thinking, adaptive, and decisive leadership was required at the outset to seize the opportunity in Ukraine. History had given us the chance to contain an emerging nuclear danger not by mutual fear but by classic diplomacy in which great care was taken that all parties benefited and were respected in their traditional national concerns—regional security, freedom as a country, and prevention of the spread of nuclear weapons and materials.

The hastily drawn agreement was soon codified. On 5 December 1994, the leaders of Russia, the United States, Ukraine, and the United Kingdom met in Budapest and formally signed the Budapest Memorandum, which formalized the agreement we had reached in Kiev. This memorandum was later signed by France and China. Under the terms of this memorandum, the signatory nations agreed "to respect the independence and sovereignty and the existing borders of Ukraine"; and "to refrain from the threat or use of force against the territorial integrity or political independence of Ukraine."[7]

(Alas, the spirit of cooperation that led to this landmark agreement did not last. Two decades later, Russia, with their annexation of Crimea, violated this agreement, with the lame rationalization that the agreement had already been violated when the United States, they claimed, instigated the popular uprising that led to the removal of then Ukrainian president Viktor Yanukovych.)

Back in Washington, I learned that the president had nominated as secretary of defense Bobby Inman, a close colleague of mine who had been director of NSA while I served as undersecretary of defense. I had great respect for Inman, believed that he would be an excellent secretary, and traveled to his office in Texas to brief him so that he could get off to a fast start after confirmation. In a bizarre turn, Inman held a press conference on 18 January 1994, and announced that he was withdrawing his name from nomination. Although I remained close to him for years after that, I have never known what was behind his withdrawal.

President Clinton called me in on Friday of that week and offered me the job as secretary. I told him I would discuss it with my wife and let him know on Saturday. Lee and I had an anguished discussion that evening and jointly decided I would turn down the offer. We valued our privacy and thought we would find distasteful the media attention that would follow our every move. Further, I had been able to perform the undersecretary and deputy secretary jobs essentially on an apolitical basis, but I feared that would be impossible as secretary. And though I was (and am) a Democrat, and fully supported President Clinton, I felt strongly that defense should be handled on a nonpartisan basis, and I believed I would be unable to avoid being drawn into partisan political issues as a cabinet officer. I called President Clinton on Saturday morning and declined his offer.

I had been closest in the White House to Vice President Al Gore, and he was aghast that I had turned down the opportunity. He asked me to come over to his residence Saturday afternoon to discuss my decision. We talked for several hours, and, in essence, Vice President Gore convinced me that I was making too much of the privacy concern. He assured me that he and the president would fully support my dealing with national security issues in a nonpartisan fashion. I found his arguments persuasive, discussed the issue with Lee once more, and decided to accept. So I called President Clinton again and told him that I would accept his nomination after all, though I would commit only to one term. The president indicated that he would announce the nomination in a few days.

On Monday I was at the CIA cochairing a meeting with CIA director Jim Woolsey on the intelligence budget. Woolsey's assistant entered the room and announced that President Clinton wanted to speak to me, so I left the meeting to take the call. The president's message was simple: he was holding a press conference in one hour to announce my nomination, and I should drop what I was doing and come to the White House. I called Lee to tell her I would pick her up in thirty minutes to go to the White House with me. Lee gasped at the short notice but was ready when my car arrived. I also invited the two of my five children who were living in the area to attend, and called to tell the other three to turn on their televisions. When I returned to the CIA meeting room, everyone stood and applauded—news travels fast in Washington, especially in the Central Intelligence Agency!

At the press conference, President Clinton took the podium, briefly extolled my virtues, announced that he was nominating me to be the secretary of defense,[8] and turned the podium over to me. I briefly acknowledged how honored I was by the nomination, and then the questions started. It was my first encounter with the White House press corps, and I was surprised that the questions had almost nothing to do with national security. Wolf Blitzer asked me if I had a "nanny problem" (referring to the fact that some previous appointees had not paid required taxes for domestic help). I said, "No." Andrea Mitchell asked whether I would continue Secretary Aspin's policy on advancing women in the military.[9] I said, "Yes." The White House media was unaccustomed to brief, on-point answers, and I was asked to expand on my answer. I said, "Secretary Aspin created many important legacies in his year—the bottom-up review, his work on all of the social aspects in the military; in particular his advancement of women in combat is one that I enthusiastically support." (Three years later, at my farewell ceremony, President Clinton commented that my answers were always made with a mathematician's precision, not a politician's artfulness. I took that as a compliment, but I was keenly aware that on occasion my direct answers had caused the White House some anguish.) I got through my first press conference with the best possible political result—no hits, no runs, no errors! As the president left the room, he gave me a big smile and a "thumbs up," and then my family and I joined him and Vice President Gore in the Oval Office for pictures.

We had been experiencing difficulties in obtaining timely confirmations, some of them being delayed for eight or nine months. But this time it was different. Senator Sam Nunn, as chair of the Senate Armed Services Committee, saw to it that my hearing before that committee was scheduled just nine days after the nomination. The confirmation process went smoothly, but it did include one surprise. When it came time for Senator Robert Byrd to speak during my hearing, he began by referring to a news article that noted disapprovingly that I was "soft-spoken." Senator Byrd obviously was not impressed with the article and intoned: "Some are born great, some achieve greatness, some have greatness thrust upon them. I hope that you will not be overly apologetic about being soft-spoken. Some of our illustrious predecessors on this planet were soft-spoken. George Washington, Robert E. Lee, Omar Bradley, Abraham Lincoln, Jesus. You stay just what you are. The reason you are going to get an overwhelming vote, if not a unanimous vote, is because you are you." Stunned, I wisely remained silent. At the end of the hearing, the committee unanimously recommended my confirmation, and the next day the Senate confirmed me by a vote of 97 to 0.[10] After all, no senator wanted to be on the wrong side of any of his constituents who might admire Washington, Lincoln, or Jesus! Lee had attended the hearing, and as we left she wryly asked me how Byrd could have been so sure that being soft-spoken would be an asset, since she imagined that he had little or no experience dealing with that quality in senators or in other cabinet officers.

Within an hour of my confirmation I was sworn in and assumed the responsibilities of the secretary of defense. The next day I flew to Munich to represent the United States at the annual European Security Conference (Wehrkunde). This would be my second opportunity to meet with my fellow defense ministers from Europe (the first had occurred the previous fall when I attended the NATO defense ministers' meeting because Les Aspin had been hospitalized). We took off from Andrews Air Force Base that evening accompanied by a few of my staff and a dozen Pentagon reporters. After we were airborne, we conducted what turned out to be a long press conference—it was the first opportunity the Pentagon press corps had to hear from me as secretary. By the time we touched down in Munich, I had gotten very little sleep.

I was met at the airport by our ambassador to Germany, Richard Holbrooke, who told me the headline news that the Bosnian Serbs had fired a shell into a Sarajevo market place killing sixty-eight and wounding two hundred. He then informed me that he had scheduled a press conference for me to respond to reporters' questions about the shelling. One of my senior staff, Bob Hall, could only see problems coming out of a brand-new secretary fielding press questions on this sensitive issue ("How will the US respond to this outrage?"), but given that the conference had already been announced, we prepared intensely for an hour. Bob's veteran advice to his neophyte secretary was, "Don't make news!" Fortunately, I didn't.

Although the conference was ill timed in being held just a few days after my confirmation, I used the occasion to create very early in my tenure working relationships with several key defense ministers and with Helmut Kohl, the chancellor of Germany. I believe that establishing trust is the key to effective diplomacy, and I wanted to start building that foundation immediately.

On the flight home, I used the time to cram for a congressional hearing the following morning on the defense budget. The cramming must have succeeded, because at the end of the hearing, Helen Thomas, a long-time reporter known for her aggressive questions, commented that it was the first time she had heard a defense secretary explain a budget so that she could understand the issues. I've never been clear as to whether this was a comment on my briefing skills or her listening skills.

On 18 February I had my formal swearing-in ceremony at Fort Myer, which my five children, their families, and many friends attended. No one puts on a more stirring ceremony than our military—the passing in review included colonial soldiers, patriotic music, and precise formations of marching units from all of the services.

After the ceremony, I hosted a long reception, the most memorable moment of which came when I met the army's senior noncommissioned officer (NCO), Sergeant Major Richard Kidd. He offered me a simple piece of advice: "Take care of your troops, and your troops will take care of you."

I had been an enlisted man, so Sergeant Major Kidd and I had an unspoken special understanding, a most personal one for me, out of a common experience. I took his advice to heart, and it was to guide me through many of the difficult decisions lying ahead.

Later in the book, I will tell you about how this new secretary of defense "took care of his troops."

*Top left:* Perry at age twelve, 1939.   *Top right:* Perry enlists in Army Air Corps, October 1944.   *Bottom left:* Perry during army basic training.   *Bottom right:* Perry in army reserves, July 1950.

*Top:* Perry with wife, Lee, and their five children, 1958.

*Bottom:* Perry as undersecretary of defense for research and engineering, describing a high-tech DoD program, 1978.

*Top:* F-117 stealth fighter. Photo by Staff Sgt. Aaron Allmon II, U.S.A.F., from Creative Commons (in public domain). *Bottom:* Sea Shadow stealth prototype vessel being tested in San Francisco Bay. Photo by Naval Sea Systems Command, from Creative Commons (in public domain).

*Top:* President Clinton nominates Perry as secretary of defense, January 1994. White House photographic office. *Bottom:* One day after being confirmed, Perry's first press conference as secretary, en route to Munich, February 1994.

(*All photos of Perry while serving as secretary of defense are by DoD photographic office.*)

*Top*: Press conference at Pentagon, 8 December 1994.

*Bottom:* Perry with wife, Lee, and chairman of the Joint Chiefs John Shalikashvili, as honor guards of each service pass in review, February 1994.

*Top:* Peering into an underground missile silo on Perry's first visit to Pervomaysk, Ukraine, March 1994. A Russian general explains details of the SS-24 ICBM and its protective silo to Perry (in dark fur hat).

*Bottom:* Russian soldiers extract missile from silo for dismantlement in Perry's second visit to Pervomaysk, April 1995.

Perry joins Russian and Ukrainian defense ministers to view destroyed missile silo, blown up on Perry's third visit to Pervomaysk, January 1996.

*Top:* On his fourth and final visit to Pervomaysk, June 1996, Perry joins Russian and Ukrainian defense ministers planting sunflowers in field where missile silos had been previously destroyed. *Bottom:* Sitovskiy family in front of their new home and garden in a housing development built as part of the Nunn-Lugar program to accommodate officers who formerly staffed Soviet ICBM sites.

*Top:* Perry and Russian deputy defense minister Andrei Kokoshin (*center*) visit Ukraine, April 1995. *Bottom:* An historic meeting in Kiev, Ukraine: the defense ministers from the United States, Russia, and Ukraine all join hands before discussion, 4 January 1996.

*Top:* Perry and Russian defense minister Grachev blow up an American missile silo at Whiteman Air Force Base, October 1995. *Bottom:* Ambassador Pickering (*left*) and Senators Nunn, Lieberman, and Lugar (*center right of Perry, l to r*) join Perry and Ash Carter (*behind Perry*) at Sevmash shipyard in Severodvinsk, Russia, to observe Nunn-Lugar program dismantlement of nuclear missile submarines, October 1996.

*Top:* Partnership for Peace joint military exercise at Fort Polk, Louisiana, 1995.

*Bottom:* "Russia + NATO = Success." Perry and Russian defense minister Grachev sign Bosnia agreement at NATO headquarters in Brussels, November 1995.

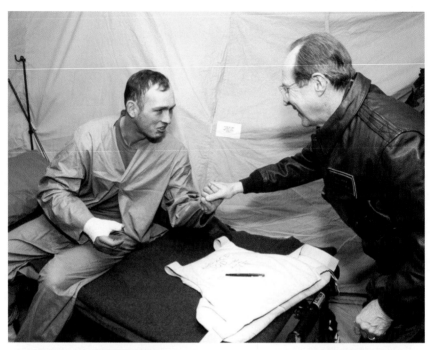

*Top:* Perry meets with US casualty from Bosnian campaign, 1996, at Tazar Air Base in Hungary. *Bottom:* Perry meets with submariners, July 1995.

*Top:* Perry talks with crewmember of USS *Eisenhower*, August 1995.

*Bottom:* Perry observes carrier landings on USS *Eisenhower*, August 1995.

*Top:* Perry meets with marine NCOs, December 1995.
*Bottom:* Perry meets with air force personnel in Saudi Arabia, 1996.

*Top:* Perry tours Khobar Towers in Saudi Arabia after attack by terror group, June 1996. *Bottom:* Perry with Senator Sam Nunn (*left*) and General John Shalikashvili at ceremony awarding Defense Distinguished Civilian Service Medal to Senator Nunn, 12 July 1996.

*Top:* Lee Perry, sponsor of the USS *Cole*, after its dedication 7 June 1996. The USS *Cole* was later the target of a terror attack on 12 October 2000 that killed seventeen sailors.

*Bottom:* Perry family with President and Mrs. Clinton after Perry's farewell ceremony, January 1997.

*Top:* Tripartite Korean policy team: Perry, Japanese ambassador Ryazo Kato (*right*), and South Korean minister Lim Dong Won (*left*) share three-way handshake after completing North Korean policy review in 2000.

*Bottom:* North Korean delegation with Perry (*second from left*) visiting San Francisco, October 2000.

*Top left:* Jeong Kim touring joint North Korea/South Korea factory in Kaesong, North Korea, 2004. *Top right:* Siegfried Hecker inspecting North Korean nuclear facility in 2008. Siegfried Hecker Photo. *Bottom:* Perry escorted across the DMZ by North Korean soldiers to attend historic concert in Pyongyang by New York Philharmonic, February 2008.

*Top:* Principals of the Nuclear Security Project: Sam Nunn, Henry Kissinger, Bill Perry, George Shultz. *Bottom:* Perry with students from the William J. Perry Project summer study, August 2013 (*left to right*: Isabella Gabrovsky, Pia Ulrich, Jared Greenspan, Daniel Khalessi, Hayden Padgett, Perry, Sahil Shah, Raquel Saxe, Cami Pease, Taylor Grossman). Photos by Light at 11B: Joseph Garappolo and Christian Pease, with permission.

*Top left:* Colonel Paul Kaminski was Perry's military assistant while Perry served as undersecretary in the 1970s; he played a crucial role in the implementation of stealth technology. *Top right:* Ashton Carter is a long-time colleague and protégé of Perry's; he played a key role in implementation of the Nunn-Lugar programs. Carter was confirmed as the 25th secretary of defense 12 February 2015. *Bottom left:* Siegfried Hecker has collaborated with Perry over many years in academic and Track 2 dialogues; he is currently senior fellow at the Freeman Spogli Institute for International Studies at Stanford University. *Bottom right:* Albert "Bud" Wheelon served as chief of CIA's technology development, and worked with Perry in the early years of the Cold War on government panels analyzing imagery of Soviet missiles. Photos by Light at 11B: Joseph Garappolo and Christian Pease, with permission.

# 13     Dismantling Nuclear Weapons and Building the Legacy of Nunn-Lugar

*The best money I ever voted for was the money that is now allowing us to work together to tear down these weapons of mass destruction.*
—Senator Sam Nunn, Sevmash Shipyard, Severodvinsk, Russia,
18 October 1996[1]

As soon as I returned from Germany and held my first press conference on the defense budget, I turned to implementing the Nunn-Lugar program. As deputy secretary, I had already arranged the necessary transfers of funds, installed a first-class team, and helped negotiate the Trilateral Statement signed in Moscow by the three presidents in January 1994. We were ready to roll! Ash Carter and I decided that to symbolize the importance of Nunn-Lugar, and to ensure the success of the weapons dismantling—its most dramatic and visible component—I would visit Pervomaysk, Ukraine, one of the largest missile sites in the former Soviet Union, which had eighty ICBMs and seven hundred nuclear warheads. I wanted to personally oversee the four stages of the process: removing the warheads to mine their fissile material; removing the missiles for reduction to scrap metal; destroying the silos; and converting the former missile field to an agricultural field.[2] Attendant to visiting the Pervomaysk missile fields, I would visit the former defense factory nearby where the Ukrainians, with our assistance, were making prefabricated houses for the Ukrainian military officers being decommissioned. Our goal was to accomplish this entire ambitious program in the three years remaining in President Clinton's first term.

We first visited Pervomaysk in March 1994. Our air force plane took us to Kiev, where the Ukrainian minister of defense, General Vitaly Radetsky, provided the helicopter that flew us to Pervomaysk. As soon as we landed there, General Radetsky led us through an armored door into a concrete bunker. There an elevator took us deep underground. We emerged into a dimly lit passageway that led to the missile control center that controlled seven hundred nuclear warheads, nearly all of them directed at targets in the United

*Nuclear Weapons and the Legacy of Nunn-Lugar*

States. At the launch console were two young officers clearly unnerved by the presence of senior American officials. But they had been directed to put on a "show and tell" for us, and they did just that. They proceeded through a practice launch sequence, stopping just short of the launch command. I had often in my career participated in simulated war games, but that had not prepared me for this experience. I was overwhelmed with the absurdity of the situation—watching young Russian officers simulating the destruction of Washington, New York, Chicago, Los Angeles, and San Francisco, and knowing that American missiles were at that moment targeting the very spot on which we were standing.

Indeed, never has the surrealistic horror of the Cold War been more vivid to me than at that moment. I stood among the first few Americans to witness the facilities and launch procedures that the Soviets had kept in readiness 24–7 for raining down nuclear warheads on American targets. The Soviet ICBM launch process, one I had never expected to see firsthand, was one dreaded stage in a full-blown attack. As I stood there watching the simulated countdown, I imagined what might have led to such an attack: it might have started as a result of miscalculation during a crisis; or because of a false alarm (such as I had personally experienced); or from an incendiary situation such as the US naval blockade challenging Soviet ships approaching Cuba. But even as I imagined those attack scenarios, my mind was riveted to that underground missile control center in Pervomaysk. And as I watched a realistic simulation of an ICBM attack on the United States, I also imagined the warning and decision stages in the US that would ensue. The NORAD false alarm of a Soviet nuclear missile attack I had experienced earlier in my career dramatized well the overwhelming decision scenario—only minutes to make what would be the most foreboding decision ever, and one that stretches the traditional idea of "rationality." That awful decision would likely be informed by a realistic understanding that there would be no successful defense. And it would be made in the full knowledge of the "overkill" size of the attacking nuclear force. The certain apocalyptic destruction on its way might evoke scenes of cities destroyed in World War II, but truly, the assault and its aftermath would be unimaginable.

After the launch simulation at the control center in Pervomaysk, we rode the elevators back up to ground level, silent and somber. General Radetsky then led us to one of the silos that contained an SS-24 missile. The large silo lid was open. We peered down into the silo to confirm that all warheads had been

92

removed from that hydra-headed missile. We were staring at one of the most dreaded weapons of the Cold War "balance of terror," now beheaded. The warheads already had been loaded on a train and sent back to the factory in Russia where they had been made and where now they would be dismantled. That was the bright side of the experience of that unforgettable day.

In April 1995 we returned to Pervomaysk to review the next stage of the dismantlement. We watched a huge crane remove an SS-19 missile from its silo. The toxic fuel would be drained from its tanks. The missile then would be transported by rail to a facility where it would be chopped into scrap metal.

We left the missile site and drove into a nearby town to see the housing complex we were building for retired missile officers. Ukrainian (and Russian) law mandated that officers discharged from military service be provided housing, but housing was not available and the Ukrainian government had no resources for building the needed houses. With the help of Senator Nunn, we had obtained a design for prefabricated homes from an American contractor and converted a Ukrainian defense factory into a plant for making them, its first task to provide houses for the retired missile officers.

We inspected the factory and then drove to the housing site, which was in an early stage of construction. The visit to the housing site ("Perrytown," so-called by wags on my staff) was one of my happier moments as defense secretary. Following an old Ukrainian tradition, we all sampled celebratory bread and salt. Then, again following tradition, Lee and I planted a tree at the housing site. An Orthodox priest blessed the site with holy water, and a delightful children's choir sang the blessing.

In January 1996, we made our third visit to Pervomaysk. The American team (myself and Ash Carter, Chip Blacker [from the White House], ambassador to Ukraine Bill Miller, and soon-to-be ambassador to Russia Jim Collins) was joined by a Russian delegation headed by Defense Minister Grachev and the Ukrainian delegation headed by the new defense minister, Valeriy Shmarov, who was also the deputy president of Ukraine. On that cold day of heavy snows, we were stalled at the Kiev airport for several hours waiting for the weather to clear. It was beginning to look as though the trip would be canceled. Finally Minister Shmarov entered the waiting room and told us we were cleared to proceed. We piled into the Ukrainian Air Force plane and took off in the snowstorm. Nearly an hour later we approached the landing field nearest Pervomaysk. In the continuing heavy snow, I could not see the ground as we made our landing approach—neither could the pilot, and he missed the runway. The plane tipped to the left, its wing plowing up a snow bank. General Grachev and I were both thrown from our seats and landed on the floor (there were no seat belts in Ukrainian Air Force planes). Somehow our pilot regained control of the plane and brought it to a stop. The badly damaged aircraft was still upright but not flyable. (The Ukrainians brought in another plane for our later return to Kiev.) We later heard that Defense Minister Shmarov, not wanting to disappoint us by calling off the trip, had decided unilaterally that it would be safe to fly. In the thousands of flights I've taken during my lifetime, this landing was certainly the most exciting I have ever experienced, or ever care to experience again.

After the excitement had abated, we drove to the site at Pervomaysk. The weather, besides being snowy, was cold and windy. All three ministers, wearing heavy coats and hats, were led to a platform that had three buttons prominently displayed—we were to make remarks and press those buttons. In that weather our speeches were mercifully short, and then we simultaneously pressed the buttons that sent a signal to a missile silo, blowing it up. Seeing the cloud of smoke arising from the silo was one of the most memorable moments in my term as secretary. Given that missile silos are constructed to withstand being blown up, we walked out to the silo and confirmed that it had been destroyed. We then held a joint, one-hour televised news conference discussing the historic significance of what we had just done. When I look back on that day, my dominant memory is not of the nearly disastrous airplane landing or of what was said by the ministers, but of the SS-19 silo disintegrating in a cloud of smoke.

Our fourth and last visit to Pervomaysk was on a beautiful day in June 1996. Again, it was a joint meeting with Minister Shmarov and Minister Grachev. The last nuclear warhead had left Ukraine for the disassembly plant in Russia on the eve of our meeting. The missiles, the warheads, and the silos were all gone, and the holes where the silos had been submerged were filled with dirt. We were about to convert a deadly missile field into a life-giving sunflower field. (To me, the sunflowers were symbolic; to the Ukrainians, the sunflowers were a cash crop.) We were each handed shovels and together we planted the first sunflowers. Later that day we celebrated a difficult and an important job very well done by joining in a three-way handshake. In retrospect, looking at that picture of the handshake, and reflecting on how much we had accomplished with a spirit of good will and cooperation, I am saddened to realize that such a scene and such cooperation are unthinkable today.

We then made a return trip to the housing site, which in the intervening months had been completed, and visited the Sitovskiy family, who had just moved into their new home. Two years later, after I had returned to Stanford, I received a letter from the Sitovskiys with a picture enclosed of the family at their vegetable garden and a note reading:

> Every time we gather the harvest we remember our warm meeting in Pervomaysk and the words you said: "I wish you prosperity and peace." We want to express our deepest gratitude for your efforts to rid the planet earth from nuclear missile fire. We hope that the seeds of peace that you planted on Ukrainian soil will grow just as wonderfully throughout the entire world. We wish you health, happiness, and peace to you and to your motherland.[3]

This moving letter symbolizes all that was good about the daunting project we undertook. It makes me all the sadder to realize that the spirit in which we jointly approached that project is now gone, and it is difficult to conceive of the circumstances that could revive it.

Three years earlier both Ash and I had set as our objective removing all of the missiles in Ukraine, Belarus, and Kazakhstan during President Clinton's first term, for there was a very real danger of backsliding in any of those countries, and we could not be certain of a second term. And we had succeeded against what sometimes seemed insurmountable obstacles. But we were tenacious, the skill and dedication of our staff were remarkable, and the Russian and Ukrainian teams working with us soon developed the same enthusiasm for the project as their American counterparts. It was one of the most gratifying experiences in my journey at the nuclear brink, seeing people rise above adversarial times and cooperate in the quest to lower the danger posed by our nuclear arsenals.

Of course, we not only dismantled former Soviet missiles; we also dismantled an equivalent number of US missiles. Russian defense minister Grachev had been criticized at home from the publicity of our visits to Pervomaysk—"You are letting the Americans disarm us, but they will keep their own missiles." So we arranged to take him to an American ICBM site and gave his visit wide publicity in Russia and Ukraine. On Saturday, 28 October 1995, Ash and I arrived at Whiteman Air Force Base with Minister Grachev and a host of American, Russian, and Ukrainian reporters. I had arranged for Minister Grachev to sit in the pilot's seat of a B-2 based at Whiteman. Since the B-2 was the newest and most exotic aircraft of our strategic forces, he was thrilled with that gesture. (Grachev later returned the favor by arranging to have me sit in the pilot's seat of their Blackjack bomber.) At the missile field at Whiteman, Grachev and I were stationed in front of buttons, and when we pressed them, a Minutemen II missile silo went up in smoke. The next day the picture of Grachev and Perry blowing up an American missile silo was on the front page of the *Washington Post* as well as newspapers in Moscow and Kiev.[4] That small gesture went far to ease the criticism Grachev and Shmarov endured for cooperating with the Nunn-Lugar program.

There are two epilogues to the Pervomaysk story.

Epilogue 1: The highly enriched uranium mined from the dismantled bombs was sent to a Russian facility that blended it down to low enriched uranium suitable for use in commercial power reactors, after which it was sent to the United States. This fuel became part of our Megatons to Megawatts project, which provides fuel for many of our commercial reactors. Said differently, the fuel for the bombs that were formerly aimed at targets in America now provides electricity for American homes and factories.[5]

Epilogue 2: The year after we planted the sunflowers, Ambassador Miller returned to Pervomaysk and, while there, collected some sunflower seeds from the fields we had planted and sent them to me. I was touched by this gesture and thrilled to receive them—it brought back poignant memories of one of the most significant actions of my life. I, in turn, gave some of those seeds to one of my grandsons to plant, a symbol of my hope that he would grow up without the threat of nuclear annihilation hanging over his head.

It is not a fantasy that we can greatly reduce the transcendental danger posed by nuclear weapons. The sunflower seeds were evidence that we had, in fact, done so—and gave rise to the hope that we could do so again.

⮑

We pursued other initiatives (which the Pentagon called the Cooperative Threat Reduction program), as part of the Nunn-Lugar program. Besides helping Ukraine, Kazakhstan, and Belarus dismantle their ICBMs, we also used funding to assist the Russians in dismantling their strategic bombers and submarines. On 4 April 1995, I joined Ash Carter and his team on a visit to Engels Air Force Base, across the Volga River from Saratov and about 450 miles south of Moscow, to witness the dismantlement underway there. Engels, well known to us from our Cold War studies of Soviet nuclear weaponry, had been the premier base for the latest and best Soviet strategic bombers, their primary mission to drop many hundreds of nuclear bombs on the United States. The

A Russian soldier watches over scrapped metal from "demilitarized" Soviet TU-95 "Bear bombers" awaiting recycling, April 1995.

bombers at Engels carried the biggest bombs ever fashioned. We never knew how the Soviets armed their bombers, but as I noted earlier, we did know of the "Tsar Bomba" with a yield of 100 megatons; a scaled-down (50-megaton) version of that bomb had been test-dropped from a modified version of the Bear bomber (TU-95), one of the bomber types based at Engels. We also knew that among the current strategic aircraft at Engels was the newest Russian bomber, the Blackjack (TU-160).

This knowledge formed our expectations as we landed at Engels. But when we deplaned, we saw what appeared to be a junkyard. Ragged stacks of scrap metal—once bomber parts—lined the runway as far as we could see. I was riveted by the sight. As we walked the taxiway, workers wielding electric saws were slicing wings and fuselages from bombers. The scrapped metal from the bombers would supply factories in Russia making commercial products. I wondered what the Russian workers at Engels thought about dismantling their nation's strategic bombers with tools provided by Americans—Americans who had recently been their greatest foes and had now come to observe their work.

After I tore my eyes from the scrap heap, I spotted a few of the modern Blackjack bombers—not, of course, included among the models of bombers being disassembled. I immediately accepted the base commander's invitation to inspect a Blackjack. Years earlier I had studied the bomber from satellite imagery taken during its test phase, trying to assess its performance capabilities—I never imagined I would have the opportunity to see it this close; indeed, from the pilot's seat.

After our inspection, the base commander hosted a reception and lunch, and I soon discovered that he meant to drink the American secretary of defense under the table. I immediately went on red alert. After the second of the vodka toasts in my honor, I invited him to meet my staff. He agreed, so I led him around the table, and one by one he made toasts to each member of my staff. By the time we returned to our seats, he had lost interest in offering me any more toasts. After lunch I made it back to our plane under my own power.

Our work on the Nunn-Lugar Cooperative Threat Reduction program initiatives continued apace. On 18 October 1996, I joined Ash's team on a visit to the Sevmash shipyard located at Severodvinsk on the White Sea. We escorted the three key senators who had made the Nunn-Lugar program possible: senators Nunn, Lugar, and Lieberman. We were there to observe the dismantlement of Soviet nuclear submarines. This dismantlement was technically challenging and environmentally dangerous because of the nuclear reactor on each of the submarines. Severodvinsk lies 30 miles from the port of Archangel, the latter used by the Allies to deliver more than 4 million tons of supplies to the Soviet Union during World War II, a feat crucial in keeping the Soviet Union from defeat by Germany early in the war. More than a hundred Allied ships were sunk and more than three thousand merchant marines drowned in the treacherous, icy waters. Winston Churchill referred to it as "the worst journey in the world."[6] That tragic history was in the fore of my thinking as we drove to the base. We arrived shortly after noon, but the bright sun was already low in the sky. Severodvinsk is near the Arctic Circle and in late autumn receives only a few hours of sun each day. The whole area was strikingly bathed in a golden glow.

As we walked onto the base, I fixated on a huge, rusting submarine in the dry dock and the towering crane poised above it, looking like a robotic Tyrannosaurus rex. These desolate hulks were the submarines of the Cold War that prowled the ocean depths with nuclear missiles targeted at the United States, and it was deeply satisfying to witness their dismantlement. The process was especially sensitive because of safety hazards with the submarines' nuclear reactors. The old, dead boats were in danger of leaking radiation in northern waters, a serious environmental risk. After some talk in Russia about simply scuttling the submarines at sea, the Norwegian government grew worried that dangerous radiation would wash ashore on their northern coast and urged us to do all we could to help organize a safe dismantlement.

To do that we had used funding from the Nunn-Lugar program to provide the Russians with some expensive specialized machinery (including the crane that resembled a Tyrannosaurus rex), and we wanted to see how well they were using it. We first toured the submarine being dismantled, then watched the reptilian crane swing large sections of removed plate metal from the submarine to a shearing machine that cut them into small pieces as readily as scissors cut paper. We entered a building that housed a machine being fed the many miles of wire removed from the submarine, separating the relatively useless insulation from the valuable inner copper. It is hard to imagine a more dramatic, real-world example of "converting swords into plowshares."

Russian and Ukrainian media accompanied us when we observed the Nunn-Lugar program in action. On this trip, Jamie McIntyre, the CNN reporter who covered the Pentagon, also came along to record interviews with each of us, the most memorable of which was with Senator Nunn. Seeing firsthand the stunning results of the Nunn-Lugar program, Nunn was visibly impressed, telling Jamie:

> I've voted for missiles; I've voted for bombers; I've voted for submarines. All of them, in my view, were necessary for our defense. But the best money I ever voted for was the money that is now allowing us to work together to tear down these weapons of mass destruction, and do it safely.[7]

After our inspection we met with the senior management of the shipyard and told them how important their work was, both for security and environmental reasons. I had thought that they might be resentful of being assigned the dismantlement task—obviously they would rather be building than dismantling. But we were surprised at the pride they took in how well they were performing this difficult and dangerous task.

Chemical demilitarization was also pursued under Nunn-Lugar. The ending of the Cold War left the United States with almost as many chemical weapons as the Soviet Union (30,000 versus 40,000 tons) stored in more than a half-dozen sites throughout the nation. Some 90 percent of the American chemical weapons have been destroyed, much of it after I left office. The few remaining chemical weapons, stored at two small sites, are scheduled for destruction by 2023.

The Nunn-Lugar program assisted Russia in demilitarizing the huge chemical arsenal of the former Soviet Union. Nearly three-quarters of the vast store of the old Soviet chemical weapons had been demilitarized as of 2013. Delays arose from a technical difference of opinion as to the best means of destruction, as well as out of the general confusion in the Russian government during the turbulent 1990s. Even without those problems, very real difficulties and expenses are entailed in destroying these deadly weapons safely. Still, Russia estimates that it will complete its chemical demilitarization by 2020.

A little known but important part of the Cooperative Threat Reduction program was directed at keeping the technology, as well as the bombs, from falling into dangerous hands. In the early 1990s, with the Russian economy suffering and with almost no government money going to the nuclear weapons labs in Russia, there was a very real danger that nations wanting to become nuclear powers—or even terror groups—would hire seasoned Russian nuclear scientists and engineers. In fact, there were a number of credible intelligence reports of such recruiting in Russia. To forestall this recruiting, we used Nunn-Lugar funds to establish a technical institute in Moscow that would employ former Soviet nuclear scientists in nonmilitary activities. This was a successful program that used relatively little of the Nunn-Lugar funds, but it may very well have saved the world from a proliferation disaster.

Besides our efforts in dismantling nuclear weapons, we also used Nunn-Lugar funds to gain better control over potentially loose fissile material in the former Soviet Union. Our intelligence was quite explicit on the extent of the danger from material, both from the weapons program and from research reactors (some of which use highly enriched uranium as fuel), which could be used for making bombs. In fact, the research reactors probably posed the greatest danger because they typically had lax security.

The most dramatic example of using Nunn-Lugar to remove loose fissile material from danger is Project Sapphire.[8] The project came into being after President Nazarbayev of Kazakhstan informed US ambassador Courtney in the fall of 1993 of a very large store of highly enriched uranium in his country at a warehouse in Ust-Kamenogorsk. The security at the warehouse was little more than a barbed wire fence, and there was real incentive for a terror group to buy or steal this uranium. President Nazarbayev, to his great credit, requested that the United States move this fissile material to a safe storage area.[9] When American technical experts got access to this warehouse in early 1994, they discovered that it held 600 kg of highly enriched (bomb grade) uranium—enough to fuel dozens of Hiroshima-size bombs. The White House assigned to the Department of Defense the responsibility of moving this material to Oak Ridge, Tennessee, with maximum secrecy and security. There it would be blended down and used to fuel our commercial reactors. Within DoD the responsibility for the project fell to Ash Carter, who set up a top-secret program, Project Sapphire, to secure the uranium, load it onto several C-5 cargo planes, and fly it to Tennessee. The project had to be carried out with maximum speed and total secrecy, because if a terror group or aspiring nuclear nation got wind of the existence of the uranium, they might try to snatch it before we could transfer it. Indeed, CIA had reported that Iranian agents were already on the trail of the uranium at Ust-Kamenogorsk.

Project Sapphire was a notable success, and demonstrates that our government actually can move swiftly and efficiently when the stakes are high, and when the project is being managed by capable and motivated people. The success of this project was the result of many people's dedicated efforts in the Department of Energy, the CIA, the State Department, as well as DoD. The organization and speed with which it was executed was only possible because of the existence of the Nunn-Lugar program; and it could not have been done without the full cooperation of the Kazakhstani and Russian governments. Still, I give the primary credit to Ash Carter for his leadership, and to his team—including Jeff Starr, Laura Holgate, and Susan Koch—for their competence and speed in planning and executing Project Sapphire.

Nunn-Lugar seems almost miraculous in the ominous history of the nuclear age. Given the foreboding times, the historic threat, the vital stakes, the precious opportunity to be seized, the imperative for international cooperation out of the common good, the dire need to demonstrate the plausibility of an idea whose time must come—the Nunn-Lugar program stands as one of the most enlightened congressional initiatives ever. Nunn-Lugar was brilliantly multifaceted, and each facet contributed to enhancing our security and finally that of civilization itself.

We worked very hard to take advantage of the unique opportunity afforded by this program, and we achieved truly remarkable results. The team headed by Ash Carter was exceptionally gifted, motivated, and energetic. But the final reflection must center on the innovative, inspired, and far-sighted Nunn-Lugar legislation and finally to Senator Sam Nunn himself. Because of Senator

Nunn's role in conceiving this program and, with Senator Lugar's assistance, pushing it through, as well as his countless other contributions to American security, some of which are recounted in this book, President Clinton authorized me to present Senator Nunn with the Defense Distinguished Civilian Service Medal. This was the only time that I presented this medal to a senator, and I was deeply honored to do so.

# 14      The Crisis with North Korea: Containing an Emerging Nuclear State

*Clamoring about "the North's nuclear weapons development," this war maniac [U.S. Defense Secretary Perry] spouted the belligerent, absurd statement that "America intends to end it even at the cost of causing another war on the Korean Peninsula."*

—Rodong Sinmum (Korean Press), 5 April 1994[1]

If time waits for no man, military and national security crises wait for no secretary of defense. They congregate and clamor. The linear presentation in this narrative of the crucial challenges I encountered belies the reality of multiple and simultaneous crises. Indeed, I had barely settled into my new office as secretary of defense when a dangerous crisis erupted with North Korea.

Since the Korean War ended with an armed truce, not a peace treaty, the Korean Peninsula, among the most heavily armed regions in the world, was surely the most volatile. North Korea believed that Korea should be reunified under its leadership, and through the years it had taken outrageously aggressive actions, most notably the Korean War, to promote that outcome.

This new crisis, stimulated by North Korea's move toward nuclear weapons, would test our resolve and our adaptability. Above all, it would require innovative thinking. A nuclear-armed North Korea would be destabilizing in Northeast Asia and could promote a spread of nuclear weapons elsewhere in the world. That alone put a high priority on this crisis. But showing the resolve needed for successful diplomacy would risk triggering another Korean War, and that diplomacy would be complicated by the fact that we had had no official diplomatic contacts with North Korea since the Korean War. So just a few months after I had taken office, it appeared that we would be confronted with a choice between two terrible alternatives: either let North Korea go nuclear, or face the risk of starting another Korean War. As I told President Clinton at the time, I feared that he might have to choose between a disaster and a catastrophe (of course, our real goal was to create a third choice, which in fact we were able to do). How had we gotten to this dangerous point?

During the first few years after World War II, North Korea and South Korea both had the goal of unification, but each wanted to be the surviving government after the unification. By the late 1940s Kim Il Sung, with major help from the Soviet Union, had built an army strong enough to defeat South Korea. At first Stalin refused him permission to attack, but after the successful Soviet nuclear test, and after the US secretary of state had indicated that South Korea was not within our defense perimeter, Stalin did give him permission, as well as additional military assistance. But, in fact, the United States did come to the aid of South Korea, defeated the North Korean army, and then, when the Chinese intervened, had to settle for a stalemate and an armistice, not a peace treaty. After the Korean War ended, the Soviet Union made major investments in rebuilding North Korea, and by 1990 the North was again a significant military threat to the South. But when the Soviet Union collapsed and the Russian economy tanked, Russia ceased aiding North Korea and became increasingly friendly with the West.

At that time, North Korea had about 20 million people, was desperately poor, but had the fifth largest army in the world: its army was over a million strong (twice as large as the American army!), most of them based near the border with South Korea, with another few million in reserve. This huge military force was deterred by a strong South Korean army (750,000) as well as American forces. The US forces deployed in Korea were a small fraction of the Korean forces, but they were backed up by highly ready and very powerful US forces in Japan, Hawaii, Alaska, and the US West Coast. We could dramatically and quickly increase our air power by flying in fighter aircraft based in Japan, Hawaii, and Alaska; B-2 bombers based at Whiteman Air Base could be over North Korea in less than a day; and the 6th Fleet, with a powerful aircraft carrier, was based nearby in Japan. Every year we scheduled an exercise called Team Spirit that entailed redeploying military forces to Korea and joining up with our South Korean allies. Our war simulations showed that North Korea would be decisively defeated should it make another unprovoked attack on South Korea. I think that North Korean military leaders have believed this as well, which has contributed to the maintenance of peace on the peninsula for the last few decades.

North Korea had never given up its aspiration for unification under its terms, but now saw that it could never hope to force that outcome with the Soviet Union gone and no hope of support from Russia. It was probably that set of post–Cold War circumstances that led them to try to make a covert nuclear breakout, understanding that they were outclassed in conventional weapons. And they were prepared to take considerable risks in achieving that outcome.

The basis for the North's covert weapons program was to be its "peaceful" nuclear power program based at Yongbyon. As a member of the Nuclear Non-Proliferation Treaty (NPT), North Korea had agreed not to make nuclear weapons, and further agreed to allow the International Atomic Energy Agency (IAEA) to inspect their nuclear facilities to ensure that they were not moving to a weapons program. But in early 1993, North Korea was in a dispute with the IAEA about special inspections that the IAEA was requesting in the belief that North Korea had already made a small amount of plutonium in an early refueling operation that had not been under inspection. On 12 March 1993, shortly after I took office as the deputy secretary of defense, North Korea announced that it was withdrawing from the NPT. On 2 June 1993, the United States and North Korea began talks to discuss the disagreement regarding the inspections of nuclear sites by the IAEA, and on 11 June North Korea suspended its decision to withdraw from the NPT. These discussions continued until early January 1994 and led to an agreement by North Korea to allow inspections at several sites. But in April 1994 (by this time I had become secretary), the diplomatic efforts stalled when the North would not allow IAEA inspectors to carry out activities essential to completing their inspection and certifying that the nuclear facilities at Yongbyon were in compliance.

What lay behind North Korea's refusal to allow inspections? The answer was disturbing. At that time, North Korea was ready to unload the spent fuel from its nuclear reactor at Yongbyon. If the North Koreans reprocessed this spent fuel, the resulting plutonium could serve as fuel for nuclear bombs.

By the spring of 1994, the dispute was reaching a dangerous level. Although the fuel was now ready to be removed from the Yongbyon reactor, the IAEA still had no inspection agreement. Alarmed, I made an unscheduled trip to South Korea and Japan in April. I had visited South Korea about a year earlier as deputy secretary, but this was my first trip as secretary. I wanted to discuss the situation with the South Korean president and military leaders, and to meet with General Gary Luck, the commander of all allied forces in South Korea. I felt the need to get a firsthand report from General Luck on how well prepared we were to respond if North Korea made an unprovoked attack on South Korea, as they had done in 1950. General Luck took me on a tour of our military forces along the DMZ (demilitarized zone), and then reviewed with me in some detail the long-standing military plan (OpPlan 5027) to repel an attack from North Korea. He told me that the American and South Korean forces in his command were well prepared and would defeat any North Korean attack, but that he could stop them sooner, and with significantly fewer casualties among South Korean civilians, if he were given another twenty thousand troops, more Apache helicopters, and a full Patriot air defense unit.

Impressed with his plan and recommendation, I agreed to move immediately with the Apaches and Patriots and told him that I would invite him to Washington to brief the National Security Council on troop reinforcements if North Korea did not back off its plan to make plutonium. After returning from that trip I made a public warning to North Korea that the United States would not permit them to make plutonium. This provoked a vitriolic assault on me from spokesmen for the North Korean government, including the assertion that I was a "war maniac."[2] On 14 May, North Korea, still not allowing full IAEA inspection, began unloading the spent fuel rods from their reactor, the final step before they could reprocess the spent fuel. This action brought the crisis to a head. If North Korea reprocessed this spent fuel, they could produce in a few months enough plutonium to make six to ten bombs, with consequences that were unpredictable but clearly very dangerous.

I asked General Shalikashvili, chairman of the Joint Chiefs of Staff,[3] and General Luck to update our contingency plan to accommodate the latest intelligence on North Korean forces, and to include a specific plan for dealing with the massive deployment of long-range artillery that North Korea had positioned within range of Seoul. I then ordered preparation of a plan for a "surgical" strike by cruise missiles on the reprocessing facility at Yongbyon. The strike option took into account that the reactor would have spent fuel in it, and even that it could be operating. Since our analysis showed no appreciable radiological plume, we deemed it "safe" to strike. The plan as presented could be executed with a few days alert and the attack would entail little or no risk of US casualties. But of course there was a possibility that such a strike could incite North Korea to attack South Korea, an outcome that could hardly be construed as "surgical." I can still vividly recall the intense feelings as Ash Carter presented the plan to a small group seated around my conference table, and the tension inherent in a decision of this import. So the strike plan was "on the table," but very far back on the table. We would proceed with diplomacy as our first and, I thought, best option.

The diplomatic plan was a classic example of coercive diplomacy, with the coercive element being a robust program of sanctions. Through Secretary Christopher's diplomacy, Japan and South Korea had agreed to join the United States at the UN in demanding that North Korea stop its reprocessing and allow the inspectors full access or face severe sanctions. North Korea's response was not encouraging: first they threatened to turn Seoul into a "Sea of Flames"; then they announced that they would consider the imposition of sanctions as an "act of war."[4] While this was probably a bluff, we could not simply shrug it off. The North Koreans, backed into a corner, might act in desperation.

I called a meeting in the Joint Chief's secure facility of US military leaders who would be involved if a military conflict broke out. General Luck flew in for the meeting, as well as the commander of our forces in the Pacific (who would be responsible for providing reinforcements if needed), the commander of our forces in the Persian Gulf (we were concerned that Saddam Hussein might take advantage of our distraction in Korea to start trouble in Kuwait), and the commander of our Transportation Command, who, in a contingency, would play a major role in rushing men and supplies to Korea. This heavily secured meeting took two days and centered on a detailed review of General Luck's plan for dealing with the possible contingencies.

During those tense days, an op-ed in the *Washington Post* caused considerable excitement. Brent Scowcroft, the former national security advisor, and his colleague Arnie Kanter (both long-time friends), wrote a column essentially stating that the United States would strike the Yongbyon reactor if North Korea did not verifiably stop its reprocessing. The key sentence was: "It either must permit continuous, unfettered IAEA monitoring to confirm that no further reprocessing is taking place, or we will remove its capacity to reprocess."[5]

Not surprisingly, that op-ed attracted a lot of attention both in the United States and in Korea. In reality, while we had a contingency plan, we were not planning to make such a strike. (Indeed, the strike would have required authorization from President Clinton and concurrence from the South Korean president, which had not yet been sought.) But I have always believed that the public call for a strike by Scowcroft and Kanter played a positive role in the crisis because it focused the minds of North Korean officials on the stakes in play. It is likely that North Korean officials wrongly thought that Scowcroft was speaking for the US government; indeed, even some Americans mistakenly imagined that I had encouraged Scowcroft to write the piece. For whatever reason, North Korea moved quickly to diminish the crisis, inviting former president Jimmy Carter to Pyongyang, where they proposed a resolution that Carter could relay to the American administration (there being no official channels of communication).

The crisis finally was resolved in the following remarkable, almost bizarre, way. On 16 June 1994, General Shalikashvili, General Luck, Secretary Christopher, and I were in the cabinet room to propose action plans for President Clinton's consideration. We were briefing the president on plans to impose sanctions on North Korea, to evacuate American civilians from South Korea, and to reinforce our troops. I began by briefing the president and the National Security Council (NSC) on OpPlan 5027 for responding to a North Korean invasion of the South, together with our options for immediately reinforcing our troops in South Korea; one option (the one I recommended) would add twenty thousand troops, an almost 50 percent increase in our deployment. The president was to choose one of the options, after which the new deployments would commence immediately. We understood that the troop additions might provoke North Korea to attack the South before our reinforcements were in place. Given that such an attack might also be provoked by the sanctions alone, I proposed to delay the sanctions by a few weeks while we got the reinforcements deployed. The new forces would increase our deterrence of North Korea and, if deterrence was not successful, would afford us the best chance of blunting a North Korean attack before it reached Seoul, the capital of South Korea, only an hour's drive from the closest point of the DMZ.

Just as the president was about to decide which reinforcement option to approve, an aide came breathlessly into the room to report that Jimmy Carter was calling the president from Pyongyang. National Security Advisor Anthony Lake was sent to take the call, and in minutes we learned that Carter had reported that North Korea was willing to negotiate their plans to reprocess the fuel if we would suspend our actions (sanctions and troop reinforcements). After a brief discussion, Lake returned to the phone with President Clinton's answer that we were willing to begin talks and suspend our actions during the talks if North Korea agreed to suspend all reprocessing activity at Yongbyon during those talks, a condition intended to preclude North Korea from embroiling us in never-ending negotiations while they continued making plutonium. In a few minutes Lake returned conveying Carter's doubts that North Korea would agree to suspend its reprocessing during the talks. President Clinton, supported by a unanimous NSC, decided to stand firm; Carter delivered that message to Kim Il Sung and he accepted. The immediate crisis was over, the reinforcement plans shelved, and the negotiations pursued, with Bob Gallucci, a highly capable foreign service officer, leading the American negotiating team.

The negotiations concluded before year's end with the so-called Agreed Framework, under which North Korea agreed to stop all construction activity on two larger reactors and suspend their reprocessing to produce plutonium from the smaller, already operational reactor. South Korea and Japan agreed to build for North Korea two light water reactors (LWRs) for producing electricity; and, until the LWRs were operational, the United States agreed to supply fuel oil to compensate North Korea for the electricity it would forfeit by shutting down its reactor. I considered this a good deal for the US: war was averted, plutonium production suspended, and North Korea gave up (permanently, it appears) their program for building the larger reactors that were under construction.

Here is the most important consideration. To understand what the North Koreans were giving up, and the nuclear peril we prevented, consider this: US nuclear experts estimated that by the year 2000 (give or take a few years), those three North Korean reactors could have been producing enough plutonium to build fifty nuclear bombs a year!

Even though this preventive measure was clearly a major one in the nuclear era, especially in signifying new imperatives for nonproliferation and for worldwide nuclear security, considerable opposition arose in the US Congress: I struggled each year for appropriations for the modest funds to supply the fuel oil to North Korea (but always was able to get them). In the meantime, Japan and South Korea began to build the LWR reactors in North Korea. For the rest of President Clinton's tenure, the United States maintained the Agreed Framework and kept North Korea free of nuclear weapons.

Then the story took a bad turn. During the next decade North Korea again threatened to break out. This time US diplomacy was not successful in stopping them, and we are now faced with a nuclear-armed North Korea, the very security danger that we had worked so hard to avoid.

This new action in the dangerous and continuing drama of North Korea and nuclear weapons forms a later chapter in which I will chronicle how this proliferation unfolded and the grave new security challenges it has created.

# 15    Ratifying Start II and Battling over the Test Ban Treaty

*Don't take my attack on you personally. It's just politics.*
—Vladimir Zhirinovsky to Perry (paraphrased),[1]
Duma hearing on START II treaty, 17 October 1996[2]

One of the continuing challenges on my journey has been the development and support of arms control agreements. It has always been a priority in reducing the nuclear danger to seek and obtain such agreements, with the Soviet Union (later Russia,) and with other nations. The state of communication and cooperation with other parties is, of course, crucial to progress. Happily, by the time I became secretary of defense, the evolving relationship between the United States and Russia appeared to be conducive to effective arms control measures, and I was an enthusiastic supporter of the negotiations carried out by the State Department.

President Clinton was intent on obtaining meaningful arms reduction agreements with the Russians. It also seemed evident that international measures such as nonproliferation and bans on testing nuclear weapons were increasingly needed. For example, the North Korean nuclear crisis had chillingly underscored a requirement to strengthen international programs to prevent nuclear proliferation.

Working with the Russians took highest priority. Together with rapid and safe dismantling of nuclear weapons specified in previous treaties, President Clinton believed it mandatory to ratify the landmark START II treaty signed by President George H. W. Bush and President Boris Yeltsin in January 1993. START II would eliminate MIRVed ICBMs and require robust verification of compliance. The president's view was strongly supported throughout the administration, certainly by myself, and in 1995 he moved on ratification. General Shalikashvili and I testified strongly in favor of ratification to the US Senate.

As we pressed in the Senate and elsewhere to seize these arms control opportunities, opportunities we had long awaited through the darkest times of the Cold War nuclear arms buildup, we were not surprised to encounter obstacles. Although Cold War tensions and enmity were showing unmistakable signs of exhaustion, some members of our Senate and some members of the Russian Duma were unable fully to believe the Cold War was over. In an odd logic, some in the United States believed that the end of the Cold War erased any threat from Russia and that consequently arms control treaties were pointless; they believed that we should retain all our nuclear weapons as a hedge against some future contingency. (They were neglecting to note that retaining those weapons could become a self-fulfilling prophecy—that is, it could actually stimulate the contingency to occur.) In sum, ratification was variously not compelling to some in the Duma and the Senate. Nevertheless, in January 1996 we won ratification in the US Senate by a lopsided vote.[3] Many of my Russian colleagues, however, advised that the Duma vote was very much in doubt.

In an unusual development, one that I cannot imagine happening today, I was invited to testify before the Russian Duma on why Russia should ratify START II. Why was I invited? I believe that there were two major reasons. First, I had immediately seized the opportunity to dismantle nuclear weapons under the Nunn-Lugar legislation. This was at a time when the Russians and officials in the new republics were looking to us for leadership and assistance in the aftermath of the collapse of the Soviet Union. Along with Ash Carter and his talented staff, I had directed the facilitating of the Nunn-Lugar programs and was seen by Russian colleagues as someone they could trust (trust, I believe, being the most valuable asset in diplomacy). They also knew by my actions that I was a determined advocate for diminishing the surreal "overkill" in nuclear weapons that was the legacy of the Cold War. There were many Russian officials and leaders who felt the same way, and they too faced old modes of thinking and resistance that would have to be opposed, and they hoped that I could make a better case for ratification than they could.

Against the advice of a colleague in the State Department less audacious (and probably wiser) than I, I accepted the invitation. On 17 October 1996 I addressed a crowded session of the full Duma and, via Moscow television, countless other Russians as well. My introductory remarks were well received, and the first few questions were positive ones from colleagues in the Duma with whom I had collaborated for many years. Then the presiding officer recognized Duma member Vladimir Zhirinovsky, a notorious ultranationalist hard-liner, well known for his strident anti-American positions. Once Zhirinovsky had the floor, he never surrendered it. He filibustered on all of the reasons the Duma should reject the treaty; he filibustered on the failings of the Yeltsin administration (an easy target); and he filibustered on why America was an enemy of Russia, dedicated to its destruction.[4] As long as the television cameras were on him, Zhirinovsky was prepared to speak. At the end of the hearing, I found myself thinking that I should have accepted the advice of my colleague in the State Department.

In a bizarre sequel, Zhirinovsky came over to speak to me privately as I was collecting my notes and preparing to leave. He was oozing with charm, but his message left me cold: "Don't take my attack on you personally—it's just politics." He invited me to come to his office the next day to discuss ways we might work together. I declined.

It is hard to judge whether my appearance before the Duma was a net gain for the cause of START II, but I would do it again. It was a remarkable experience. And I may have won over some Russians who, unlike Zhirinovsky, had been sitting on the fence. At the very least it did no harm. Indeed, I continue to believe that reasoned and serious dialogue is an essential step in the continuing quest to prevent a nuclear catastrophe. One thing is certain: my appearance in the Duma was far from a traditional approach. The nuclear crisis, it seems clear, calls for bold, new approaches.

But even the hard-fought victories of arms control don't ensure success. The Russian Duma finally ratified START II almost four years later in April 2000, but the treaty never really took force. It was hobbled by Russia's negative reaction to NATO's war in Kosovo and by Russian concerns over US plans to deploy a BMD system in Europe. In June 2002, President George W. Bush withdrew the United States from the ABM treaty, and the following day Russia declared START II null and void. A few years later, no longer restrained by START II, the Russians began building a new class of MIRVed missiles, a huge step backward in reducing the danger of nuclear weapons.

When I think of the history of arms control initiatives in our time, I have considered the deeper significance of Zhirinovsky's comment to me about his almost primal attack in the Duma on ratification of START II. His attack reflected some very old patterns of human behavior to include extreme nationalism and tendencies toward isolation. He said: "It's just politics." In other words, "politics-as-usual." This comment, traditionally presented as rueful but wise humor, has a more sobering significance in the nuclear era—a triumph of ancient predispositions over reason. In an era that has become the very antithesis of the "usual," it sublimates the most staggering new historical realities. Arms control and the more general imperative to mitigate the nuclear danger often founder exactly on "politics-as-usual." This pattern, it seems to me, demonstrates how much we need greater public awareness of the unprecedented dangers that face us from the nuclear threat.

Other arms control battles have continued on for years without resolution, such as the effort to get the US Senate to ratify a Comprehensive Test Ban Treaty (CTBT). In August 1995 President Clinton announced that he supported a true, zero-yield nuclear test ban. The United States had been observing a moratorium on testing since September 1992. I believed that if we signed, other nations were prepared to sign as well; and it seemed clear to me that signing was in our best national security interest. We had conducted more than one thousand tests,[5] possessed the best scientific capability in the world for simulating weapon performance, and hence were better able than anyone to live with the restrictions of the treaty. Moreover, our failure to sign would give other nations an excuse to test, an outcome I judged weakened our security. I knew, however, that we must have the full support of the Joint Chiefs of Staff and the directors of the nuclear labs for any chance of winning the needed two-thirds vote in the Senate, so I worked closely with General Shalikashvili to obtain that support. We scheduled a series of meetings in which the issues could be debated fully with the lab directors and outside experts. The Chiefs of Staff were invited to the meetings so that they could hear the same arguments we heard.

After a number of meetings over several months, General Shalikashvili told me that the chiefs would support the signing if the United States would make several unilateral statements to accompany the treaty. The most important unilateral action was for the president to agree to tie to the treaty a directive requiring US lab directors to make an annual assessment to validate that our arsenal remained at the readiness necessary to carry out our deterrence mission. Of course, the treaty had the standard clause allowing the president to withdraw should our supreme national interests be threatened by it. However, the chiefs were afraid that should our nuclear force be failing because of the ban on tests, a president might nevertheless feel bound by politics not to withdraw from the treaty unless confronted with an explicit warning from the nuclear lab directors.

Finally, after much study, discussion, and several unilateral declarations, the chiefs agreed, and on 24 September 1996 President Clinton signed the CTBT. Sadly, three years later, after I had returned to Stanford, the CTBT failed to receive enough Senate votes for ratification. Notwithstanding, each year the nuclear lab directors send an assessment letter to the president.[6] All assessments have been positive, although the letters grow longer each year.

# 16    NATO, Peacekeeping in Bosnia, and the Rise of Security Ties with Russia

*I spent most of my career doing detailed planning for a nuclear strike on NATO forces. I never dreamed that I would be standing here at NATO headquarters, talking with NATO officers, and planning a joint peace-keeping exercise!*

—A Russian general at NATO headquarters to Perry (paraphrased)

Beyond formal arms control initiatives, new opportunities for cooperation developed between NATO nations and European nations who had constituted the Warsaw Pact. Within a few years the cooperation in joint training exercises evolved into joint peace enforcement operations, of which Bosnia was the prime example. As secretary of defense, I was deeply involved in these activities. They created important opportunities to overturn the hostility during the Cold War; but I understood that management of the new relationships would carry not only great opportunities but also great risks.

During the Cold War, NATO was key to deterring the Soviet Union in its territorial ambitions. One deterrent was NATO's threat to use tactical nuclear weapons against the Red Army should it invade Europe. The grim prospect of exploding nuclear weapons on allied soil was over-ridden by the determination to repel a Soviet attack. To manage these conflicting concerns, NATO created a nuclear planning group called the High Level Group (HLG) to develop tactics and strategy for the use of nuclear weapons. By the time I became defense secretary, the NATO alliance had a very different aspect—so changed that we commonly had Russians attending NATO meetings. NATO continued to maintain the HLG (Ash Carter was its chair when I was secretary), but now its highest priority in the post–Cold War period was the safety and security of nuclear weapons.

That transformation was among the signs of a growing realization, a more realistic view beyond traditional military thinking, of the threatening legacy of the "overkill" buildup in nuclear arms during the Cold War. In short, amassing nuclear arms was now being increasingly seen as a policy not enhancing security but raising the common danger, a danger that must be diminished.

But at the same time there was another key development. Also visible now was a heightening groundswell of interest among the Eastern European nations to join NATO.

NATO had been created to provide a military force that could deter or defeat the Red Army, so it is easy to understand how NATO had long been a "four-letter word" in the Soviet Union and Warsaw Pact. But with the end of the Cold War, we saw NATO as the best vehicle for folding into the European security organization the new republics of the former Soviet Union and the former members of the Warsaw Pact. To achieve this historic broadening of cooperative security we would have to overcome these former antagonists' traditional view of NATO as their foe. From my experiences as a soldier in the Army of Occupation working with Japanese immediately after World War II through my later interactions as a senior defense official interacting with Russians, Chinese, and other former and present foes, I knew that views could change to allow substantial cooperation. In the present case, the Warsaw Pact nations and new republics had become democracies (some were rather shaky democracies); their military establishments, trained in an ideological Warsaw Pact atmosphere, had no idea how the military should behave in a democracy; and they wanted to become members of NATO to find out.

In short order, a pivotal situation emerged: with the growing interest in Eastern European nations of membership in the alliance, NATO soon discovered itself presented with a great opportunity and a great challenge for which it had no experience. The new collaboration with Eastern European nations was welcomed but at the same time it was impossible immediately to overcome long-standing suspicions and mistrust on both sides.

Most significantly, NATO had no plan for dealing with what, in my view, was a premature interest by the Eastern European nations in joining the alliance—one most understandable and heartening, but unless managed and paced with wise diplomacy, an aspiration that posed certain long-term risks. Russia's traditional outlooks on regional security, together with her historical influence in Eastern Europe, needed to be taken into account. A stampede by Eastern European nations to join NATO could remove the opportunity to work with a cooperative Russia to reduce the threat from nuclear weapons.

How could the goal best be achieved?

To satisfy both the challenges and the opportunities, a remarkable and creative initiative was undertaken known as the Partnership for Peace (PFP). The PFP was the inspiration of Joe Kruzel,[1] my deputy assistant secretary for Europe and an exceptionally creative, visionary, and energetic staff officer. (Joe was later to die in a tragic accident in Bosnia.) Joe had a simple, brilliant, and measured idea: all of the former Warsaw Pact nations, and all of the new republics of the former Soviet Union, hungry for security in their new freedom, would be invited to join the PFP, an auxiliary of NATO. PFP nations could send representatives to some NATO meetings (without voting rights); they could participate in the relevant NATO committees; and they could conduct joint training with NATO on peacekeeping exercises. Their senior officers would work with senior NATO officers, and the former would gain crucial experience in joint operations at the heart of NATO's effectiveness and solidarity. In time, the participating nations would be eligible to join NATO, an outcome nearly all wanted and many would attain in the next ten years. In 1993, DoD established the Marshall Center at Garmisch, Germany, where selected officers and senior defense officials of these countries "went to school" with NATO officers.[2] I considered this center a vitally important part of our strategy to create a broad European security structure that included nations once enemies of NATO. (I went on to create an Asia-Pacific Center for Security Studies in Honolulu,[3] and proposed a Center for Hemispheric Defense Studies in Washington,[4] which was activated shortly after I left office. I am particularly pleased that these centers have been continued by my successors.)

Of all the Eastern European nations in the PFP, Russia was treated as the first among equals. I had met the Russian defense minister, Pavel Grachev, at the NATO meeting in 1993, when I was sitting in for Secretary Aspin. I had then visited him in Moscow and become much better acquainted, particularly as we worked together to set up the implementation of the Nunn-Lugar program. So attendant to the NATO defense ministers' meeting in the fall of 1994 I hosted a dinner in his honor with all the NATO defense ministers. The dinner went remarkably well; all the European ministers were very interested in getting to know the Russian minister. This dinner meeting preceded the NATO meeting, to which Grachev was invited as one means of establishing positive connections between NATO and Russia. Besides the PFP, in which Grachev agreed to participate, NATO established a Russian comembership that entailed the Russian defense minister attending NATO meetings (without the right to vote), and Russia appointing a senior officer to be resident at NATO and serve as a liaison officer between Russia and NATO. Grachev took this quite seriously and chose a first-class officer for the job. This officer later told me: "I spent most of my career doing detailed planning for a nuclear strike on NATO forces. I never dreamed that I would be standing here at NATO headquarters, talking with NATO officers, and planning a joint peacekeeping exercise!"

Peacekeeping exercises were the most visible activities of the PFP. While I was secretary, there were five major exercises, two in the United States, two in Russia, and one in Ukraine. I attended three of these exercises and concluded that they were achieving even more than we had hoped. Carried out with the care and rigor I had come to expect of US military exercises, they additionally engendered great enthusiasm from the Warsaw Pact military units, who admired the professionalism of our military and forged personal bonds with US personnel that would last for years. Besides the PFP peacekeeping exercises, we scheduled a US-Russian disaster relief exercise. Ships from the Russian Navy and Marines joined ships from the US Navy and Marines in a disaster relief exercise in Hawaii, where we simulated recovery from a devastating tidal wave. This exercise was conducted very professionally and with a mutual goodwill that is hard to imagine today.

The PFP peacekeeping exercises, staged with an impressive degree of realism, were remarkably valuable learning experiences for all involved. Indeed, we were soon to face a real peacekeeping operation. In December 1995, when we went into Bosnia on a peacekeeping mission—not a peacekeeping exercise— most of the Eastern European nations went in with us.[5] I was thankful that the PFP had motivated them to do so, and even more thankful that the PFP exercises had increased their professionalism and fostered their interoperability with US forces.

The Bosnia peacekeeping mission was the largest military action during my tenure. Two days after I was sworn in as secretary of defense, an artillery shell landed in a Sarajevo marketplace, killing sixty-eight civilians. It was widely believed that this shell came from one of the many Bosnian Serb artillery positions on the hills overlooking Sarajevo, just one of the many atrocities carried out by the Bosnian Serbs in the savage Bosnian War. That war, breaking out in 1992 during the last year of the George H. W. Bush administration, was a latter-day awakening of the historical animosities among the Bosnian mixed population of Orthodox Serbians, Catholic Croatians, and Muslims (called "Bosniaks"). Serbian president Slobodan Milosevic stimulated the war through speeches comparable to Hitler's, firing up religious animosity and a soon-to-be-deadly nationalistic fervor. His apparent motive was to annex into Serbia the predominantly Serbian part of Bosnia. No simple division was possible, since Serbs lived throughout Bosnia, especially in the capital, Sarajevo, intermingled with Croatians and Bosniaks, having lived together with them peacefully for many generations. Yet Milosevic's fervent nationalistic oratory roused the different populations and sparked a raging civil war.

The European nations declared the Bosnian crisis to be a regional matter they would resolve without US help. President Bush was happy to accept that judgment. The United Nations established a peacekeeping force without US participation and deployed it to Bosnia. The UN Protection Force (UNPRO-FOR) was woefully unsuccessful, for by the time I had become defense secretary, war casualties, according to media reports, had exceeded 200,000, mostly Bosniaks, with many more Bosniaks routed from their homes and imprisoned in concentration camps. Because the UN force was too weak and operating under very restrictive rules of engagement, it could not stop the atrocities.

By 1995 the American public had become outraged over the continuing atrocities in Bosnia, and many advocated US intervention. Three alternative forms of intervention were being debated in the media: sending US forces to augment the UN peacekeepers; "lift and strike"; and creating a new military force under NATO strong enough to enforce a peace. I opposed the first, for it merely doubled down on a losing strategy, especially the restrictive rules of engagement. I likewise found the "lift and strike" option unfavorable. "Lift" meant lifting the arms embargo and sending arms to the Bosniaks, and "strike" meant conducting selective air strikes against the Bosnian Serbs—a cheap option but as the European nations reasonably argued, one that would endanger their peacekeeping forces already deployed. I believed that curtailing the tough and disciplined Bosnian Serb army required US "boots on the ground." However, my option of choice—that US forces would intervene as part of a NATO force—was out of step with the widespread fervent support for saving the Bosniaks through the "lift" strategy of sending them arms, which many mistakenly thought would be cheap, easy, and effective.

In June I was giving the graduation speech at Stanford University, and as I spoke a plane flew over the stadium trailing a sign that read, "Perry—Send arms to Bosnia." The next month I spoke at an Aspen conference along with former prime minister Margaret Thatcher, who favored "lift and strike." She analogized to World War II when Churchill promised Roosevelt, "Give us the tools, and we will finish the job."[6] In my talk, I reminded the audience that we had indeed sent Great Britain the "tools" (arms, ships, and aircraft), but that to "finish the job" we subsequently had to put several million "boots on the ground." Although I favored the third option—the deployment of US ground forces—I did so on the basis that American forces would be part of a NATO force, and operate under more robust rules of engagement than the UN force.

The key NATO heads of state, most notably President Clinton, would need to agree to the option before it could be enacted. But the European powers were committed to the support of UNPROFOR, to which they had supplied military forces. Then in July 1995, the Bosnian Serbs captured Srebrenica, rounded up some eight thousand Bosniaks, mostly men and boys, marched them out of town, executed them, and dumped their bodies into a mass grave, a horrific atrocity known as the Genocide of Srebrenica, inflicted as the UN force based in that city sat by helplessly. The European members of the UN force could no longer maintain that the UN force was sufficient or that much stronger military action was not glaringly needed.

Just ten days after the Genocide of Srebrenica, key foreign ministers, defense ministers, and military chiefs of the United States, NATO nations, and Russia met in London. When we returned to Washington, we met with President Clinton and his national security team. At that meeting Secretary of State Warren Christopher and I were authorized by President Clinton to take a strong position with our NATO allies for NATO intervention, and I gladly did so. Other NATO ministers joined us, resulting in a joint ultimatum to the Bosnia Serbs: stop your army (on its way to Gorazde, the neighboring city to Srebrenica) and stop all shelling of cities, or we will intervene militarily with a major air strike against your bases.[7]

Given the recent history of ineffectual resistance to them, the Bosnian Serbs were contemptuous of the ultimatum, ignored it, continued their ground attacks and shelling operations, and, in extreme defiance, took several hundred UN peacekeepers hostage. NATO air forces, led by the United States, demolished several Bosnian Serb bases. For the first time facing superior military opposition, the Bosnian Serbs backed down. They ceased military operations and agreed to negotiate an agreement (the Dayton Accords) by which the UN peacekeeping forces were replaced by NATO peace enforcement forces.[8] (The remarkable story of those negotiations at Wright-Patterson Air Force Base in Dayton, Ohio, is detailed in chief negotiator Richard Holbrooke's book, *To End a War*.)[9]

The Dayton Accords, concluded in November 1995 and signed later that year in Paris, led to a NATO force of almost sixty thousand troops, more than

Secretary of State Warren Christopher (*left*), Perry, and General Shalikashvili at NATO meeting on Bosnia in London, August 1995, seen as the turning point for intervention in Bosnia.

twenty thousand of them Americans, being deployed to Bosnia by the end of the year. An American admiral, Leighton Smith, commanded the overall NATO force, and General George Joulwan, US commander of our European forces, stood up the American force with great skill and energy. The core of Joulwan's force was the 1st Armored Division, based in Germany, and commanded by Major General Bill Nash, who also commanded a Russian brigade, a Turkish regiment, and a Nordic brigade. The Nordic brigade included Baltic troops who had been trained by Danish forces under the PFP program. The Russian defense minister authorized one of his best-trained paratrooper brigades to join the NATO peacekeepers.

How the Russian government decided to deploy one of its crack brigades under the command of an American general remains a remarkable story (and one that I cannot imagine being repeated today). In their participation in the London NATO meeting that defined dramatic new actions to stop Bosnian Serb atrocities, the Russians offered to contribute a brigade as part of the peace enforcement operation to Bosnia, but they were unwilling that it be under NATO command. The NATO commander quite reasonably insisted that a divided command would not work. President Clinton and President Yeltsin agreed at a meeting in October 1995 that their two defense ministers should figure out how to make it work—easy for them to say!

Russian defense minister Grachev and I were to have three meetings over the next two months to figure out how to "make it work." Our first meeting in Geneva was a total failure. Toward the end Ash Carter salvaged the process by arguing that we should write off that hopeless discussion and instead push for an agreement to meet again at a specified place and time. We set the next meeting for a few weeks later in the United States. During the first day in my cavernous conference room in the Pentagon we made absolutely no progress on the Bosnia command issue: Grachev unwaveringly insisted that his brigade could not report to a NATO commander. Finally, to clear the air, I took Defense Minister Grachev on a tour of Fort Riley, where he rode one of our ceremonial cavalry horses, and then to Whiteman Air Force Base, where he sat in the pilot's

Russian defense minister Grachev rides ceremonial cavalry horse at Fort Riley, October 1995.

seat of a B-2. The atmosphere began to thaw, and at our last meeting I finally "broke the code." Grachev would allow his brigade to report to an American commander but not a NATO commander! We reached a provisional understanding that General Grachev could accept the Russian brigade commander being under the "national command" of Russia, the "operational control" of General Joulwan, and the "tactical command" of General Bill Nash. I guess the moral of this story is that words matter. A few weeks later Grachev and I met at NATO headquarters in Brussels and signed the agreement that formalized the understanding we had previously reached. We conducted the signing beside posters that read: "NATO + Russia = Success."

Against this background, I believed that we were finally taking the right steps in Bosnia, but General Shalikashvili and I were called before Congress numerous times to testify and, during one hearing, were warned by a congressman that if we sent troops into Bosnia, it would result in hundreds of body bags (US military fatalities) each week. Neither General Shalikashvili nor I agreed, though we surely understood that our troops would be in harm's way and planned to take all reasonable precautions to minimize the danger. I met privately with President Clinton to give him my assessment of the dangers our troops would face, and what provisions we were making to minimize those dangers. He said he understood that his decision to intervene with a significant military force, if it went wrong, could result in the end of his presidency, but that he believed it was the right thing to do, and authorized me to go ahead.

In November, a few weeks before our forces entered Bosnia, I visited the 1st Armored Division at their main base in Germany to explain to the troops why we were sending them and what they would be facing. Then I visited a special training base General Nash had set up to simulate conditions the troops would face in Bosnia: frigid weather, roadside mines, guerrilla operations, terrorist attacks on outposts, and black-marketeering. General Nash had left nothing to chance, and required that every battalion deploying to Bosnia undergo this special training—"The more you sweat in peace, the less you bleed in war."[10] Accordingly, the year the troops spent in Bosnia was remarkably successful. They completely controlled the section of Bosnia for which they were responsible; they made significant progress in resettling Bosniaks and in rebuilding a functioning infrastructure; and they suffered remarkably few casualties.

I visited these troops as they crossed into Bosnia, and four times in 1996. The first time I flew to their staging area in Croatia and walked with them across the

President Clinton and Perry discuss sending American troops to Bosnia, November 1995. White House photographic office.

pontoon bridge they had built over the Sava River. Halfway across the bridge, General Shalikashvili and I were stopped by one of the combat engineers still working on the bridge. He told us that his enlistment was to expire that week and that he wanted us to swear him in then and there for another four years. So in the freezing rain and mud, suspended over the Sava River, General Shalikashvili and I administered his oath. That display of our troop's esprit and confidence reinforced my view that we would be successful in Bosnia.

Later that spring, on my second trip, I visited the Russian and Baltic brigades as well as the American troops. I pinned a DoD medal on the Russian

Perry and General Shalikashvili crossing the Sava River on a pontoon bridge into Bosnia constructed by army engineers, January 1996.

brigade commander at the request of General Nash, who said that the Russian commander's performance had been outstanding and that the Russian participation in the foot patrols had saved needless casualties because the Bosnian Serbs peacefully accepted those patrols.

On the third visit I spent Thanksgiving Day with the troops. My final visit was to their home base in Germany, to which they had returned with a true sense of accomplishment and, remarkably, with fewer casualties than during their peacetime deployment in Germany the previous year. (I was told that the casualties in Germany were primarily from autobahn accidents.)

The Bosnian operation was for me a defining demonstration of the skill and professionalism of the American military, exemplified by General John Shalikashvili, General George Joulwan, General Bill Nash, and all the others who made the mission a model peace enforcement operation. It also demonstrated the clout of NATO and how effective the PFP had become in just a few years.

The Bosnian operation also demonstrated how much more effective NATO was as a pan-European alliance; in particular, how it was so much better to have Russia working with us, not against us.

As I reflect on our efforts to form a pan-European security alliance, I think

Russian and US soldier, part of NATO team, observe a
local disturbance from the perimeter of their checkpoint
in Bosnia, 1996.

about the key role of the PFP, and the original rationale for forming it. History
provides an instructive context for the PFP. With the ending of World War II,
the United States had carried out the Marshall Plan,[11] a self-enlightened key
to the peace and prosperity of Western Europe for decades and central to the
grand strategy of containment. At the end of the Cold War and the new strategic opportunity this brought for enhanced pan-European security in the nuclear age, many of us advocated some version of a Marshall Plan for the Eastern
European nations with desperate economies and whose fledgling democratic
governments were at substantial risk. Obviously, collapses of these nations
would threaten our emerging prospects for a grand security.

The new Marshall Plan did not materialize, but fortunately we were able to create the PFP, through which we promoted some of our strategic security goals in Eastern Europe. Crucially, the PFP created in the Eastern European military officers a high regard for their Western counterparts and a desire to emulate them. And the PFP experience dramatized that the role of the military in a democratic society is to support elected leaders, not conduct coups against them. Indeed, the new experience of working effectively with the NATO military was profoundly valuable in a broad peacekeeping dimension—for example, in the pan-European conduct of the Bosnian War. From a strategic aspect, the PFP ensured that we would not in the foreseeable future face a military confrontation with Eastern European nations. Importantly, it also was a basis for our military working with Russia. Indeed, without PFP, I do not believe that we would have succeeded in getting Russia's full participation in the Bosnia operation; certainly we could not have had a Russian brigade under the tactical command of an American division commander.

But the success of the PFP brought its own special problem. Most of the participants were there primarily because they saw it as the doorway to NATO membership—all wanted to be part of the Western security team. I greatly favored this aspiration, but I believed that extraordinarily sensitive long-range strategic issues, issues at odds with short-range politics, must pace the timing of NATO membership. Timing was all. A cooperative security solution in our era would depend on it.

Accordingly, I spent considerable time visiting Eastern European capitals, explaining the criteria of NATO membership, counseling patience, and promoting continued robust PFP participation by those nations during the waiting period. I discovered everywhere that the PFP was not only a great success, it was almost too great a success. After three years in the PFP, all of the Eastern European nations, including the Baltic nations recently independent from the dissolved Soviet Union, wanted to join NATO. Not five years from now, not three years from now, but now!

The strategic imperative for a measured approach on expanding NATO was absolutely crucial in relations with Russia. As general enthusiasm for the PFP was growing, Russia was becoming an active PFP member and a participant in NATO meetings, but at the same time it found itself caught in a contradiction: its traditional opposition to the Eastern European nations, especially those on its periphery, joining NATO. Russia still saw NATO as a potential threat—one that could no longer be buffered by Eastern European nations. Yet at that pivotal moment, the Russians were positive about these nations participating in the PFP; indeed, they themselves were active participants. And after all, we had made a major breakthrough with the Russians in getting them to send that crack brigade to operate under an American division commander in the Bosnian mission. But I was certain that the Russians had not undergone a quick conversion to an entirely new perspective on their regional security. I did not believe that the timing was right to push for NATO enlargement. Most important, we needed to keep moving forward with Russia, and I feared that NATO enlargement at this time would shove us into reverse. I believed that a regression here could squander the positive relations we had so painstakingly and patiently developed in the opportunistic post–Cold War period; it could reverse for an indeterminate period the promising course on which we were finally moving, a course whose stakes in the nuclear era could not be greater. I knew that NATO membership would, and should, eventually come to the Eastern European nations; but I believed that we needed more time to bring Russia, the other major nuclear power, into the Western security circle. The over-riding priority was obvious to me.

When Richard Holbrooke, then an assistant secretary in the State Department, proposed in 1996 to bring into NATO at once a number of the PFP members, including Poland, Hungary, the Czech Republic, and the Baltic nations, I actively opposed his proposal. My specific thinking was this: I wanted to delay that initiative for two or three years, after which I thought the Russians would be comfortable with their place in the Western security circle and not perceive this as a security threat.

But Holbrooke was irrepressible and his proposal moved forward. I went to President Clinton, explained my concerns, and asked for a full meeting of the National Security Council to air my concerns and my arguments for a delay. The president called a meeting of the NSC dedicated to the issue, and I made my case for delaying NATO membership for a few years. I was amazed by the dynamics of the meeting. Neither Secretary of State Warren Christopher nor National Security Adviser Anthony Lake spoke out. The opposing arguments were made instead by Vice President Gore, and he made a forceful argument in favor of immediate membership, an argument more persuasive to the president than mine. The president agreed to immediate membership for Poland, Hungary, and the Czech Republic but delayed the membership of the Baltic states for later consideration. Vice President Gore's argument was based on the value of bringing Eastern Europe into the European security circle, with which I fully agreed. He believed that we could manage the problems this would create with Russia, with which I disagreed. I continued to connect the maintenance of a positive relationship with Russia with the delaying of NATO expansion for several more years. And again and most fundamentally: when I considered that Russia still had a huge nuclear arsenal, I put a very high priority on maintaining that positive relationship, especially as it pertained to any future reduction in the nuclear weapons threat.

In the strength of my conviction, I considered resigning. But I concluded that my resignation would be misinterpreted as opposition to NATO membership for Poland, Hungary, and the Czech Republic, membership that I greatly favored—just not right away. In the end, I decided not to resign, hoping that my continued involvement would help to mitigate the growing mistrust. President Clinton had given me just what I had requested—an opportunity to state my case—and unfortunately, I had not been persuasive enough.

When I look back at this critical decision, I regret that I didn't fight more effectively for delay of the NATO decision. Prior to the National Security Council meeting called by President Clinton, I could have had intensive one-on-one meetings with Warren Christopher and Tony Lake, trying to rally support for delaying the decision to expand NATO. I could have written a paper carefully laying out my case, and asked the president to make this paper available to all members before the meeting. Or I could have followed up on my consideration to resign. It is possible that the rupture in relations with Russia would have occurred anyway. But I am not willing to concede that.

The year 1996 was the high point in relations between the United States and Russia. That positive, constructive relationship was clearly in the best interests of both countries, and we should have been able to sustain it. But in the succeeding years, as I will describe later in the book, the relationship turned almost as negative as it had been during the Cold War. We now face an uphill battle to try to restore an atmosphere in which our two nations can cooperate at least on those security issues that are of greatest mutual importance to us, of which preventing nuclear terrorism and regional nuclear wars are highest on the list.

# 17

# The "Immaculate Invasion"
# of Haiti and Forging Ties for
# Western Hemispheric Security

*These principles guide our relations within our own Hemisphere, the*
*frontline of defense of American national security. Our goal remains a*
*hemisphere fully democratic, bound together by good will, security coop-*
*eration, and the opportunity for all our citizens to prosper.*[1]

—*National Security Issues in Science, Law and Technology,*
CRC Press, April 2007

Maintaining US-Russia relations was certainly key to reducing traditional nuclear dangers, but new nuclear security issues such as nuclear terrorism were
emerging, and dealing with those issues would require closer security ties with
many countries, including those in our own hemisphere. Historically, the Pentagon had largely neglected those ties.

In hindsight, the reasons for the neglect were several. An unintended consequence of the Cold War was that US security concerns were focused on the
Soviet Union and the regions where the Soviets were trying to extend their influence. As a result, we had more than 200,000 troops based in Europe and almost 100,000 in Asia, plus a powerful Pacific fleet. Except for Canada, a strong
member of NATO with significant troop deployments in Europe, the Pentagon
paid little attention to the Western Hemisphere. No sitting defense secretaries
were deeply involved with the nations there, nor did they see it as a priority to
establish ties by visiting those nations. But that was about to change. In part the
change was owing to the ending of the Cold War. But the change also reflected
my own view that security begins at home.

Even if I had not held this view, a hemispheric security problem suddenly
took shape and was immediately dropped in my lap. As I was being sworn in
as secretary of defense, a security crisis was coming to a head in Haiti. In 1991,
a Haitian military junta had overthrown the democratically elected president,
Jean-Bertrand Aristide. The junta appointed a puppet president, but the real

power resided with the head of the junta, General Raoul Cedras, who had imposed a harsh military rule. The United States demanded Cedras step down and allow President Aristide to regain his legitimate office.[2] When Cedras refused, we threatened military action, and I was told by President Clinton to prepare an invasion plan. I directed Admiral Paul David Miller, commander-in-chief of the Atlantic Command, to develop the plan and assemble the invasion force.

Admiral Miller showed remarkable ingenuity in designing and assembling the force: units of the 82nd Airborne Division would muster at Pope Air Force Base, which served Fort Bragg, North Carolina, for airdropping into Haiti; units of the 10th Mountain Division would be stationed on aircraft carriers and helicoptered in after the airdrop to serve as peacekeepers.[3] Haiti had no air force, so Admiral Miller ordered the commanders of the aircraft carrier to move their fighter aircraft to a ground base and moved the helicopters and troops of the 10th Mountain Division onto the carriers. I do not have to tell you that the carrier pilots were not pleased with the idea of sitting out a naval invasion at an army base! The day before the planned invasion, I flew to one of the aircraft carriers based a few tens of miles from Haiti, to review the force deployment. I was deeply impressed with Admiral Miller's brilliant plan, and was confident of its success.

But we were hoping that diplomacy might forestall the need for an invasion. Former president Carter, Senator Sam Nunn, and recently retired general Colin Powell—a unique and remarkable diplomatic team—accepted General Cedras's invitation to negotiate a settlement. President Clinton sent them to Haiti with a non-negotiable demand that Cedras turn the presidency back to Aristide. President Carter reported back that Cedras refused, so we set the invasion plan in motion.

On Sunday, 18 September 1994, the day we had set for US troops to enter Haiti, I went to the Oval Office to keep the president informed of our troop movements, and was alarmed when I heard that the American diplomatic team, apparently slow-rolling President Clinton's instructions to come home and not realizing the details of our invasion plan, had remained in Haiti and were with Cedras. Former president Carter was on the phone with President Clinton saying that they had agreed with Cedras to stay for one final discussion, and he was confident that they would reach an agreement. Since the conversation was over an open line, President Clinton couldn't explain his concern; but he directed President Carter to get his team out immediately. Carter, clearly dis-

President Clinton meets with cabinet officers in the Oval Office to discuss Haiti crisis, 1994. White House photographic office.

appointed, was about to break off the talks when an aide rushed into Cedras's office, shouting that the US airborne force had just left Fort Bragg—evidently Cedras had agents on the ground observing Fort Bragg and the nearby Pope Air Base. Hearing that news, Cedras relented and agreed to step down. So President Carter did get the agreement he sought, but we will never know whether he would have gotten it absent the invasion news reaching Cedras. I immediately ordered our airborne forces to return to Fort Bragg and directed Admiral Miller to convert the imminent helicopter invasion into a peaceful landing the next day. Our forces entered Haiti as peacekeepers, with no loss of American or Haitian lives. The landing came to be called "The Immaculate Invasion."

This story has a happy ending, but it also reflects the vagaries and dangers of coercive diplomacy. It is all too easy to imagine a very different—and not so happy—ending if the communications had been just a little different. Indeed, history is replete with examples of military conflicts, or even wars, that started because of poor communications between the parties, or simple miscalculations about the other party's intent. In the nuclear era, these are miscalculations of unimaginable consequence.

A few days later, General Shalikashvili and I flew to Haiti, met with General Cedras, and explained that we had arranged safe haven for him in a Central

American country. Cedras was at first unwilling to leave Haiti and tried to negotiate an alternate plan. We then had to tell him that we were not negotiating, we were directing!

Two months later, on Thanksgiving, Lee and I and General Shalikashvili and his wife, Joan, Ambassador Madeleine Albright, and Congressman John Murtha and his wife, Joyce, met with President Aristide in Haiti, and afterward enjoyed Thanksgiving dinner with our troops. When we arrived at the airport, we were shown Haitian babies who were being treated by US military doctors. At the Thanksgiving celebration, the now-restored president Aristide presented me with a live turkey—everybody except the turkey (and the American secretary of defense) seemed to think that was pretty funny!

The peacekeeping operation went smoothly under the control of competent and well-trained American troops, now joined by troops from our ally, Canada. Happily for the United States, the UN officially took over the peacekeeping responsibility in March 1995, with Canadian troops composing the bulk of the UN force, freeing up American troops for the emerging Bosnian crisis.

Although the peacekeeping operation in Haiti was my initiation into hemispheric security, I knew that my interest in the hemisphere would become much broader. It was a new period. The Cold War had ended but the nuclear crisis had not—it was taking on added forms. We could no longer operate with the mindset that the US-Russian nuclear standoff was de facto the almost exclusive focus of concern. We needed new, adaptive thinking, and immediately. If you read the emerging signs in the turbulence of the early post–Cold War period, signs such as the growing need for enhanced security for nuclear materials and facilities in many locations, it was clear that we needed to pay more global attention to security interests, and prominently those unique to our own hemisphere.

I decided to seize that opportunity. Just three months after I was sworn in as secretary I visited our hemispheric neighbor, Canada. I then planned to follow that up with a visit to our other hemispheric neighbor, Mexico, but was discouraged by the State Department, which cited the historical unpopularity of the US military in Mexico.

I found that argument unpersuasive. As I have noted throughout these pages, my own experience has frequently shown me that people formerly or currently contentious could come together effectively in a common interest, especially on the gravest issues. So I did my own investigation of the question of opening up a conversation on issues of defense with Mexico, including meeting with the Mexican ambassador to the United States. I soon decided that a fresh start in discussion and planning about matters of defense among our hemispheric neighbors might yield good results, and I invited the Mexican minister of defense to visit the US. He accepted, and the visit was substantive and cordial. He then invited me for a reciprocal visit to Mexico, which I gladly accepted.

Amazingly, this was the first time an American secretary of defense had ever visited Mexico. The visit was a great success, both politically and with regard to mutual security concerns.

I decided to push on and schedule visits to Brazil, Argentina, Venezuela, and Chile. During those meetings, the defense ministers and I jointly concluded that a meeting of all defense ministers of the Western Hemisphere would be beneficial, and I set about to organize one. In July 1995, thirty-four defense ministers (all except Cuba) met in Williamsburg, Virginia, for a substantive discussion of mutual security interests (combating drug trafficking and its violence was a priority). The Argentine minister (originally a skeptic) was perhaps the most enthusiastic about the meeting's outcome. He proposed biannual meetings and committed Argentina to host the next meeting. The meetings have continued to be held since then, and the renewed American interest in our hemispheric neighbors resulted in the establishment of the Center for Hemispheric Defense Studies. (I was honored when the 2013 Defense Authorization Act called for that center to be renamed the William J. Perry Center for Hemispheric Defense Studies.)[4]

# 18    The "Iron Logic" between Military Capability and Quality of Life

*Take care of your troops, and they will take care of you.*
—Sergeant Major Richard Kidd, Senior NCO, US Army, to Perry
(paraphrased), February 1994

The advice of Sergeant Major Kidd had stayed with me long after he offered it at the reception following my swearing-in ceremony. In the ensuing months, I reflected on it often and became determined to follow it on a large scale. I believed that the training and morale of our troops were key to all aspects of our military capability, and I knew that I had inherited military forces that were the best in the world; perhaps, for their size, the most capable military ever. I recognized this, but even more important, so did the military leaders of all the world powers. An important concomitant value of the US capability in conventional forces is that it minimized the importance of nuclear weapons, reduced the likelihood of their use or even threat of use, and gave us the freedom to pursue agreements to reduce the number of nuclear weapons in the world. The importance of this in the present nuclear era cannot be overemphasized.

The US military superiority had been demonstrated dramatically in 1989 during Desert Storm, the first war with Iraq, and I knew that I could count on it in Haiti and Bosnia, where, indeed, it was demonstrated again, although in very different circumstances. I knew that I must be the steward of this remarkable capability: I was responsible for maintaining the quality of our military and passing it on to my successor.

But how to do it? A key part of the capability of our conventional forces stemmed from their uniquely superior weapon systems, and I had played an important role in developing and fielding this "offset strategy" when I had been the undersecretary for research and engineering in the late 1970s. I also believed that capable, motivated, and well-led soldiers were at least as important, but here I had no comparable experience. Pondering how to exercise my responsibilities in this field, I judged that the leadership experience I had developed in industry would be useful, but that there would be unique factors involved in developing highly motivated soldiers.

"Take care of your troops" was the good advice I received from Sgt. Major Richard Kidd, and although I immediately recognized the value of his advice, it wasn't clear to me how to follow it. However, I did have a starting point—my own experience as an enlisted man; my perspective on the value of every soldier's well-being was personal.

Everywhere I went in each branch of the military I saw top-notch talent among our noncommissioned officers (NCOs). My senior military assistant, Major General Paul Kern, said that the quality of our NCOs was our "unfair competitive advantage" over other countries' military forces, perhaps as important as our superior technology, and he argued that I should make its maintenance a top priority. With downsizing, budget cuts, and deterioration of facilities taking their toll, General Kern recommended that I get out and see for myself how the enlisted men and women lived. I readily accepted his recommendation. My visits and direct talks with thousands of enlisted personnel taught me a key lesson, what I call the "iron logic": the quality of our fighting forces is tied to the quality of life of their families. During those visits and talks, I came to understand very clearly the "iron logic" and how to act on what I learned.

To begin my education, General Kern set up a series of meetings with the senior NCO of each service, first separately,[1] and then in groups, and I asked for their advice. We followed this with quarterly visits to different military bases—the "rules of the road" were that the senior NCO at each base plan and organize the tour, taking me to see what *he* thought was important—no officers involved. Again, this was to be the military equivalent at full stride of my practice of "management by walking around," that fundamental approach I had found to be so successful earlier in my career.

At each base, the commanding general would greet us, then turn us over to the senior NCO of the base, who had organized a program with the enlisted personnel. The programs always included some "show and tell," but invariably I learned the most in discussions, usually in small groups, with enlisted personnel. Over the course of my term as secretary, I had open talks with thousands of enlisted personnel—at first I thought they would be too nervous to talk frankly with the secretary of defense, but that was never a problem. On the return flights, General Kern and I would discuss with the senior NCOs what we had learned, and take in their critiques. Over these many visits and discussions

I came to understand in-depth the most pressing issues facing our military personnel, and began formulating a plan for what I must do to maintain the "unfair competitive advantage" we enjoyed because of the superb quality of our military personnel.

I saw that the US military's intensive training program is fundamental to the superior capabilities of our NCO corps. This training program goes on intensively throughout an NCO's career. There is nothing like it in any other military in the world; for that matter, there is nothing like it anywhere in industry. (The closest approximation is the training program carried out by IBM for several decades after the end of World War II, a time when IBM believed they would get a good return on their investment in training because IBM engineers and sales personnel typically stayed at IBM throughout their careers, a condition holding until the computer industry grew and other companies began to hire the engineers IBM had trained.) For the US military to realize the full advantage of its expensive and intensive training program, we needed a high percentage of NCO's to re-enlist. What I learned by listening to the enlisted men and women is that soldiers enlist, but families re-enlist. The relationship between high re-enlistment rates and satisfaction with military family quality of life was irrefutable.

Having concluded that an "iron logic" tied the fighting quality of our armed forces to the quality of life of their families, I proposed to President Clinton a special supplemental appropriation of $15 billion to make needed improvements at military bases around the world. And, to the surprise of many cynical Pentagon observers, he approved that proposal. We made very good use of that money in items like daycare centers that were especially important to military families. But beyond the value we got from tangible programs, we got perhaps even greater value from the strong perception that grew among military families that someone was listening—someone cared about their problems.

But those funds were only a start in overcoming the biggest quality-of-life issue, inadequate and antiquated family housing on bases. Each annual defense budget had included an appropriation for new base housing, typically a few billion dollars. But the actual cost of needed new housing was estimated to be several hundred billion dollars. Hence each year, instead of catching up, we were falling further behind. And many of our military families—NCOs and officers—were living in substandard housing. On my base tours, I was embarrassed to see just how poor the housing was; but beyond my subjective reaction was the objective fact (the "iron logic") that if we didn't fix this problem it was going to defeat our priority goal of maintaining high-quality fighting forces.

Determined to improve this situation, I asked my assistant secretary for economic security, Joshua Gotbaum, to find a way to use private capital for base housing instead of depending on the insufficient congressional appropriations for that housing. I envisioned that private contractors would build houses on military bases using their own capital. They would then rent these houses to military personnel for rental fees equivalent to the soldier's monthly housing allowance. This would result, I imagined, in superior housing without using appropriated funds. Josh got encouragement from deputy service chiefs—all of whom reported that housing was a major problem and agreed to contribute personnel to developing a solution—so he organized a family housing working group, with representation from all military departments. In early 1995 this group proposed a range of new authorities and more flexibility to use existing authorities, the "Military Family Housing" proposals.

As a complement to Josh's efforts, I appointed the Marsh Task Force on Quality of Life, chaired by Jack Marsh, formerly secretary of the army. The Marsh Task Force gave me its report in the fall of 1995, which was fully supportive of the working group's proposals.

Satisfied that we were on the right track, I took our new proposal to senior members of the congressional authorization and appropriations committees in a series of breakfasts. Josh then testified and negotiated the legislation, which was enacted in 1996. The legislation allowed for a five-year provisional use, to be followed by a permanent authorization. To get the program off to an early start, Josh set up a temporary office, later replaced by the "Residential Communities Initiative." This program was enthusiastically adopted by the services and has been used since to refurbish virtually all military family housing in the United States—some 200,000 houses.[2] After leaving office, I have had occasions to visit military bases and, while there, toured the new housing. I am enormously proud of both its extent and quality. It has far exceeded my early expectations, and I have always been grateful that my successors have seen its value and enthusiastically carried it forward.

Another lesson I learned by listening to our enlisted men and women was the "iron logic" connecting the quality of our military forces to the GI Bill. I knew well its critical importance to my own education, as well as to a whole generation coming out of service after World War II (almost 8 million veterans of World War II used the GI Bill to their benefit and, ultimately, to the great benefit of our American economy, our global competitiveness, and our standard of living). During my base visits I asked countless younger soldiers why they had enlisted, and the answer most often was a variation of: "I couldn't afford a college education, so I enlisted to get the GI Bill. When my service is done, I'm going to get a college degree." Thus, the GI Bill was a major draw in attracting high-quality, ambitious young men and women to the military. When these enlistees returned to civilian life, many of them took advantage of the GI Bill. Some of the enlistees appreciated the excellent military training programs, re-enlisted, and pursued their higher education while remaining in the service. In both scenarios, our country benefited. I was so impressed with the importance of the GI Bill to the quality of our active military forces (as well as its great value to our civilian society) that I awarded the Defense Distinguished Civilian Service Medal to Congressman "Sonny" Montgomery, who had been a leader in the passage on Capitol Hill of the new GI Bill.

These were a few of the lessons I learned on how to sustain the superb quality of our fighting forces, even during a drawdown and an era of budget reductions. Looking back, the lessons seem obvious, but had it not been for General Kern's wise guidance, I might not have learned them in time to act. Making change in a bureaucracy the size of the Pentagon requires time, focused action, patience, and unrelenting follow-up—and choosing the battles worth fighting. I remain convinced that this battle was worth fighting.

Reflecting on my effort to achieve a better quality of life for our soldiers, I recognize the key role played by my time-tested "management by walking around." Indeed, I would generalize that this approach has been basic to all my institutional management and international relations endeavors. For example, it embodies much of my style of international diplomacy, a style based on being effectively disarming through honesty and collegiality, and a style that—based on long experience—assumes that most people, including those contending with one another in even dire circumstances, can come together and collaborate in the interests of a vital common need. There is nothing complicated about the approach itself. It is critically important to meet with and respectfully and openly listen to the other parties—who they are, what they most fundamentally believe, and what they are seeking. The effect of the style is to be disarming because it is conducted in the interests of closing expeditiously on a transcendent common view of the problems and especially of the desired prospects. This closure on the common good can aid in putting parochial concerns, including perceived military and economic threats, in a proper perspective.

Another reflection on my efforts to improve the quality of life for our military personnel: On many of my visits to bases, my wife, Lee, joined me. Typically, she would be taken on a tour by spouses at the base. During the tour, she got an earful from them, mostly about quality of life issues, with military housing invariably topping the list. She never failed to take advantage of that opportunity to learn, so I got my lessons on quality of life directly from the soldiers and indirectly from their spouses. Lee also had ideas on how to attack some of the most serious issues, and she would pursue them with me when time permitted, or with members of my staff when it did not. That was noted by military leaders, and at my farewell ceremony, Lee received a medal from the military services citing her support of military families and her aggressive support for initiatives to improve the quality of their lives. Her compassion also extended to our military families who were at overseas bases, many of which she visited.

On one occasion, it extended to military personnel of another country. On a visit to Albania in 1995, Lee was taken on a tour of their military hospital and was appalled by the primitive standards and unsanitary conditions. When we returned home, she worked with my staff to see whether we could help in any way. She and General Kern's wife, Dede, hit upon the idea of inviting one of the state national guards to take their summer tour in Albania, working to bring that hospital up to sanitary standards. The results were remarkable, and led to Lee being awarded the Mother Teresa Medal by the president of Albania, a medal named for one of the most famous Albanians. I am as proud of the medals Lee has received as any of my own.

# 19                    A Farewell to Arms

*It was said of Omar Bradley that he was the GI's general. Well, surely Bill*
*Perry has been the GI's secretary of defense.*
—General John Shalikashvili, Farewell Ceremony at Fort Myer,
Virginia, 14 January 1997[1]

A few days after the 1996 presidential election, I met with President Clinton,
congratulated him on his re-election, and reminded him that I had agreed only
to one term and would be stepping down on 20 January. We had a long discussion about my successor, and I made several recommendations, including John
Deutch and John White, both of whom had served very ably as deputy secretaries of defense. The president then asked me what I thought about appointing
someone with a political background, perhaps a former senator. I named three
senators I felt had a deep enough background in national security to come up
to speed in the job quickly: senators Sam Nunn, Richard Lugar, and William
S. Cohen. He noted that if the secretary was a senator, especially a Republican
senator, he might be able to smooth over our often contentious dealings with
the Senate, at that time controlled by Republicans, and asked me to call Senator
Cohen to explore the idea. I pointed out that the secretary of defense, unlike
other cabinet officers, had a daunting task of managing a department with 3
million people and an annual budget of $400 billion, and that senators typi-
cally did not have experience in managing such a complex enterprise. But he
felt that he could deal with that problem by appointing a deputy with significant management experience. I reflected (but only to myself) that historically
this strategy had not always worked out as hoped. The next day I called Senator
Cohen, who expressed real enthusiasm for the job. I reported that to President
Clinton, who in time talked to Senator Cohen and made the nomination on 5
December 1996.

I had very mixed feelings about leaving. I felt a real sense of fulfillment in my
time as secretary, and had developed a very special relationship with our military, from the enlisted personnel and the senior NCOs to our military leaders,
especially the commanders of our unified and specific commands and the Joint
Chiefs. I was especially close to General Shalikashvili, whom I believed to be one

of our greatest chairmen. My direct staff, the key members of OSD (Office of the Secretary of Defense), had served me exceptionally well. In particular, General Kern, General House, Commander Abrashoff, General Mattis, Melba Boling, and Carol Chaffin had become like family to me. I knew I would really miss them. Also I had several key initiatives that were not yet completed, and I feared that they might be dropped by my successor. These included the military housing initiative, the special program of bonding with the senior enlisted personnel, the centers we had created (the Marshall Center, the Asia-Pacific Center, and the Center for Hemispheric Defense Studies), the Partnership for Peace, and my personal efforts to keep harmonious the relations between the United States and Russia. On the other hand, one of my highest priorities—the dismantlement of nuclear weapons in Ukraine, Kazakhstan, and Belarus—had been completed on the accelerated schedule that Ash Carter and I had set.

But I knew that I must acknowledge the issue of staying power. I would be turning seventy later in the year, and while my energy was still high, I could not be sure that it would hold up for four more years.

Finally, and very subjectively, there is an inauspicious storyline surrounding second-term secretaries of defense: none has ever finished his second term, each having been asked by the president to leave before the term was over. I believe that this is not coincidence; that there is something about this particular job that causes it to go sour before eight years elapse. Perhaps it is the pressure of signing the deployment orders that send our military personnel on dangerous missions from which they might not return. (I always approached this signing in a highly personal way, trying to understand how things could go wrong, and how military families would be affected; to keep a close personal tie to this awesome decision, I insisted on using my real signature—no auto-signing.) Perhaps it is the highly emotional meetings with the families of soldiers killed while performing a mission at your direction. Or perhaps it is the tendency to catch "Potomac Fever"—the affliction that, in time, leads defense secretaries to believe that all the attention they are getting is because of who they are, rather than the position they hold, and sometimes fostering an inability to maintain a sense of proportion while dealing with the enormous power they exercise. Whichever of these reasons—or combination of reasons—is the culprit, the history is compelling. So I believe that I left at the right time. Lee and I were heading back home to California two weeks after the new secretary was sworn in—and we never looked back.

I was proud of what I had accomplished, but I was also energized about returning to Stanford to teach, to continue the unofficial diplomacy begun before my term in office, and to explore and think at length and with sustained focus about new challenges emerging in the nuclear era, such as regional nuclear conflicts. I had been in the trenches of the nuclear crisis as defense secretary, dealing with the most immediate issues of prevention, and now I would be able to assess apparent new dimensions of the threat I had become very aware of but was unable to examine as fully as I had wished.

With these thoughts coming to mind, the last two months in office saw Lee and me attending many farewell parties. We were especially moved by the parties given us by the senior enlisted NCO from each of the services, and the special mementos from them that we still cherish. My staff also held a "last supper" for us that we found exceptionally moving.

My formal farewell ceremony, held on 14 January at Fort Myer, was memorable. President Clinton proffered that I was the best secretary since George Marshall, and presented me with the Presidential Medal of Freedom. General Shalikashvili spoke of how close I was to our soldiers, saying, "It was said of Omar Bradley that he was the GI's general. Well, surely Bill Perry has been the GI's secretary of defense." Shali, for whom I had the greatest admiration and respect, could have said nothing more meaningful to me. I ended my farewell speech by talking about my profound pride in the soldiers whom I served, and who served me so well. I received medals from each of the services. Lee received a medal from the Joint Chiefs for her dedicated support of military families. Then I received a surprise that really touched my heart: the senior NCOs presented me with a special award never before given, saying that I had done more for the enlisted personnel and their families than any secretary in history. In many ways, that award is more meaningful, and certainly more personal, than any other award I have ever received, including awards from more than a dozen nations.

The ceremony concluded with a military chorale singing some of our favorite songs, including, of course, "California, Here I Come!" Afterward my family and I walked outside with President and Mrs. Clinton to view a spectacular flyover, most impressively a B-2 swooshing over at low altitude. That evening our neighbors held their own farewell party, and as Lee and I left the party, they stood on a balcony and conducted their own flyover, sailing paper airplanes over our heads!

On 24 January, my last day in office, I attended Senator Cohen's swearing-in ceremony at the White House. As I walked down the steps of the Pentagon to where my car and driver were waiting, hundreds of my Pentagon colleagues were gathered on the steps applauding. I wish I had taken a few minutes to thank them and say "Goodbye," but I was too choked up to do more than smile and wave.

Cohen's White House ceremony was brief and to the point. Afterward, I looked for my car and discovered that it had already departed with Secretary Cohen. It was, of course, not "my" car. It was the car assigned to the secretary of defense, which I no longer was. So I caught a ride back to the Pentagon with a colleague, and by the time we got there, my official photo had already been replaced with that of Secretary Cohen. Though sudden and rather jarring, this was as it should have been. In our great democracy, cabinet officers do not "own" their cars and the perks that attend to their positions. They are privileged to serve the American people for a term—hopefully serving them well— then returning to private life. And Lee and I were ready to do so.

Two weeks later Lee and I were on the road home, once again returning to our beloved California, this time for good. As a way to decompress and hasten our transition back into civilian life, we decided to drive rather than fly, taking a deliberately meandering southern route to avoid the worst of winter weather. For the first few days, Lee did most of the driving—after four years of being transported by Pentagon security, my driving skills needed an overhaul! We drove west by way of Fort Bliss, Texas, to visit General Paul Kern, my former senior military assistant (then commander of the army's 4th Infantry Division, Mechanized), and his wife, Dede. After a delightful visit, we prepared to leave the next morning and found that our car wouldn't start. As the garage owner was telling us that our car would have to be towed to another town for repair, I noticed over his shoulder a new Chevy Blazer sitting on his lot. In an inspired moment, I said, "I'll trade you my broken Cadillac for your new Blazer." Within an hour we were headed west again, arriving in Palo Alto three days later in our bright red, brand-new Blazer.

Back in Palo Alto, I met with Condoleezza Rice, now the provost of Stanford, who asked me to resume my position at Stanford, but now full time, half in the Engineering School and half in the Center for International Security and Cooperation (CISAC). Mike Berberian had offered to establish a chaired professorship, the Michael and Barbara Berberian Chair. (I had known Mike when we both served on the board of Jim Spilker's company, Stanford Telecommunications, Inc.) So I rejoined the Stanford community with ease and felt as though I was truly "back home."

I would need assistance in pursuing my planned new agenda at Stanford. In the Pentagon I had a team of very competent assistants, military and civilian, who helped me achieve a daunting schedule. They were my "force multipliers," without whom I could never have accomplished the broad extent of programs I undertook. I had ambitious plans for my new program at Stanford, so I was looking for a similar "force multiplier" there, but my chair funded only one position, instead of the team I had had at the Pentagon. I hired Deborah Gordon, who quickly rose to the occasion and became a one-person "force multiplier."

Had my cabinet post in the Clinton administration given me special stature at Stanford? A week after my return I was walking on campus and ran into an old friend. Looking at me with puzzlement, he asked, "Hi, Bill! I haven't seen you around lately. Where ya been?"

A week later, when I was traveling to Washington, an excited young marine stopped me in Dulles Airport to ask, "Mr. Secretary, may I have your autograph?" As I was signing, he whispered to his wife, "Honey, I can hardly wait to introduce you to the former secretary of defense, Dick Cheney!"

My excellent re-education continued. At Stanford the dean of engineering, John Hennessey (later president of Stanford), asked me to oversee the merger of my department with another department in the School of Engineering. I naively accepted the assignment, only to learn that the fierce academic politics unleashed in merging those departments made resolving the Bosnian crisis seem easy. After eight months of often contentious discussions, the merger was approved along the lines we recommended; the new department, Management Science and Engineering, continues to thrive.

I resumed teaching my class on the role of technology in national security and started a seminar on current security dangers. But first and foremost, I intended that my research at Stanford extend the work I had done as defense secretary in reducing the dangers of nuclear weapons. Ash Carter had returned to Harvard's Belfer Center, and we formed a Stanford-Harvard joint project called Preventive Defense,[2] the name I had given to the nuclear threat reduction work we did in our Pentagon days under the Nunn-Lugar program. When I was secretary I chose that name to make clear to Congress that appropriations to dismantle missiles in Ukraine were not done as a favor to the Ukrainians but to prevent the possible need for US military efforts that could cost American blood and treasure. Ash and I undertook as our early project to cowrite the book *Preventive Defense*, published in 1999, which chronicled, made the case for, and drew out the future policy implications of our Pentagon programs and activities to reduce nuclear dangers.[3]

Since that time and up to the present day I have devoted a majority of my time to a series of Track 2 diplomatic dialogues on nuclear and national security issues with Russia, China, India, Pakistan, North Korea, and Iran. These efforts, described in the chapters ahead, have been ongoing and often overlapping for more than fifteen years, occasionally yielding breakthroughs and other times stalling out. In spite of the sometimes frustrating outcomes, I have never questioned the ultimate value and purpose of these efforts. To find common ground and to keep a dialogue going in spite of profound differences point the way forward through our thorniest security challenges.

# 20    The Fall of Security Ties with Russia

*I think it [NATO expansion] is the beginning of a new Cold War. I think the Russians will gradually react quite adversely and it will affect their policies. I think it is a tragic mistake.*

—George Kennan, quoted by Thomas L. Friedman,
*New York Times*, 2 May 1998[1]

At the time I left the Pentagon, our relationship with Russia was still good, but there were dark clouds on the horizon. Fearing that we could begin a downward spiral in that relationship, Ash Carter and I put a high priority on maintaining the close relationships we had formed with Russians before and during our time at the Pentagon. As part of our Preventive Defense program, we established ongoing dialogues held in Russia and the United States. But the decade of the 1990s was terrible for most Russians. They were going through a deep economic depression, lawlessness was rampant, President Yeltsin's behavior on the international scene was embarrassing, and they felt disrespected by other nations. Russians considered this a decade of humiliation. Many Russians blamed their problems on their new democracy or on the United States—feeling that we were taking advantage of their weakness to grind them down. Some Russians even yearned for the "good old days" of the Soviet Union.

In the next few years we saw the passing of power from Yeltsin to Putin, the erosion throughout Russia of democratic institutions and practices, the ascendancy of their new security organization (built around Putin's former colleagues in the KGB), restoration of order, and a significant improvement in the Russian economy. The Russian people apparently credited Putin with the restored order (which was true, but with a concomitant loss of freedom) and the improvement of the economy (which was not true, since the economy was lifted primarily by the rise in international oil prices to levels of more than $80 a barrel). In this atmosphere, Putin encouraged a strident nationalism, coupled with anti-American rhetoric.

As US-Russia relations continued to sour, our meetings in Russia grew more discouraging. Russia considered the expansions of NATO underway in 1997–99 a threat, and they regarded the later inclusion of the Baltic States as "marching the NATO threat up to their border." In what was less than enlightened conduct, the United States and NATO generally acted as if Russia's concerns were inconsequential. Particularly galling to Russians were NATO's actions in Kosovo, in the deployment of a ballistic missile defense (BMD) in Europe, and in the continuation of NATO expansion, including the Baltic states, which had been a part of the czar's Russia and, for a few decades, the Soviet Union. Subsequently, NATO started the early processing of Georgia and Ukraine for NATO membership. Now Russia distanced itself even further from NATO and showed increased resentment of the US, believing that the US displayed no regard for Russian feelings and interests, concluding that we would do whatever suited us best, leaving Russia to cope as best it could.

With great difficulty the United States had worked out a cooperative Bosnian peacekeeping operation with Russia in 1995, but we were unable to do the same for Kosovo in 1998. The NATO military intervention against the Serbs, never brought before the UN for authorization, had the important and positive objective of preventing a likely slaughter of Muslim Kosovars comparable to the slaughter of Muslim Bosnians (Bosniaks). However, Russia, as a traditional ally of Serbia, strongly opposed NATO intervention, and would have blocked any UN authorization for it. Could we have reached an agreement with Russia that protected the Kosovars? We don't know, but I don't think NATO tried very hard. NATO knew that the Russians could not stop their incursion into Kosovo and decided it would be done in spite of Russian concerns. However, the Russians could and did build a resentment that would manifest itself in later actions.

A notably serious aggravation to deteriorating US-Russia relations was our deployment of a BMD system in Europe. Since the early days of the Cold War, BMD systems (aka ABM systems) had been a contention between the United States and the Soviet Union. BMD became a dead issue after SALT was signed, because one of the treaty provisions substantially limited ABM deployments. But when the George W. Bush administration withdrew the US from the ABM treaty with the Russians in order to deploy a BMD system in Eastern Europe directed against Iranian missiles, grave tensions with Russia built up.

The original and fundamentally incisive idea behind enshrining the ABM limits in the SALT Treaty was that offensive and defensive nuclear weapon systems are inseparably linked. Even if the Russians doubted the effectiveness of the new American defense, they felt that they could not safely decrease offensive systems without also limiting our defense. In short, the Russians believe that the new BMD system in Europe is directed against *their* missiles and could, as it expands, weaken their deterrence. Further, the Russians emphasize that the Iranians presently have no ICBMs or nuclear warheads, that it would take them many years to obtain them (if they ever do), and ask why the Iranians, even if they had a few ICBMs, would fire them at the United States with our arsenal of thousands of retaliatory nuclear warheads. In the context of these arguments, Russia has appealed to the US to stop the European BMD program or, at the very least, build it cooperatively with the Russians—Iranian missiles presumably threatening Russia as much as the US. There seemed to be no prospects that the two governments might reach agreement, and so Track 2 diplomacy trying to find a viable approach sprang up.

In 2009, my Track 2 partner, Ash Carter, accepted a position in the Obama administration as undersecretary of defense (in 2011 he was promoted to deputy secretary, resigning in December 2013; in February 2015 he was confirmed as secretary of defense). I then became a Track 2 partner with Siegfried Hecker, former director of the Los Alamos National Laboratory (LANL) and a Stanford professor and coteacher of our Stanford course on technology and national security.[2] Having met with Russians on strategic issues hundreds of times, the first time when he was the director of LANL, Sig has many Russian contacts and brings a most salient background to our meetings. We have sought an approach to the European BMD issue that mitigates Russian concerns yet credits the potential danger from the Iranian nuclear program, but we have found no viable opening yet. In the meantime, Russia, concluding that no satisfactory agreement would be reached, proceeded with "appropriate actions" as though the United States were threatening its ICBMs. They began to rebuild their offensive forces and started new ICBM programs that would arm their missiles with multiple warheads, MIRVs being the least expensive increase in offensive ability. I feared that we were drifting into a new version of the Cold War nuclear arms race. I have seen this movie before; I didn't like it the first time, and I like it even less this time.

Understanding the seriousness of this offensive arms buildup underway, President Obama, just one month after taking office, declared that he was going to "press the reset button" on US-Russia relations. This was a good idea, and for a while it seemed to be working. Medvedev had succeeded Putin as president (Putin became prime minister) and seemed to be open to improving US-Russian relations. New START was signed, a treaty that limited nuclear weapons and provided for intrusive verification; Medvedev concurred in the UN resolution endorsing the goal of zero nuclear weapons and made a visit to the United States (including a visit to Stanford and a dinner hosted by George and Charlotte Shultz). The "reset" seemed to be in full swing. Then at the end of Medvedev's four-year term, he announced that he would not seek a second term, but would step aside in favor of Putin (Putin, having termed out four years earlier, was now eligible to run again).

Putin won the election, but not without charges of "ballot-stuffing." Amazingly, Medvedev told the press that when he had run four years earlier, he had made a deal with Putin to step down after his first term in favor of Putin. Many Russians were outraged and expressed their ire in a protest demonstration in Red Square that attracted more than 100,000 Russians. That demonstration was followed by a pro-Putin demonstration attended by a few hundred orderly marchers carrying neatly printed signs. I was at a meeting in Moscow at the time and watched this demonstration from the window of our conference room. One of the Russians in the meeting remarked (with typical Russian sardonic humor) that he was surprised that the government couldn't afford to hire more demonstrators.

Early in President Obama's administration, he indicated that he intended to resubmit the Comprehensive Test Ban Treaty (CTBT) for ratification, but after the tough fight to secure the ratification of New START, he decided against submitting it during his first term. As of the writing of this book, it seems unlikely that CTBT will be ratified during President Obama's second term.

Perhaps no arms control failure troubles me more than our failure to ratify the CTBT. That treaty has always seemed to be so unassailably in our national security interest that I cannot fully credit the impassioned opposition to it. Ratifying this treaty is such a clear imperative to me that I tend to impute purely political motives to the opposition. That attitude, of course, makes it hard for me to deal effectively with this opposition. Nevertheless, my essential appraisal of the CTBT is that, besides being an effective arms control measure, it is supremely in the US national security interest. After all, failing to ratify it gives other nuclear powers—in particular, Russia, China, India, and Pakistan—a pretext to test, and therefore an opportunity to develop new nuclear weapons. Indeed, I believe it is likely that Russia will soon restart testing of nuclear bombs to validate the new weapons they are now designing. And they will use our failure to ratify the CTBT as their rationale. I also fear that the Russian tests will open a floodgate of testing: China, India, Pakistan, and, not to be outdone, the United States. It is absolutely clear to me that whatever benefits to our security the United States would gain by testing our nuclear weapons—and there are some—they are more than offset by the detriment to our security of other nations developing new nuclear weapons.

After Putin's re-election and the demonstrations, US-Russian relations seemed to enter free fall. Putin saw the demonstrations as the first stage of a "color" revolution, designed to overthrow his regime, and he apparently believed that they were being organized and financed by the US government. When the new US ambassador, Mike McFaul, arrived in Moscow a few months later, he was greeted with headlines in the Moscow papers that he was sent over with instructions from President Obama to help overthrow Putin. Some greeting for a new ambassador! Contributing to this (erroneous) belief was the fact that McFaul's previous job had been as director of Stanford's Center for Democracy and the Rule of Law.

In this turmoil, the Obama administration was looking intently for a way to get relations with Russia back to a better state, but not finding much purchase. Some Russian scholars now believe that by this time Putin had "written us off" and was pursuing his own aggressive agenda without regard to our concerns, believing that we were powerless to stop him. Putin was, in a sense, reversing his feeling during the 1990s of being powerless to stop our actions.

Putin continued his attempt to instill a traditional sense of Russian prominence as a great power. In 2012, Russia hosted the Olympics and put on a spectacular show, designed to announce that Russia was back as a major power. Immediately after the Olympics the Russians began military operations in Crimea, resulting in the effective annexation of Crimea to Russia. Subsequently, after the Ukrainian president, Viktor Yanukovych, was overthrown by demonstrators in Maidan Square in Kiev, Putin supported a break-off of the largely Russian-speaking provinces in Eastern Ukraine, at first using thinly disguised Russian troops to support the local insurgents, and later not bothering with the disguise. The United States led the NATO response, consisting primarily of economic sanctions. The sanctions have been effective at the economic level, and will continue to hurt as long as the price of oil stays significantly below $80 a barrel. But the sanctions have not been effective at the political level: they have not curtailed Russian support of the insurgents.

The story I have related is sad, if not tragic. It is a parable of how quickly relations can sour, and how much damage can be done when two powerful nations operate in opposition to each other. In less than fifteen years the relations between the United States and Russia went from positive to an all-time low. It is particularly sad when one believes, as I do, that we had the opportunity in the 1990s to build a long-lasting cooperative relationship with Russia. The descent down the slippery slope began, I believe, with the premature NATO expansion, and I soon came to believe that the downsides of early NATO membership for Eastern European nations were even worse than I had feared.

President Putin has been building his popularity by promoting ultranationalism in Russia, fueled by anti-US rhetoric; the Russian military has embarked on a major arms program, most importantly in building new generations of nuclear weapons—ground-based, sea-based, and air-based—and Russian government officials have trumpeted how these weapons are the key to their security; arms reduction talks have been pushed to the side while some Russian commentators are arguing for withdrawal from New START. One popular commentator on government-controlled TV has even boasted that Russia is the only country capable of "turning the US into radioactive ash"![3] And while all this unfolds, the US government is leading an international effort to impose heavy sanctions on Russia.

How should we take stock? How should we analyze the key factors in this extremely undesirable downturn in US-Russia relations? Certainly it is one of the most unfortunate crises in the larger and longer pursuit of reducing the nuclear peril. There is no question that actions by the Russian government have contributed to these sad results; and certainly, NATO expansion did not by itself cause them. But NATO expansion was the first step.

Again, following that decision there occurred the series of other American and NATO actions that Russia found threatening: most prominently, the American deployment of BMD systems in Europe, the NATO military action against Serbia, and the proposal to offer NATO membership to Ukraine and Georgia. No one of these was decisive; but together they were interpreted by Russia as a sign of disrespect for Russia's interests—a sign that the United States did not see Russia's views as important.

It is a troubling turn of affairs that has the potential of becoming very dangerous.

# 21      Seeking Common Ground with
          China, India, Pakistan, and Iran

*The greatest leverage—the first-order and most seminal preventive mea-
sure—seems not diplomatic but economic: stimulate a major increase in
trade between India and Pakistan: again, not MAD but MAED (mutual
assured economic destruction).*

—Findings of a Track 2 US-Pakistan Dialogue, Stanford University,
23–24 August 2012[1]

As described in the previous chapter, US-Russia relationships are at an all-time
low since the ending of the Cold War, and neither our official diplomacy nor
our Track 2 programs have had much traction in turning this unfortunate situation around. But even as we looked for new ways to work with Russia, we
could not ignore the potential danger from other nations with nuclear programs—China, Iran, India, Pakistan, and North Korea.

Although I am often impatient with the obvious difficulty in making the
discussions lead to real governmental action, I truly believe that Track 2 efforts,
even though they do not encompass the authority I had when in office, are
worth my time. In the case of the China/Taiwan Track 2 work, we did succeed
in influencing some important governmental decisions.

⌒

Our Preventive Defense program placed the priority of talks with China
just below that of talks with Russia. We recognized that China had a large and
growing economy, and a significant nuclear program that it could readily and
swiftly increase should it choose to do so. China was certain to be a pivotal nation on the international scene in the coming decades.

In 1997, we met in China with my old friend and sometimes poet, Jiang
Zemin, now president of China. He agreed that we set up a long-term Track 2
initiative to improve US-China relations, saying that it should focus on cross-
strait relations with Taiwan; he appointed as head of the Chinese delegation

Wang Dao-Han, mayor of Shanghai prior to Jiang, someone whom Jiang regarded as his mentor. On our part, Ash Carter and I partnered with the National Committee on US-China Relations, which appointed as their representative Jan Berris, who had been working with the Chinese since "ping-pong diplomacy" and was fluent in Chinese. Alternating between China and the United States, we met annually, stopping in Taiwan on most of our China visits.

The Track 2 diplomacy with China and Taiwan occurred in a familiar context. For years we had focused on easing tensions between China and Taiwan, tensions that could have pulled the United States into a disastrous military conflict. But there were clear constraints on our diplomacy. Early in our Track 2 dialogue, it was evident that we could not meaningfully affect the old and deep sovereignty disagreement between China and Taiwan. Furthermore, there seemed no traditional ideas that could promise success. So we improvised with a new way of thinking: we adapted as a strategy a newer idea of deterrence, one that fit the particular period—namely, to leverage the growing prosperous economic interaction between China and Taiwan. We focused on narrowing the possibility of military conflict by promoting increased contact—business, social, and familial—across the strait, which we believed would help prevent flashpoints from leading to war. And we picked a specific issue of intrinsic leverage for our strategy: influence both sides to agree to normal civil air traffic across the strait. And indeed, such traffic finally was agreed to in 2008, after which it quickly expanded, prompting significant increases in business transactions and greatly expanding social and family connections as well as tourism.

I believe that our talks with both governments were instrumental in bringing about this agreement. There was even a prominent public sign of our influence: one of my Track 2 colleagues, Ta-Lin Hsu, reported that the Taiwan airport displayed a huge mural showing our delegation with President Ma Yingjeou. That picture was taken at our meeting in Taipei just prior to Taiwan's reaching an air traffic agreement with China.

Importantly, China's and Taiwan's businesses today are so closely intermixed that a military conflict would be disastrous for both countries, no matter the military outcome. During the Cold War, the United States and the Soviet Union were deterred from attacking each other militarily by the fear of mutual assured destruction (MAD). But times had changed, regionally and globally. Today, China and Taiwan are deterred from military conflict because of their fear of mutual assured *economic* destruction (MAED). Deterrence can be rethought with new ideas appropriate for changing times.

Along with this good news comes bad news: a growing mistrust, even hostility, may be gaining strength between the United States and China. Groups in both countries sound alarms that the other is becoming a military threat, with war inevitable, even though the long-time assumption that the China-Taiwan conflict would be the trigger has diminished. New triggers are arising to take the place of Taiwan. The long-simmering dispute over China's claim to ownership of islands and reefs in the South China Sea affects not only the other claimants but also the United States, which sees it as a challenge to freedom of navigation in the South China Sea. And the long-quiescent dispute over the ownership of some obscure islands raises the potential of a conflict between China and our ally, Japan.

I was discouraged during our Track 2 meeting with China in November 2012, held just before the 18th Party Congress. Many Chinese had worked themselves into a nationalistic fervor over the Japanese purchase of an unpopulated set of islands (Senkaku or DiaoYu) located between Taiwan and Okinawa. (The Japanese government states that they bought the islands from a Japanese citizen who they feared would undertake actions provocative to China.) I was not in Japan to witness them, but strong nationalistic sentiments were displayed there as well. China and Japan both claim to own the islands (as does, for that matter, Taiwan). There are no islanders to favor any of the claimants. Nor does there seem to be a compelling economic value to the islands, a sharp contrast to the contested islands in the South China Sea. Yet neither of these conditions cools the nationalistic fervor in play. Japan has called for the United States officially to support their claim, including asserting that our defense treaty with Japan covers the islands.

The South China Sea dispute took a dangerous turn in 2014 when the Chinese raised the stakes by first dredging the coral reefs and then in 2015 building an airbase on the Spratly Islands. This unilateral action caught the Philippines, one of the long-time claimants to the Spratlys, by surprise, confronting them with an accomplished fact. The Chinese used their military to guard their construction activity, effectively daring the Philippines or the United Sates to take any action. I find this profoundly disappointing, since it seems to indicate that China plans to realize its territorial claims by military force rather than by diplomacy. Reason dictates that these disparate claims be resolved by mediation or through an international court, or simply an understanding to maintain the status quo, but it seems that the Chinese government is preparing itself to resolve them militarily if they deem it necessary.

In 2015, the Chinese government released copies of its new military strategy, which announced their plans to build a "blue water" navy, a major departure from their present navy, which is oriented around coastal defense. Additionally, they are making a major increase in their nuclear forces, modernizing their ICBMs by adding a new ICBM with MIRVs. This represents a significant change in the capability of Chinese strategic nuclear forces. Both of these military build-ups are especially unsettling because they are coincident with China's increased aggressiveness in regional disputes. Of course, any military conflict between the claimants for any of these islands would be a major disaster for the countries involved, and, were the United States to join the conflict, a world disaster. It would be the first war between two nuclear powers, and I believe that all parties concerned understand that there would be no winners, only a global catastrophe. Yet history teaches that we should never underestimate the ability of a country to act against its own self-interests, especially when passions are high.

꙳

Another pressing issue was the growing concern over Iran, its nuclear activities, and the prospect that it would enrich its uranium and develop nuclear weapons. During the George W. Bush administration, the European Union negotiated fruitlessly with Iran to forswear enriching its uranium. When the Obama administration took office, it actively joined in those talks—a good idea—but the talks remained stalled. I thought this impasse the highest priority for Track 2 talks, and Sig Hecker and I, invited to Geneva to talk with the Iranian national security advisor, hoped that we might find an opening that could be useful to American official negotiators.

From 2007 to 2012, I was involved in four Track 2 meetings with Iranian officials, my objective to speed progress in official discussions held to prevent an Iranian nuclear arsenal. The first two meetings, one in Geneva and one in Amsterdam, were with the Iranian national security advisor; the last two, held in New York City, were with the Iranian foreign minister and were held in the margins of his UN meetings. All were organized by Bill Miller, with whom I had worked closely when I was the secretary of defense and he was our ambassador to Ukraine. Early in Bill's career as a foreign service officer, he had served five years in Iran, so he brought relevant experience, not to mention great passion, to US-Iranian issues. Alas, no tangible results have yet ensued.

The way forward, I believe, is for the European Union and the United States to accept Iranian enrichment, but limit the degree of enrichment under a reliable verification regime, which conceivably Iran would accept. If Iran is determined to build a bomb, that negotiating strategy would fail, but without seriously putting it to a test we cannot know.

Outrageous anti-Israel statements by Iranian officials have magnified the Israeli fear that Iran would attack them if it had a nuclear arsenal. Should the Iranian nuclear program come to be viewed by the Israeli government as an existential threat, there is every possibility of Israeli air strikes to destroy or set back the Iranian program. Aside from the genuine difficulties of such strikes, it is clear that they would lead to unintended consequences, all of them bad and some of them potentially very serious.

My past motivation to remain a part of a Track 2 dialogue on the Iranian nuclear program has been my belief that an Iranian nuclear arsenal could lead to a catastrophe, but the Track 2 talks have been (thankfully) replaced by serious official negotiations. As of the writing of this book, the US-European negotiating team has reached an agreement with Iran. But this agreement has powerful detractors in the United States, Israel, and Iran. The detractors in the United States and Israel are driven by the fear that the treaty provisions are too weak and Iran will exploit the treaty to build a nuclear arsenal (as North Korea exploited their IAEA membership). The detractors in Iran are apparently driven by the fear that the treaty is too strong and will succeed in preventing Iran from building a nuclear arsenal. Both of course cannot be right, and in fact I believe that neither is. They are simply reflecting the common problem of treaty negotiation—any compromise solution that is accepted by both sides of the negotiation is destined not to satisfy the extremists on both sides. If I were the American negotiator, I could easily negotiate a treaty that would satisfy all factions in the United States—but only if I were able to sit on both sides of the negotiating table! If this agreement were to fail because of domestic opposition in the United States, the outcome would be no restraints on the Iranian program and no cooperative monitoring of what they are in fact doing in their program. The extremists in Iran would undoubtedly like that outcome, but it is hard to see how any American or Israeli can think it a desirable one.

This danger of Iran going nuclear emphasizes that we are now in a new chapter in the perilous nuclear age. Two long-familiar dangers are growing—nuclear proliferation and inadequate security at too many of the far-flung nuclear facilities throughout the world. The nuclear security challenges differ much from those of the Cold War and present their own grave complexities and a steeply mounting imperative for vigilance and international cooperation. In the nuclear crisis with Iran, time is not on our side.

⌐

In the increasingly complex international picture of nuclear concerns, India and Pakistan are growing in importance. The two countries have fought three wars since their separation, all of them "won" by India, with its considerably larger economy, population, and military force. Kashmir has been a primary issue in each conflict, and since that territorial issue remains unresolved, a fourth war hardly seems remote—and now it would match two nuclear powers. Many Indians and Pakistanis, however, believe that their nuclear arsenals, with their inherent deterrence power, make the occurrence of a fourth war improbable. Both nations finally would be deterred from regional war because it might turn nuclear, a terrible escalation for both countries and, considering the possible spreading of the war and the certain contamination beyond the region of the inevitable nuclear fallout, a terrible calamity for the world at large, bringing significant casualties in many countries. But deterrence here is by no means certain. My fears of a regional nuclear war in South Asia have been raised by Pakistan's recent initiative to deploy a "tactical" nuclear weapon.

Understanding the gravity of this situation, my Stanford colleague, former secretary of state George Shultz, and I have sponsored Track 2 talks at Stanford, some with Pakistanis and some with both Indians and Pakistanis. In the margin of one meeting, a retired Pakistani senior military official confided to me his grave fear of a coming regional nuclear war. Groups in Pakistan are planning a "Mumbai 2" attack, he believes, which the Pakistani government probably cannot stop. He speculated that following another such terrorist attack against India, the Indian government, no longer showing the restraint they demonstrated during the 2008 Mumbai attack, would conduct a punitive Indian military assault into Pakistan. The outnumbered Pakistani army, in turn, would be tempted to try to repel the Indian invasion with the Pakistani "tactical" nuclear weapons. This desperate logic assumes that the Indian government, because the nuclear attack occurred only within Pakistan, might not respond in kind with Indian nuclear weapons. The retired Pakistani general and I both saw this assumption as remarkably dubious, fearing that a Pakistani decision to use "tactical" nuclear weapons could very well escalate to a full-scale nuclear war.

The chief hope in this dangerous situation is the work of serious people in both countries, in and out of government, who understand the dire risk and understand that they cannot depend on nuclear weapons deterring another war, especially with some terror groups in Pakistan possibly seeking to stimulate just such an apocalypse. In our Track 2 meetings, we have found no direct avenue to a solution of the simmering Kashmir dispute and its historical enmities. But we have discovered some indirect ways of lowering the probability of another war with its danger of a nuclear escalation. The greatest leverage—the first-order and most seminal preventive measure—seems not diplomatic but economic: stimulate a major increase in trade between India and Pakistan: again, not MAD but MAED (mutual assured *economic* destruction). Here the obvious analogy is to China and Taiwan, where the prospects of military conflict have been substantially lowered by the extensive trade and joint enterprises between Taiwan and the mainland, for the two nations have become so economically interdependent that a war would be mutually destructive.

Perhaps in yet another parable of awareness, this one especially important in the spirit of today's "globalism," grand deterrence strategy must assume a much broader popular awareness of the dangers of nuclear weapons and the need to diminish them. Economic risk, as the world economy becomes more internationally intertwined, seems far more constant and universal, far more of a continuing awareness among individuals and peoples and societies, than does a seemingly remote military danger for the most part hidden away in two superpowers and deployed in remote badlands and beneath the seas.

So our Track 2 talks have continued to focus on actions to increase trade and joint enterprises between India and Pakistan. There have been encouraging results in 2011 and 2012, and our abiding hope is that the two countries will continue to build on these mutual interests.

But for all of my concern about a regional war erupting between India and Pakistan, my grim experience with North Korea when I was secretary had alerted me to the great dangers of a nuclear North Korea. North Korea had had nuclear aspirations for decades, and I knew that they had the technical capability and the single-mindedness to realize those aspirations—they had for many years been within a few months of having enough plutonium to make six to ten nuclear bombs. As the last Stalinist regime in the world, they are unpredictably dangerous compared with the democratic regimes in India and Pakistan.

# 22    The North Korean Policy Review: Triumph and Tragedy

> *United States policy must, therefore, deal with the North Korean government as it is, not as we might wish it to be.*
> —North Korean Policy Review to President Clinton,
> President Kim Dae Jung, and Prime Minister Keizo Obuchi, 1999[1]

The last crisis with North Korea, which occurred in 1994 just after I became the secretary of defense, had been resolved by the Agreed Framework, a bilateral agreement between the United States and North Korea. Under that framework, North Korea agreed to shut down their nuclear facilities at Yongbyon, which were posed to make plutonium from the graphite-moderated reactor there; the Japanese and South Koreans agreed to build two light water nuclear reactors (LWRs) in North Korea that would provide a total generating capacity of 1,000 MW(e), and the United States agreed to furnish fuel oil until the LWRs could provide electricity. Other countries joined as well to support the effort, all of which was under the leadership first of Ambassador Steve Bosworth and then of Bob Gallucci. Everything seemed to be going well: Yongbyon remained shut down (it could have provided enough plutonium for many dozens of bombs during that period); the LWR was under construction (although behind schedule); and the US was supplying fuel oil annually.

In North Korea, however, things never go well for long. A new crisis arose in 1998. North Korea was producing, testing, and deploying the NoDong, a medium-range ballistic missile able to reach South Korea and parts of Japan. Further, North Korea was developing the Taepo Dong 1 and Taepo Dong 2 long-range missiles, both using a modification of the NoDong as their first stage. The Taepo Dong missiles, when their development was completed, would be able to reach targets in parts of the United States, as well as South Korea and all of Japan. As a result, these missiles raised concerns in both countries, particularly since intercontinental missiles make no military sense unless they carry nuclear warheads. This concern reached a crisis stage on 31 August 1998, when North Korea flew a Taepo Dong 1 over Japan in a failed attempt to launch a satellite. (The first successful Russian and American satellites had been put into orbit by military rockets.) Provoking both US and Japanese outrage, this test flight brought calls in the US Congress and the Japanese Diet to end the funding for the Agreed Framework. Yet were the Agreed Framework to have been terminated, North Korea would doubtless have reopened its nuclear facility at Yongbyon, allowing the North to produce the plutonium needed to install nuclear warheads on those missiles.

During this dangerous period, the US Congress called for, and President Clinton agreed to establish, an outside North Korean Policy Review. President Clinton asked me to lead this review, and I felt obliged to accept. I believed that the review was called for by the new risks that had arisen in the four years since we had resolved the last crisis with the Agreed Framework—new risks in which the stakes had become even higher. I scaled down to half time at Stanford so that I could spend the other half of my time on the policy review.

I would need a strong team, and I immediately asked my long-time colleague, Ash Carter, to be the deputy director of the review. He agreed and similarly scaled down his work at Harvard. I also needed strong State Department support, potentially problematic because State traditionally resented presidential appointees intruding into its business. But as secretary of defense, I had worked closely with Madeleine Albright,[2] then our UN ambassador and now the secretary of state. I told her that with a first-class State team I had a good chance to succeed, and I pledged to work closely with her. She asked Wendy Sherman, one of her strongest deputies, to serve as codeputy with Ash; and she assigned Evans Revere, the department's foremost expert on Korea, and Philip Yun, a young Korean-American who was a rising star at State. We were also fortunate that the White House loaned us Ken Lieberthal, an expert on Asian policy with whom I had worked before.

My next challenge was Congress. I set up briefings for the relevant committees, which went well, and I met one-on-one with key members. These meetings also went well save for my meeting with Senator John McCain, an opponent of the Agreed Framework, who was opposed to further dialogue with the North Koreans. It helped some that I had gotten along well with Senator McCain in my days as secretary of defense, but it was clear that he would not be supportive of this project.

Finally, I believed that it was vitally important to bring the Japanese and South Korean governments on board, each a problem and differently so. Kim Dae Jung, the South Korean president, feared that my North Korea review would upset his ongoing "sunshine policy" with North Korea, while Keizo Obuchi, the Japanese prime minister, feared that I would ignore what he saw as Japan's main issue with North Korea—securing the release of Japanese citizens who had been abducted by North Korea several decades ago and were still held in that country. I traveled to Asia, met with Prime Minister Obuchi and President Kim Dae Jung, promising each that I would take seriously their respective guidance and represent their full interests. I asked each to help me keep my promise by appointing to the review a senior representative of his government, with the three of us acting as codirectors of a "tripartite" project. This request surprised and disarmed both, and they made superb appointments to our review team. From this point forward I made no decision without the support of ambassadors Ryozo Kato and Lim Dong-Won. This approach slowed our start more than I would have liked, but in the end it paid a large dividend when we needed approval of our final report. This collaborative process (dubbed the "Perry Process" in Japan and South Korea) was widely popular in those countries, and remains so even to this day.

I believe that this collaborative approach is a model of how governments should work together on many important issues in our increasingly global times with their worldwide security concerns, especially regarding the perilous nuclear question. I believe in the collaborative process because my experience has shown me that individuals and nations, even those with a history of conflict and competition, can cooperate to important ends under a policy of mutual trust and respect. Undeniably, the North Korean crisis was an ominous portent. The nuclear weapons crisis, historically and by nature, must inevitably be a global crisis. It is in the urgent common interests of individual nations to collaborate in the diplomacy of creating international programs and processes to mitigate the threat.

In that spirit, and along with South Korea and Japan, I also held information meetings with Chinese and Russian government officials to get their advice and to keep them informed of our progress, even though they were not part of the formal approval process for the review.

With this collaborative foundation in place I started the review. During the next five months our tripartite group met six times: once in Washington, once in Tokyo, two times in Honolulu, and two times in Seoul. The meetings got off to a slow start because of the traditional suspicion between Japan and Korea, but as I had anticipated, our Japanese and Korean codirectors soon rose above that; thereafter the meetings went smoothly, and we quickly arrived at a consensus.

Our tripartite project team recognized that the strength of our coalition military forces was solidly in our favor in the power balance, a fact understood as well by the North. Our deterrence was not only strong, we concluded, but would remain so barring the North's introduction of nuclear weapons, which could occur if North Korea restarted Yongbyon and began producing plutonium. We were keenly aware that North Korea could restart operations at Yongbyon in just a few months.

We noted that our governments were balancing two fundamentally different strategies, one new and one traditional. The new and preferred strategy was to make step-by-step progress to comprehensive normalization and a peace treaty (technically we still remained in a state of war, since the Korean War had ended in a truce), while the North Koreans dismantled their facilities capable of making nuclear weapons.

The more traditional alternative was a coercive strategy, applying successively stronger sanctions against North Korea, attempting to coerce them into giving up their nuclear facilities. For the coercive approach, we recommended first strengthening our deterrence forces, including adding key units to our Seventh Fleet, deploying additional troops to South Korea, and accelerating the deployment of ballistic missile defense (BMD) systems there.

Since the second strategy would be expensive, dangerous, and could all too easily slide into war, we put our focus on achieving the first. But we emphasized that none of our individual governments could unilaterally implement that strategy, for it would need the support of each of our legislative bodies and the full cooperation of the three allies (for which the tripartite meetings cleared a path). Most important, North Korea would have to agree to cooperate with our preferred strategy and the conditions it imposed on them. If it did not, we would have to fall back to the coercive strategy. All three leaders of our governments approved our recommendation and authorized me to visit Pyongyang to see if the leaders of the North would accept our preferred strategy. President Kim and Prime Minister Obuchi gave me letters authorizing me to speak for their countries, as well as for the United States. There was essentially full (even enthusiastic) agreement on our plan of action, a testimony to the tripartite process by which it was drawn up. We did not at this stage seek approval from our legislative bodies, although we knew that such approval would be necessary if I were able to get an agreement with North Korea.

The North Korean government permitted my team to fly into Pyongyang on a US military aircraft, a good sign that they took our mission seriously (as well as a great convenience over the alternative of flying to Beijing to wait for one of the infrequent flights to Pyongyang). I have to confess that I was somewhat nervous when our military aircraft crossed into North Korean airspace—had the ground-based air defense battery received word of our permission to fly in? Evidently so. We were met at the airport by a North Korean delegation that escorted us to our guest houses for a rest, after which we met that evening with the president of the Supreme People's Assembly, a cordial but largely ceremonial affair, since Kim Jong Il, in fact, held the real power in North Korea. I looked over the schedule he gave me and pointed out that it showed no meetings with military leaders. Reminding my host that I had been the US secretary of defense, I asked to meet with a military leader. I also told him that we had brought medical supplies and would like to deliver them to the Children's Hospital in Pyongyang. He agreed to both requests.

The next morning we were escorted to a conference room and, as we assembled, a North Korean general entered leading a delegation. The conversation went something like this:

> "This meeting was not my idea," he said at once. "I was directed to meet with you. I don't think we should even be talking about giving up nuclear weapons."
>
> I replied, "Why do you think you need nuclear weapons?"
>
> "To defend ourselves from aggression!"
>
> "Aggression from whom?"
>
> "From *you* [pointing at me]! We will develop nuclear weapons. Then, if you attack us, we will use our nuclear weapons to destroy your cities—not excluding Palo Alto!"

I appreciate candor in diplomacy, but this was, perhaps, overdoing it! In any event, I knew exactly where we stood with the general. In spite of the rocky beginning, the ensuing discussion proved to be interesting and useful. One indicative side note about North Korean intergovernmental relations came when the representative of the North Korean foreign minister made a point and the general interrupted to tell us, "You don't have to pay any attention to these 'neckties.' They don't know anything about military matters!"

Our experience the following day was much different. We visited the Pyongyang Children's Hospital, where the chief physician at the hospital received us graciously. When we presented her with the medical supplies, including a large supply of antibiotics, she was almost in tears. She told us that children died needlessly there every day because there were no antibiotics. She invited me to visit with some of the children, and then paused, saying apologetically, "I have to warn you. This morning I told them that you were coming, and they asked me if you were here to kill them." Could there be a sadder commentary on the warping of minds caused by hateful propaganda? North Koreans have no access to news except via government radio and television, which bombards them 24–7 with warnings about American "fascist war mongers." (During the 1994 crisis, for example, the North Korea media called me a "war maniac.")[3] Nevertheless, the visit went without incident, and the children were delightful.

We spent most of three days negotiating with Kang Sok Ju, the senior North Korea diplomat, and the discussions were entirely without bluster. The North Koreans obviously valued their missiles, and saw them as providing deterrence, prestige, and cash from foreign sales. But they understood that giving up long-range missiles as well as nuclear weapons was the path to normalization of relations. Most important, they obviously wanted normalization, which, after decades of insecurity, could finally lead to a secure, stable, and prosperous Korean Peninsula.

Before we left Pyongyang we toured the city, including the famed Juche Tower. While there, a bus stopped below and its passengers disembarked, joined hands, and began dancing in a desultory manner. All the surrounding streets were otherwise empty, prompting us to ask about the dancers. Our guide said that these were "spontaneous, popular masses."

On our return flight home, the consensus of our team was that North Korea was ready to accept the cooperative strategy we had presented.

In the year following our Pyongyang meeting, everything pointed to normalization. The two Korean teams marched together in the 2000 Sydney Olympics; Kim Jong Il, in a trip to Shanghai, visited the stock exchange and a Buick plant; North and South Korea held a first-ever summit meeting; and Japan and North Korea began planning a summit meeting. During that heady period, Lee and I traveled to Seoul with our son, David, and his son, Michael, a native Korean. We wanted Michael, adopted when he was less than a year old and now fifteen, to be reintroduced to his native country. When we arrived late one evening at Seoul airport after a long flight, we were swarmed by reporters and camera operators from Seoul's television stations, each clamoring for an interview with Michael and me. US ambassador Steve Bosworth, there to meet us, managed to shield the barely awake Michael from the cameras and whisked us to the ambassador's residence. Over the next three days, Lee and I took David and Michael on a tour of South Korea, including a train ride to see the ruins of the Silla dynasty tombs. We were recognized everywhere by Koreans who wanted to speak with us, and who invariably tried to use Michael as an interpreter, but Michael did not speak Korean.

On our last evening in Seoul, we were invited to attend a soccer match between Brazil and South Korea—the game of the year in Seoul. The teams were well matched, and with the score 0–0 in overtime, the Korean left wing intercepted a Brazilian pass, raced down the length of the field, and scored the winning goal—Michael and I jumped to our feet and an alert photographer a few seats in front of us snapped a picture of us waving our arms and cheering. The next morning, the Korean paper *Chosun Ilbo* ran the picture on its front page headlined, "Perry and Oldest Grandson Heartily Cheer Soccer Match."[4] What a memento for Michael! The next morning, just before we left for the airport, we took Michael to a souvenir shop where he chose a sweatshirt. As he reached for his wallet, the clerk told him, "You are Michael Perry—you don't need to pay!" Neither Michael nor I will forget that incident. It showed the true warmth and hospitality of the Korean people; I also believe it was a tangible demonstration of how deeply their citizens wanted peace in their divided and war-scarred country.

The "sunshine policy" continued forward. In October 2000, Kim Jong Il in-

"Perry and Perry Cheer Korea on to Victory." Perry with grandson Michael Perry (*right, with raised arms*) at soccer match between Korea and Brazil, March 1999. From *Chosun Ilbo.*

dicated his support for our proposal by dispatching his senior military official, Vice-Marshal Jo Myong-Rok, to Washington. On his way, he stopped off at Stanford to visit me. Kim Jong Il had told him to ask me to take him to some Silicon Valley companies, so I organized a motor trip around the San Francisco Bay Area during which we visited three high-tech companies. Marshal Jo's visit coincided with Fleet Week in San Francisco, an annual celebration of naval tradition in the Bay Area, and we were entertained on our drive across the Bay Bridge by the Navy's Blue Angels flying overhead in tight formation, while a parade of ships down in the bay featured cruisers, destroyers, and aircraft carriers. The marshal probably thought the show of military might had been organized for his benefit!

That evening I hosted Marshal Jo for dinner at Stanford's Encina Hall and invited three Korean-American businessmen to join us, including my friend Jeong Kim,[5] a senior technology officer for Lucent who later became the president of Bell Labs. Earlier in the day, Jeong had given Marshal Jo a tour of Lucent's advanced optical lab. Although Marshal Jo did not understand the technology, he did understand that it was decades ahead of anything in North Korea. At dinner, our three Korean businessmen could not only talk to Marshal Jo in his own language but they served as examples of how successful Koreans can be in the free market system, which we (and North Korea's Chinese colleagues) were encouraging the North to consider.

The next day Marshal Jo flew to Washington to meet President Clinton and other government officials, and gave the president an invitation from Kim Jong Il to visit Pyongyang. On his last evening in Washington, Secretary Albright held a banquet for Marshal Jo, which I attended, sitting beside him. The banquet coincided with my birthday, and Secretary Albright led the traditional "Happy Birthday" song. Marshal Jo learned in the ensuing table discussion that I was three weeks older than he, whereupon (in the North Korean culture greater age implies greater wisdom) he rose and toasted my advanced years, to the general amusement of all the Americans in the room. The warm feelings in the room that night, along with the developments of the previous year, made us all hopeful that the threat of a nuclear North Korea was behind us. But that was not to be.

By then, President Clinton had only three months left in his second term. The two major foreign policy issues he wanted to address before leaving office were North Korea normalization and an Israel-Palestine peace treaty. He held both in high priority, believed that he had a chance to achieve one, but did not have time for both. He chose to spend his remaining time on a Mideast peace treaty, and almost succeeded but ultimately fell short when Yasser Arafat developed cold feet at the last minute. So sadly then, despite a determined and creative effort, President Clinton lost on both issues.

Colin Powell,[6] who was the chairman of the Joint Chiefs when I joined the Clinton administration, was now the designated secretary of state in the George W. Bush administration. I brought him up to date on our negotiations, and he told me that he planned to follow up on our negotiations with North Korea and try to bring them to a successful conclusion. Just six weeks after President Bush's inauguration, South Korean president Kim Dae Jung visited Washington for reassurance that the new administration would follow through on the North Korea negotiations that I had started. Secretary Powell apparently gave him that assurance, which led to the next morning's *Washington Post* headlines reading: "Bush to Pick up Clinton Talks."[7] That same afternoon, when President Kim met with President Bush, the latter told Kim flatly that he was breaking off all dialogue with North Korea, and for two years there were no discussions with the North. I was confused and angry as I saw our long and carefully conducted diplomacy being summarily rejected. And I was despondent at what the future would bring in Korea as this opportunity for diplomacy slipped away. I appealed to my long-time friends in the State Department, Colin Powell and Rich Armitage, but they had no real option but to comply with the president's decision.

In October 2002, Assistant Secretary of State James Kelly visited Pyongyang and told North Korean government leaders that our intelligence had discovered another nuclear processing activity underway in North Korea, this one to enrich uranium (Yongbyon in its active days produced plutonium, which entails an entirely different process for making nuclear fuel). The facts behind this assessment have never been made public, but it does appear that in 2002 North Korea was in the early stage of a uranium enrichment program. The meeting ended in acrimony, and shortly after the meeting, the United States, Japan, and South Korea issued a joint statement ". . . that North Korea's program to enrich uranium for nuclear weapons is a violation of the Agreed Framework, the Non-Proliferation Treaty, North Korea's IAEA safeguards agreement, and the South-North Joint Declaration on Denuclearization of the Korean peninsula."[8] The outcome was that both the United States and North Korea withdrew from the Agreed Framework. The US stopped delivery of fuel oil; Japan and North Korea stopped work on the LWRs; North Korea responded, as I expected, by reopening Yongbyon and beginning once again to produce plutonium (the activity behind the crisis in 1994). The Bush administration called this action "unacceptable" but took no effective actions to stop it.

In 2003, China, alarmed by the growing danger in the region, established the so-called six party talks with North Korea, South Korea, Japan, China, Russia, and the United States. These talks seemed like a good idea, but apparently unrelated to "facts on the ground," were getting nowhere. Indeed, during the talks, North Korea completed the reprocessing at Yongbyon and, on 9 October 2006, conducted its first nuclear bomb test. I was critical of the administration for not insisting that progress at Yongbyon be suspended while the talks were underway, a critical condition that President Clinton had insisted on in 1994 before he began talks with the North Koreans.

Frustrated by the official failure, I began to engage in unofficial Track 2 diplomacy with North Korea. In February 2007, I made my first visit to the joint North-South special economic zone at Kaesong in North Korea near the border with South Korea. There, more than a dozen modern manufacturing facilities were complete with many more planned. Under the Kaesong business model, the North supplies the land and labor and the South supplies the capital and management. What I saw there impressed me, and I believed that it could be a precursor to the Korea of the future. The South Korean companies had done a first-rate job of establishing facilities for making low-tech, high-quality products. The working conditions were excellent, and the North Korean workers productive. My friend, Jeong Kim, joined me on that visit, and I benefited from his experience with manufacturing and his Korean language skills.

In January 2008, my Stanford colleagues John Lewis and Sig Hecker visited North Korea and were given an extensive tour of the nuclear processing plant at Yongbyon, where they were shown that those facilities were being dismantled. It seemed as though we might have again reached a negotiating path with North Korea.

A month later I went to South Korea for the inauguration of President-elect Lee Myung-Bak. In President Lee's remarkable inauguration speech, he challenged North Korea to give up its nuclear program and offered to help build up their economy if they would do so. Some weeks before, North Korea, to the world's surprise, had invited the New York Philharmonic to give a concert in Pyongyang. To *my* surprise, I was invited by the North Korean government to attend and, while there, to meet with their negotiators for unofficial bilateral nuclear talks. The concert was 26 February, just a day after President Lee's inauguration, and I was forced to decline because there was not enough time to fly to Pyongyang from Seoul by the only permitted air route to North Korea— through Beijing. Unexpectedly, the North Korean government told me that if I agreed to attend the concert, I would have their permission to travel directly from Seoul to Pyongyang by crossing the DMZ in an official car. I immediately accepted.

Crossing the DMZ was both a unique and eerie experience. The North Korean government sent a car to pick me up, but because it had snowed heavily the night before, the road had to be cleared. To my astonishment, the government had dispatched thousands of workers with brooms and shovels to clear the road to Pyongyang on which we were the only car. The road is only occasionally used, even in good weather, and then only by officials, because ordinary North Korean citizens did not have cars. After I had crossed the DMZ, the Korean colonel who was my escort, and who had until then favored me with a forbidding expression on his face, broke into a big grin and joked: "I would offer you some ginseng, but it would be wrong because your wife is not with you!" (The "joke" is based on ginseng's supposed aphrodisiac properties.) Even though lame, the joke served to break the tension. Once in Pyongyang, my nuclear discussions with North Korean officials produced little, but the concert that evening was memorable.

I expected the musical performance to be outstanding, and the New York Philharmonic rose to the occasion; what I didn't expect was to see the American flag on stage and to hear the American national anthem performed. But the greatest surprise was the standing ovation the North Koreans gave the American musicians. It was a magic moment. I have never seen such an emotional outpouring of people-to-people friendship. A few US senior administration officials had been invited to the concert but declined; in my view, that was another missed opportunity. The event was not just a concert, any more than "ping-pong diplomacy" with China in 1971 was just a ping-pong game. That concert and its aftermath were opportunities to explore an entirely new relationship with North Korea, potentially leading to a significant improvement in security on the Korean Peninsula.

I had hoped that the concert might have created another opening for positive dealings with North Korea. But the next American action was to tighten its sanctions. From that point, North Korea has launched one provocative action after another. They conducted a second and, according to US intelligence, probably successful nuclear test in 2009; they launched a satellite that failed before it entered orbit; and in 2012 they successfully put a satellite in orbit. A previous UN resolution had enjoined North Korea from launching long-range missiles, but their satellite, in a flouting of the resolution, used as its first two stages the Taepo Dong long-range missile, after which the UN ordered imposed sanctions on North Korea. Undeterred, North Korea conducted a third nuclear test in February 2013. Statements from the North Korean government in response to the sanctions were remarkably vitriolic, even by their standards:

> We do not hide that a variety of satellites and long-range rockets which will be launched by the DPRK one after another and a nuclear test of higher level will target against the US, the sworn enemy of the Korean people.[9]

In 2000, we had the possibility (not a certainty) of reaching some degree of normalization with a North Korea that appeared ready to give up its nuclear aspirations for economic revival. By 2015 we faced an angry and defiant North Korea that had armed itself with six to ten nuclear bombs, was producing fissile material for more bombs, and was testing the components of long-range missiles. Based on those outcomes, this is perhaps the most unsuccessful exercise of diplomacy in our country's history.

# 23          Fiasco in Iraq: Then and Now

*President George W. Bush's decision to invade Iraq in 2003 ultimately may come to be seen as one of the most profligate actions in the history of American foreign policy.*[1]

—Opening sentence, *Fiasco*, Thomas E. Ricks, 2006

Although my priorities in my Track 2 work have always been focused on nuclear issues, and therefore focused on nuclear powers or aspiring nuclear nations, I found it impossible to ignore Iraq. First of all, Iraq's alleged nuclear capability was a primary rationale for the war. Was there a possibility that along with North Korea, Iraq now presented an authentic case of nuclear concern? As it developed, Iraq did not then have a viable nuclear weapons program.

But even beyond that question it was impossible to ignore a war that soon began entailing large casualties and difficult moral issues. Furthermore, the war in Iraq was brought home to me in a very personal way when one of my grandsons, Nicolas Perry, enlisted in the marines, eventually serving three tours in Fallujah—one of the most dangerous spots for American troops. So I soon found myself being drawn into the contentious debate on Iraq.

As 2006 began, America was being torn apart by the war in Iraq. Words like "fiasco" and "quagmire" were typical descriptors, recalling the Vietnam War, one of the saddest periods in recent American history. After the magnitude of the Iraq disaster had become clear, the US Congress, alarmed at the increasingly dangerous US entanglement, commissioned an independent bipartisan study, the Iraq Study Group (ISG), charged to reach consensus on a way forward in Iraq. James Baker and Lee Hamilton, named cochairmen, each chose four other members from his own party, and I was selected as one. Additionally, Baker and Hamilton recruited forty expert advisors; neither the members nor the advisors received compensation (except the standard government allowance for travel). We met two to three days each month from March to August of 2006, talked with the selected experts on Iraq from in and out of government, and deliberated among ourselves.

As we gathered perspective and began to develop recommendations, I concluded that we were dealing with a large error in US foreign policy composed of numerous smaller errors. I discuss those errors below because I believe they constitute a negative blueprint for behavior in today's increasingly dangerous world. The missteps fall into two sets. The first set has to do with the rationale for invading Iraq; the second with the execution of the invasion and subsequent occupation.

Among its stated reasons for the Iraq invasion, the George W. Bush administration foremost trumpeted an imminent danger from weapons of mass destruction (WMD) programs in Iraq. Military action to stop an illegal nuclear program, which would have been warranted, should have targeted nuclear facilities, not entailed occupation of Iraq. There was, however, no imminent or even gathering danger from Iraqi nuclear weapons or other WMD. The reports of the UN inspectors appear to have been correct in their prewar assessment.

The second dubious justification by the administration was an alleged imminent danger to the United States from an imputed support of Al Qaeda by Iraq. Military action to defeat Al Qaeda, which could have been justified just as in Afghanistan, foundered here because Al Qaeda, which used Afghanistan as a training area, had no significant presence in Iraq before the US invasion, and it had no important relationship with Iraq's government.

The third reason to invade Iraq advanced by the administration was that it would bring stability to the Middle East by creating a democratic government in Iraq. Obviously a democratic government there could be a blessing to Iraqis and a boon to the region, but spreading democracy by the sword turned out to be hugely more difficult than the administration imagined. Could any strategy have fully succeeded in bringing a democratic, stable government to Iraq? Since the administration's attempts were burdened with serious and fundamental errors, we will never know.

In particular, four errors in execution were the most consequential:

The administration failed to obtain support from regional powers and from key allies. US forces constituted almost 90 percent of the coalition forces, as opposed to about 70 percent in Desert Storm and 50 percent in Bosnia.

The administration sent in too few troops to maintain security after the Iraqi army was defeated. With the Iraqi army scattered and the breakout of massive looting throughout the country, the United States lacked the resources to impose order, ironically giving the insurgency ample opportunity to establish a growing presence.

The administration disbanded the Iraqi army and dismissed most civil servants a few weeks after the Iraqi army was defeated. About 400,000 unemployed and angry young men, many still armed, were loosed on Iraqi towns, and Iraq had no security force except the undersized coalition military.

The administration pressured the Iraqi provisional government to write a constitution and to hold elections, but in a faulty process careless of minority rights, fueling a bloody power struggle between Shias and Sunnis.

The cumulative effect was a disastrous failure of security in Iraq. Every month about a hundred US military personnel and thousands of Iraqis were killed or wounded. As the violence trended up and coalition forces could not stop it, well over a million Iraqis left the country, among them large numbers of Iraqi professionals.

It was at this time, with the situation spinning out of control, that the US Congress established the Iraq Study Group. Crucial to our fact-finding were discussions with the Iraqi government. In September we spent four days in Baghdad meeting with the top government officials and with our military commanders, the meetings chaired by either Jim Baker or Lee Hamilton, both superb diplomats. We found ourselves impressed by the dedication and competence of our diplomatic teams and those of our allies. Iraqi governmental leaders clearly were out of their depth, hardly a surprise given that there was no history of democratic institutions in Iraq. We found a high level of competence in American military leaders, and American troops exhibited a high level of training and performance. We found a low level of competence and dedication among Iraqi military leaders and troops.

Neither of those findings on the military surprised me. I had my own personal "boots on the ground" assessment from my grandson, Lance Cpl. Nicolas Perry, serving with the Marine Expeditionary Force in Iraq. He was on his second of three tours conducting foot and mounted patrols in Fallujah, then a notoriously dangerous area. Our study group's assessment coincided with Nick's: the American troops were first-rate, but the Iraqi troops had no concept of discipline or of the purpose for which they were fighting. Even those Iraqi troops sent through the training program we had set up would think nothing of going AWOL for a few weeks to go home; and many were more loyal to their tribal groups than to their company commanders. The following year, Nick's third tour, he was assigned to conduct on-the-job training of an Iraqi battalion by patrolling the streets of Fallujah with them. Given what I knew of the Iraqi military, I was intensely worried about his safety on that

Lance Corporal Nicolas Perry in Iraq.

assignment. (The above insights into the poor capabilities of the Iraqi military were signals of the later battlefield failures of those units to preserve the new post-Saddam political regime after the US forces had departed. This illustrates that while training is important—and the United States did provide extensive and expensive training to the Iraqi army—motivation is at least as important. Training must be done in the context of the military's relationship to the nation's culture and to the soldier's quality of life, both in question in Iraq.)

Returned from Iraq, we spent five intensive days seeking consensus. That we succeeded is a tribute to our extraordinary cochairmen. We were all motivated by the seriousness of the Iraq conflict for our country and knew that to help we must reach a bipartisan consensus. The ISG report was released to the public on 6 December 2006. It counseled to change the mission, to reinvigorate diplomacy in the region, to strengthen the Iraqi government, and to begin redeploying US and coalition troops.

The change in mission was key. An emphasis, we concluded, should be on strengthening the present Iraqi government's ability to prevent a full-scale civil war. We should continue our efforts to defeat Al Qaeda in Iraq, which although insignificant in Iraq before the war, now had a strong foothold and was specializing in mass killings, a major sign of future problems should Iraq become even more unstable. Co-opting the insurgents, we advised, could turn the insurgency in Anwar Province, and that strategy was already starting to be pursued, with encouraging results. This was proving to be an effective strategy because Al Qaeda leaders in Iraq had badly overplayed their hand in Anwar Province, turning most of the tribal leaders against them. We believed that we should continue to support Iraqi forces with intelligence, logistics, and air support. And we needed to provide both positive and negative incentives for the Iraqi government to accelerate the reconciliation process and to implement the sharing of oil revenues so that the Sunnis had a stake in a stable Iraq. An important negative incentive was for the administration to establish a pullout date so that the Iraqi government would understand that they had to take responsibility for their own security sooner rather than later.

A week after receiving our report, the president proposed a new way forward in Iraq that differed from the ISG recommendations in two important ways: adding about thirty thousand combat forces, the bulk to be used in securing Baghdad (the ISG had considered such a recommendation but had not been able to reach a consensus on it); and not agreeing to set a pullout date. I thought then that President Bush was doubling down on a losing game by keeping the same strategy and the leaders responsible for the fiasco. But it soon turned out that my assessment was wrong. Within a few weeks, President Bush replaced Defense Secretary Donald Rumsfeld, the architect of our Iraq strategy, with Bob Gates,[2] a member of the ISG and, incidentally, a long-time friend dating back to our service together in the Carter administration. Bush further replaced the US military leaders in Iraq with a team focused on counterinsurgency operations as detailed in a new army manual authored by General David Petraeus, with special emphasis on bringing the Sunnis in Anwar Province to our side. I granted this new approach a good chance of success, considering it a better strategy than the one we had recommended in the ISG. In retrospect, the real value of our ISG report is that it probably forced the president's hand and accelerated his decision to change leaders and strategy in Iraq.

After years of conflict and a terrible price in blood and treasure, the United States finally reached the point where it was able to withdraw its occupying military forces from Iraq owing to a tenuous period of reduced violence among rival Iraqi groups in the postwar period. But not surprisingly, the relative quiet did not persist. Hopes for, and even some apparent signs of, a political turn in Iraq toward a relatively stable democratic politics, an *inclusive* politics that could bring more stability and peace than in the past and over an indefinite period, were abruptly quashed as highly traditional sectarian violence rose again. Indeed, since the departure of the US forces, Iraq has been increasingly torn by bloody conflict between Sunni and Shiite factions, joined opportunistically by other aggressive groups, conflicts that seem almost impossible to resolve, at least in the near term.

As I write this book, in fact, Iraq seems to be on the verge of breaking apart. In 2014, extremist Sunnis formed ISIL, a new "state" dedicated to returning the caliphate to the Mideast, and began attacking government forces in Iraq and Syria, which had governments dominated by Shiites and Alawites. In 2015, ISIL military forces, showing impressive strength and discipline, scored major victories against Iraqi government forces that in fact outnumbered them, calling in question the will of the government forces to fight for their country. Sunni tribal leaders in the Anwar Province, who had played a key role in defeating Al Qaeda when American forces were still in Iraq, apparently did not join the fight against ISIL. It appears that the failure of the Shia-dominated government in Iraq to give the Sunni minority an equal role in the government was now playing out in these terrible consequences. The Iraqi government responded by forming Shia militias to try to turn the tide of battle, but this only exacerbates the Sunni-Shia divide. Allied forces attempted to turn the tide by limited air strikes on ISIL forces, but in the absence of competent Iraqi ground forces, such support cannot be decisive. The American goal of building a democratic Iraq was giving way to a civil war that could lead to a new division of power in the Mideast along Sunni-Shia lines, destroying former national boundaries and leading to a region in perpetual civil war between regions controlled by Shiites and regions controlled by Sunnis. In that environment, only the most radical versions of those religions could prevail. As of the writing of this book, American and allied forces were considering a change in military strategy, but the reluctance to get re-involved in a ground war in Iraq is profound, so the outcome of this conflict is uncertain. What is certain, however, is that America's quixotic adventure in Iraq was a major disaster; still to be resolved is the extent of the disaster.

In a world in which we must control the spread of nuclear weapons to terror groups and other aggressive actors, Iraq is a prime example of how not to succeed in achieving this critical objective.

# 24    The Nuclear Security Project: Former "Cold Warriors" Offer a New Vision

*I state clearly and with conviction the commitment of the United States to seek the peace and security of a world without nuclear weapons.*

—President Barack Obama, Prague, 5 April 2009[1]

On 11–12 October 1986, an historic summit meeting was held in Reykjavik, Iceland, between US president Ronald Reagan, accompanied by Secretary of State George Shultz, and USSR general secretary Mikhail Gorbachev, accompanied by Minister of Foreign Affairs Eduard Shevardnadze. Remarkably, they discussed dismantling all of their nuclear weapons—an agreement Reagan and Gorbachev both wanted but were unable to reach. The stumbling block was that Gorbachev, citing the link between offensive and defensive nuclear weapons, sought a provision by which the Americans would "limit the SDI program to the laboratory." This was a condition Reagan would not accept, ending those talks without an agreement.

The importance of Reykjavik in the dark nuclear era is immense. The Cuban Missile Crisis, one might argue, was the most dangerous episode in this unfolding history of our time when erratic humankind, in the words of Henry Kissinger, now possesses "the fire of the gods." Certainly the Cuban Missile Crisis, hardly the only close call of the nuclear era, brought us to the brink of a world catastrophe. And as I noted earlier, we may have avoided a disaster through considerable luck. "Luck" is a dishearteningly unreliable deliverer from nuclear conflagrations. Indeed, the decades of the Cold War nuclear arms race—its unthinkable surreal "overkill"—surely have done nothing to curb a deep pessimism that the eventual outcome might be the end of our civilization. But suddenly, at Reykjavik, in an inspiring burst of radically new thinking, the nuclear powers met in a spirit of dismantling their nuclear forces! It was not the first appearance of that enlightened idea. And certainly there was reasonable skepticism about the plausibility of follow-through had there been an agreement. But Reykjavik may be thought of as a beacon that affirms the well-being of new ways of thinking and the positive possibilities they inspire in our quest to prevent further use of nuclear weapons and ultimately eliminate them.

On their return to Washington, Reagan and Shultz were harshly criticized for even discussing the elimination of nuclear weapons, most notably by Prime Minister Thatcher, who made a special trip to Washington to unleash a scathing rebuke to Shultz, and then, more diplomatically, to express her concern to Reagan. Notwithstanding these criticisms, George Shultz understood very clearly the positive significance of Reykjavik and continued to work to contain the transcendental danger of the world's nuclear arsenals.

Nearly twenty years later, Shultz reflected that the Reykjavik Summit was a uniquely important moment in history and deserving of commemoration. He discussed this with Stanford physicist Sid Drell, who suggested hosting a seminar at Stanford's Hoover Institute to revisit the Reykjavik Summit on the day of its twentieth anniversary. Sid and former ambassador Jim Goodby[2] took on the considerable task of organizing the meeting and commissioning appropriate papers to pursue the lessons of Reykjavik from a twenty-year perspective.

The seminar produced a robust discussion.[3] One of the participants, Richard Perle, who was the DoD representative at the original Reykjavik meeting, said bluntly that complete nuclear disarmament was a bad idea in 1986 and remained a bad idea. But a majority of the attendees thought it should be re-examined, the most eloquent advocate being Max Kampelman,[4] the veteran American diplomat. Kampelman stressed the humanistic importance of establishing "oughts." He drew an analogy to the Declaration of Independence, ". . . all men are created equal." Although obviously not true in practice in America when the Declaration was signed, most of the signers believed that it *ought* to be. By declaring the "ought" as a vision, our nation was able to work toward that condition, if over much time and sometimes (as in the Civil War) with enormous pain. Without the "ought" as an ideal, our progress toward that vision would have been doubtful. With Kampelman's analogy as a touchstone, most of the seminar participants concluded that the idea of a world without nuclear weapons, if premature in 1986, was now an idea whose time had come. We ought to have a world without nuclear weapons.

The conference was a turning point in my own thinking, bridging my growing concern over nuclear danger and presenting a catalyst to move forward, guided by a vision of a world without nuclear weapons. Because of my unique vantage point I had for several decades been deeply concerned about the dangers posed by nuclear weapons, but it seemed that total disarmament was impractical—that we could not uninvent nuclear weapons. Instead I focused my efforts on facilitating steps that could reduce the dangers they posed. After decades, I could see that our success had been very limited—there were still tens of thousands of nuclear weapons in the world and new nations were taking steps to build their own. Any meaningful success had to be at an international level, and most nations were not willing to take seriously the US preaching to them that they did not need nuclear weapons when they saw the United States and Russia demonstrating that nuclear weapons were vital to their security. Although I believed then—and now—that progress toward zero would be very difficult and very slow, I concluded after the conference that it would never succeed, even to reach its limited goals of reducing nuclear dangers, unless the international efforts were tied to eventually reaching a goal of zero, and that it was paramount to have that vision as the propelling force. Perhaps I was more impressed by Max Kampelman's "ought" than I was by the arguments of traditional arms controllers.

Encouraged by the substance and momentum of the meeting, George Shultz, Sid Drell, Sam Nunn, and I agreed that we should schedule a follow-on meeting for the next anniversary of Reykjavik. In the interim, we decided to write an op-ed that would call the world's attention to the great dangers posed by nuclear weapons, call for increased urgency in taking steps to reduce those dangers, and advocate that we begin moving toward a world without nuclear weapons. George noted that our group was composed of three Democrats and one Republican, and quite rightly observed that reducing the danger of nuclear weapons was a nonpartisan matter and that our proposition should be seen from the outset as nonpartisan. After an invitation from George, Henry Kissinger joined our group and Sid volunteered to leave his name off the article to ensure that it would be seen as nonpartisan. George submitted this fateful op-ed to the *Wall Street Journal* in January 2007.[5]

We expected little response other than the usual commentary from security specialists, so we were surprised to be swamped with letters and news posts from around the world, most agreeing that the time was overdue for a serious re-evaluation of nuclear arsenals and postures. Buoyed, we scheduled meetings with senior government officials and former officials in other countries. For the next several years we were on a nonstop travel schedule, attending conferences dedicated to examining the ideas outlined in our op-ed, and meeting with government and NGO officials in Russia, China, India, Japan, Germany, Italy, Norway, and the United Kingdom.

Our op-ed quite naturally attracted the interest of the community of specialists who had been pursuing nuclear disarmament for many years. Some of them were querulous, saying in effect, "What took you so long?" But most saw our op-ed as a golden opportunity to advance the cause they had pursued unsuccessfully for so long. It seemed that the "Peaceniks" were being joined by the "Cold Warriors," giving more credibility to their cause, now a common cause.

In a sense that was true, but differences remained. A long-time colleague, Bruce Blair, who had long advocated nuclear disarmament, took the opportunity to form a new organization, called Global Zero, which had an appealingly simple goal: to seek an international treaty banning all nuclear weapons. Each of the members of our group had discussions with Bruce and other Global Zero members to see if we should somehow collaborate, but these efforts failed. While we agreed on the end goal, we had vastly different ideas about how to achieve them. Rather than seeking a world treaty banning nuclear weapons, we believed that a more realistic approach was to proceed step by step to reduce the dangers of nuclear arsenals, and to clearly articulate why we believed this and how to go about doing so. As Sam Nunn has described so effectively, we were at a base camp not even halfway up a mountain and saw our goal as reaching the top of the mountain, which was obscured by haze. We could only proceed step by step, understanding that it would be a long, difficult journey, but knowing that each step up would make our world safer, even if we never reached the top.

I regret that we were not able to find more common ground with Global Zero, especially since they have been successful in forming advocacy groups in many colleges around the country. Certainly any long-term success is going to require a far better understanding of nuclear issues than now exists among the generation of Americans who were born after the end of the Cold War.

A year later we wrote a follow-on op-ed that appeared in the *Wall Street Journal* in January 2008,[6] describing how to accomplish the goals articulated in the first op-ed. All of the steps we outlined were consistent with moving toward zero, but each, by itself, improved our security even if we were never to reach zero. Further, ours was now a global perspective. We were past the Cold War with its strong emphasis on the bipolar nuclear arms race between the United States and the Soviet Union: now we were in a period in which the mitigation of the threat from nuclear weapons should be seen more closely than ever as a worldwide dynamic.

In the series of op-eds we wrote, coming to consensus among the four of us was a dynamic process, endlessly fascinating and always instructive. Behind the scenes, Sid Drell and Jim Goodby at Stanford and Steve Andreasen and others at the Nuclear Threat Initiative collaborated in the drafting process. The first draft always generated a blizzard of emails over a several week period before we arrived at a final version we could all agree on. This was never easy; indeed, it is a small miracle that we were able to reach consensus. Surprisingly, the differences were never *partisan*—that is, there was never a Republican view versus a Democratic view—but they did reflect the different positions we had held in government. As secretaries of state, George and Henry had much more experience in international diplomacy than either Sam or myself. Both were remarkably gifted in articulating their views, which had typically been the last word on earlier policy papers they signed. Now they were seeking consensus on gravely important issues where giving equal weight to the views of their partners was integral to the process. In each case they did so, strengthening the message and the bond that united us.

I considered George to be the informal leader of our group, but he carried his mantle of leadership lightly. When one of us sought a revision to his text, he would seriously consider it and either persuade us to accept his version or gracefully accept the requested change. We all gave special weight to Henry's views because of his vast experience in diplomacy, his great fluency in writing, and the respect with which he is held by international leaders. Sam invariably had a well-reasoned view, but when disagreements arose, he would draw on the well-honed skills he had developed as a Senate committee chairman to craft an intelligent compromise (a talent sorely lacking today in the US Senate). For me, it was a uniquely valuable experience, debating ideas of such moment with three of the world's most gifted and experienced practitioners of international policy.

It is remarkable that collaboration on such a critical enterprise could be successful considering our vastly different backgrounds and the challenge of geographic separation. The power of technology aided us immensely, giving us many options for communicating our ideas and ironing out our differences—we met in person only several times a year. But most important was the deep respect we had for each other and the trust that enabled us to express our views openly.

In response to our op-eds and visits, other former officials around the world began speaking out for a world without nuclear weapons. Similar groups of former officials from thirteen countries joined together across party lines—including in Britain, France, Germany, Italy, Russia, and South Korea—to write like-minded op-eds in support of our initiative and to help spur actions by their own governments. We traveled to many of these countries to coordinate strategies and messages with the newly formed groups, and met with national leaders.

Considering the deep moral issues, religious leaders also began to speak out. During the Cold War, Catholic bishops and evangelicals had written papers that questioned the moral justification for the use—or even the threat of use—of weapons so deadly. Most prominent at that time was a treatise from a group of Catholic bishops concluding that nuclear deterrence could be justified under the "Just War" doctrine. Now religious groups were re-examining that question. The Catholic bishops and evangelicals were reviewing their earlier work, and a new interdenominational group (United Religions Initiative), founded by Bill Swing, began studying the issues.

Each of us, acting individually and collectively, became deeply involved in speaking, writing, and attending conferences worldwide. We called ourselves the Nuclear Security Project (known informally as the Four Horsemen, the Quartet, or the Gang of Four). Our work was coordinated and supported by the Nuclear Threat Initiative (NTI), an organization founded by Sam Nunn and Ted Turner and on whose board I have served since its inception in 2001. NTI designs and implements projects that directly reduce threats and show governments how to reduce threats faster, smarter, and on a larger scale. It has also used its voice to raise awareness and advocate solutions.

One such step of especially urgent importance in the post–Cold War period has been to assume the leadership in improving the security of stored fissile material. One notable example was catalyzing the removal of a large store of fissile material from Serbia. The project leveraged the creation of a major US government program to remove and eventually blend down vulnerable nuclear material around the world. With major financial assistance from Warren Buffett, NTI has played a key role in setting up a nuclear bank at the International Atomic Energy Agency to reduce the risk of proliferation. In 2012, NTI published the first-ever report that grades the effectiveness of the fissile material security provisions of every nation. NTI also produced a movie, *Last Best Chance*, to educate the public about the dangers of nuclear threats.[7] Outside the nuclear field, NTI has performed highly significant work designed to improve the early warning of biological pandemics, arising either from natural causes or through biological terrorism.

In 2009, the Nuclear Security Project decided to support a documentary movie articulating our views, believing that a well-made film would reach a wider audience than we could reach through op-eds and speeches. NTI agreed to produce the movie—one that would graphically depict nuclear dangers and include interviews with each of us. Directed by Ben Goddard, narrated by actor Michael Douglas, and introduced by General Colin Powell, *Nuclear Tipping Point* was released in 2010[8, 9] and my colleagues and I organized screenings in cities all over America, taking questions after each showing. At the screenings we passed out DVDs of the movie and invited recipients to organize showings in their own communities and to initiate dialogue on these issues. We were supported in our efforts by governments, experts, other nongovernmental organizations, friends, and family members.

Our op-eds attracted the attention of Phil Taubman, a *New York Times* editor and author of *Secret Empire*. He proposed to write a book that told the story of how the five of us (the op-ed signers plus Sid Drell) had arrived at our present thinking about nuclear weapons after years as "Cold Warriors." (*The Partnership* was published in 2012.)[10]

During the 2008 presidential elections, Senator McCain and Senator Obama both spoke in support of Ronald Reagan's vision of a world without nuclear weapons. By the end of 2008 public support and momentum were growing, but we knew that unofficial Track 2 initiatives could carry only so far—governments must take the actions that make a real difference. Up to that point, none had.

Then, in 2009, barely ten weeks after he was inaugurated, President Obama delivered a speech in Prague that included the now-famous line: "I state clearly and with conviction the commitment of the United States to seek the peace and security of a world without nuclear weapons."[11] The crowd in Prague roared its approval. Watching the speech at home on my television, I was overcome with emotion. Could this really be happening? Since then I have often replayed a recording of this speech, deeply moved each time.

A few months later, at a summit meeting in Moscow, President Obama and Russian president Medvedev jointly declared their support for a world without nuclear weapons and made a commitment to move forward on a new arms reduction treaty. Then in September, President Obama chaired a UN Security Council summit meeting in which a resolution supporting nuclear disarmament was amazingly approved 15 to 0.[12] I had the privilege of attending this historic meeting together with Shultz, Kissinger, and Nunn and consider this one of the high points of our work together. As momentum built, governments all over the world began to weigh in. Japan and Australia formed an International Commission on Nuclear Non-Proliferation and Disarmament, of which I was the American commissioner.[13]

It would seem that 2009 was a genuine "Annus Mirabilis," a Year of Miracles. The term traditionally describes two miraculous breakthrough years in science: 1666, when Newton published his landmark papers on the theory of gravitation and optics; and 1905, when Einstein published three landmark papers, including his paper on the theory of relativity. I can remember Czechoslovakian president Václav Havel calling 1989 an "Annus Mirabilis," when all Eastern European nations gained their independence very nearly bloodlessly, a year culminating in the fall of the Berlin Wall.

If 2009 was a year of miracles, 2010 would be a year of action. That action exploded in one memorable week in April. On Tuesday, 6 April, President Obama released his eagerly awaited Nuclear Posture Review, which explicitly diminished the role of nuclear weapons in American military strategy. That evening he hosted the premier showing of *Nuclear Tipping Point* in Washington, DC, at the White House theater; his guests included the four of us who were speakers in the movie and our spouses, key officials from NTI, and the president's national security team. The president introduced the movie by saying that our views on nuclear weapons had guided his own thinking and actions, and urged his security team to be guided by them as well.

On Wednesday, the president left for Prague to meet with President Medvedev. On Thursday, the New START arms control treaty was signed by Russia and the United States, followed by a bilateral meeting between Obama and Medvedev. That weekend, forty-nine world leaders arrived in Washington and on Monday and Tuesday convened the first Nuclear Security Summit to strengthen worldwide measures for the control of fissile material.

Then on 29 April, the Senate Foreign Relations Committee held its first hearing on the New START treaty, with the first two witnesses being former secretary of defense James Schlesinger and myself. The hearing was generally friendly—the chairmen and ranking members, senators John Kerry and Richard Lugar, could not have been more gracious. But there was formidable opposition to the treaty in the Senate, led by Senator Jon Kyl. It was hard to imagine this deeply divided Senate coming together with the two-thirds majority needed for ratification. But on 22 December 2010, the Senate, in a lame-duck session, and against the expectations of many astute political observers, ratified the treaty with seventy-one favorable votes, an outcome made possible by thirteen Republicans voting against their leadership and for ratification. Had the Senate not ratified New START, the United States would have forfeited its world leadership and the global nuclear disarmament effort would have dissipated. The Russian Duma also voted for ratification.

All this was deeply satisfying. But soon a counter wave of events began to unfold. Progress on diminishing the nuclear dangers started to stall out and even reverse. Except for the second and third Nuclear Security Summits held in Seoul (2012) and The Hague (2014), it is fair to say that the United States and Russia began a long backward slide in 2011. Old modes of thinking began to reassert their power and block the transcendent vision that mitigating the nuclear threat serves the common good. It is sobering but educational to chronicle the setback.

To begin with, the ratification of New START, which I had thought would be noncontroversial, was in fact so politically contentious that President Obama decided not to offer the Comprehensive Test Ban Treaty (CTBT) for ratification during his first term. (CTBT had been signed by President Clinton in 1996, when I was still the secretary of defense, but it went to the Senate for ratification in 1999 and was defeated on a near party-line vote.)

Meanwhile, North Korea was building and testing nuclear weapons, and Iran began actions that appeared to be heading in that direction. It was clear that if North Korea and Iran could not be stopped from building nuclear arsenals, other nations would likely follow, and the Nuclear Non-Proliferation Treaty would become impotent.

At the same time, Pakistan and India were creating more fissile material and bombs. Most ominously, Pakistan has developed a "tactical" nuclear weapon—that is, a weapon for use in battle, not as a deterrent. These events inexorably increase the probability that a nuclear bomb will be used, either by a terror group or in a regional war.

And with President Putin replacing President Medvedev in Russia, together with the continued installation of the US BMD system in Europe, Russia showed no interest in a follow-on treaty to New START.

The response of the Nuclear Security Project to this parade of disheartening events was to re-energize its efforts to move the United States and the world back to serious efforts at reducing nuclear dangers. We began reaching out to leaders in the religious community, asking them to spread the urgent message to their members. We observed that our counterpart groups in Europe have extended their reach by forming a European Leadership Network and encouraged NTI to form a similar group for North America called the Nuclear Security Leadership Council, which includes members a generation or two younger than we. Similar networks have been formed in the Asia-Pacific and Latin America. Even if the world is not yet ready to move seriously toward a world without nuclear weapons, it must move seriously to reduce the very real and very great dangers they pose today.

In 2013, we (Shultz, Perry, Kissinger, and Nunn) wrote our fifth *Wall Street Journal* op-ed,[14] which lays out in some detail steps that should be taken to reduce significantly those dangers. The most important of the steps are:

*Changes in nuclear force posture to increase decision time for leaders.* I described earlier a false alarm of a nuclear attack that I had personally experienced—one that could have triggered a nuclear holocaust. That was not the only false alarm during the Cold War. Scott Sagan's landmark book, *The Limits of Safety: Organizations, Accidents, and Nuclear Weapons*, documents the disturbing reality that the likelihood of a catastrophic accident increases with technological complexity—and nuclear weapons are among the most complex systems known to mankind.[15] A recent book by Eric Schlosser, *Command and Control: Nuclear Weapons, the Damascus Accident, and the Illusion of Safety*, reveals chilling stories of nuclear accidents and near-accidents, most not known to the public.[16] Those stories about false alarms have focused a searing awareness of the immense peril we face when in mere minutes our leaders must make life-and-death decisions affecting the whole planet. Arguably, short decision times for response were necessary during the Cold War, but clearly those arguments do not apply today; yet we are still operating with an outdated system fashioned for Cold War exigencies. It is time for the United States to make clear the goal of removing all nuclear weapons everywhere from the prompt-launch status in which nuclear-armed ballistic missiles are ready to be launched in minutes.

*Accelerated nuclear reductions under New START.* The United States could speed up the already agreed upon reductions in nuclear weapons under New START and announce that it is prepared to go below those levels as a matter of national policy. The US also could announce support for consolidating and reducing US and Russian tactical nuclear weapons in Europe, which I believe are more of a security risk than a military asset both to NATO and Russia. Over the longer term, the United States and Russia should seek to make large reductions in their nuclear forces, including the thousands of theater and tactical nuclear weapons not covered by present treaties, and the thousands of weapons in reserve or storage, also not covered by present treaties. But clearly any progress in nuclear arms reduction will require the United States and Russia to resolve other security issues now creating mistrust and fear.

*Verification and transparency initiative.* Nuclear weapons reduction agreements cannot be reached without reliable verification and transparency, essential for building cooperation and trust. In 2014, the United States took the lead, in collaboration with NTI, in a new verification initiative that would involve its nuclear weapons laboratories and other global scientific experts in developing key technologies and innovations for reducing and controlling weapons and materials.

*Securing nuclear materials to prevent catastrophic nuclear terrorism.* The materials required to build a nuclear bomb today are stored at hundreds of sites in twenty-five countries around the globe, down from more than forty countries just ten years ago, an important measure of progress. But many of the remaining sites are still not well secured, leaving the deadly materials vulnerable to theft or sale on the black market. The commitments to secure nuclear materials and improve cooperation made during the Nuclear Security Summits are crucial; the process has the potential to improve security for generations to come. Yet despite the growing importance attached to nuclear security by world leaders, there is still no global system in place for tracking, accounting for, managing, and securing all weapons-usable nuclear materials. World leaders should cooperate to close this gap by committing to develop a comprehensive global materials security system to secure all weapons-usable nuclear materials from unauthorized access and theft. Such a commitment could be a very positive outcome of the 2016 Nuclear Summit.

In sum, 2007 to 2010 was a heady period of measurable progress in nuclear disarmament and real enthusiasm for moving toward a world free of nuclear weapons, followed by 2011 to 2014, a discouraging period when progress slowed and then stopped. But those discouraging developments were only a prelude to the disastrous turn of events beginning in 2014 when Russia sent its troops into Ukraine. The United States called this an "incredible act of aggression" and organized international sanctions against Russia. The sanctions have been effective economically, but not politically. Russia went on to annex Crimea, and continued to support separatist forces in Eastern Ukraine.

As a result, in 2015 relations between Russia and the United States sank to their lowest level since the depths of the Cold War. And, far from continuing the nuclear disarmament that has been underway for the last two decades, we are starting a new nuclear arms race. Russia has underway a massive rebuilding program in nuclear weapons. They are building, testing, and deploying two new ICBMs, equipped with MIRVs (which had been outlawed under the treaty negotiated by President George H.W. Bush). They are building and testing a new generation of nuclear submarines, along with the attendant SLBMs. And they are building shorter-range missiles to intimidate their neighbors in Eastern Europe. All of these new programs motivate Russia to test new warheads for their new missiles, and, on our present course, I expect them to soon withdraw from the CTBT and begin those tests.

In case we don't fully understand what is at stake here, the statements of Russian officials make it clear. They have rejected their long-standing policy of "no first use" of nuclear weapons and stated that they are prepared to use nuclear weapons to respond to any threat to their security, whether or not it is nuclear. They have explicitly threatened Eastern European nations with an attack by their Iskander missiles based in Kaliningrad. And they have implicitly threatened the United States: on 16 March 2014, Dmitry Kiselyov, the Russian media head appointed by President Putin, published the following remarkable statement: "Russia is the only nation capable of turning the United States into radioactive ash."

While all of these provocative statements and actions are going on, the United States has been considering how to modernize its nuclear arsenal. The obvious choice is to respond in kind, leading to expenditures of perhaps a trillion dollars over the next twenty years, and to match Russian nuclear testing with testing of our own. Certainly that is more likely than choosing to ignore the Russian actions and statements.

We can only hope that our leaders will make every effort to find a third choice—a choice that would require diplomacy with the Russians with a level of skill we have not demonstrated in several decades. The challenge to do so is daunting, but the failure to do so could be catastrophic.

Despite this serious regression, the Nuclear Security Project will continue its work. The consequences of failure—nuclear bombs being used by terrorists or in a nuclear war—are too catastrophic for any lapse in determined action. We will continue to pursue concrete measures that lessen the danger of nuclear weapons. And while the present international climate is not conducive to moving to a world without nuclear weapons, we will not abandon that vision. Indeed, we believe that the practical steps we propose to lower nuclear dangers will not gain full international support unless they are attached to a vision of ultimately eliminating nuclear weapons; likewise, we believe that this vision will never be achieved in one grand move, but in a step-by-step process, each step of which makes us safer.

# 25  A Way Forward: Hope for a World without Nuclear Weapons

*I believe that man will not merely endure: he will prevail.*
—William Faulkner; Nobel Prize acceptance speech, 10 December 1950[1]

This book tells the story of my efforts over many decades to reduce the possibility of a nuclear catastrophe, including several times when the world was at the nuclear brink.

I hope the story of my journey at the nuclear brink will resonate with young men and women everywhere. Even now some are coming forward who will take up the same dire challenge that I first recognized as a young a soldier in 1946 amid the rubble of postwar Japan, witness to the unprecedented devastation of modern war. I would come to be haunted by the disasters visited by a sudden new fire in the sky, a fire now a million times more powerful than before. World War II's weapons destroyed cities. Today's weapons could destroy civilization itself.

Those voices in our time that are optimistic—that human violence is declining; that global political trends, if fitful, may be signaling an eventual broad establishment of humanistic governance; that a global free-market economy rescuing millions of people from wretched poverty is plausible—are heartening. This upward progress is indeed hopeful, but nuclear conflict could in a blink of history be the ultimate reversal of all such outcomes.

Our chief peril is that the poised nuclear doom, much of it hidden beneath the seas and in remote badlands, is too far out of the global public consciousness. Passivity shows broadly. Perhaps this is a matter of defeatism and its cohort, distraction. Perhaps for some it is largely a most primal human fear of facing the "unthinkable." For others, it might be a welcoming of the illusion that there is or might be an acceptable missile defense against a nuclear attack. And for many it would seem to be the keeping of faith that nuclear deterrence will hold indefinitely—that leaders will always have accurate enough instantaneous knowledge, know the true context of events, and enjoy the good luck to avoid the most tragic of military miscalculations.

Is there reason to believe that we can take serious actions to reduce the deadly nuclear dangers in the face of this public passivity? Years ago, in the darkest days of the Cold War, when the barriers to progress in mitigating the danger from nuclear weapons were even greater than today, President John F. Kennedy urged us to believe that we *can* succeed:

> Too many of us think it is impossible. Too many think it is unreal. But that is a dangerous defeatist belief. It leads to the conclusion that war is inevitable, that mankind is doomed, that we are gripped by forces that we cannot control. We need not accept that view. Our problems are man-made—therefore, they can be solved by man.[2]

And so it is today. Facing the danger from nuclear weapons is daunting, but we must recognize the threat and devote ourselves to diminishing it. To be sure, as long as nuclear weapons are deployed by nations as a part of their war plans, we can never be certain that they will not be used in a regional war or by a terror group. Even a single nuclear detonation would entail casualties a hundred times greater than those suffered on 9-11; beyond that, there would be economic, political, and social consequences that could destroy our way of life. But we can take actions that greatly reduce the probability of such a catastrophe, and taking those actions should become our highest priority.

We must do everything in our power to ensure that nuclear weapons will never be used again.

In the preceding chapter I described how, after two years of great progress in reducing nuclear dangers, progress has faltered, and now has begun to regress. The problems are the traditional ones: politics as usual, parochial economics, nationalism rather than international cooperation, and failures of imagination regarding the nuclear danger.

These familiar obstacles are deeply discouraging, but we must not give up. Our response need not be passivity and defeatism and illusion. There is enough promising history—some of it I have described in this narrative—to offer fact-based hope that mankind will be able to rise to the ultimate threat posed by nuclear weapons today; that we will take the actions necessary to reduce the danger and, ultimately, to eliminate it.

I have described the ongoing and encouraging work of the Nuclear Threat Initiative and the Nuclear Security Project, focused on specific steps that reduce the danger of nuclear weapons, even as there are still thousands of them in the world. We must take heart in the fact that world governments already have taken important measures to make us safer from nuclear weapons. Consider the following.

In the international actions resulting in the denuclearization of Ukraine, Kazakhstan, and Belarus, we demonstrated the hopeful reality, very soon after the animosities of the Cold War, of successful cooperative efforts to mitigate the nuclear danger.

In our op-eds of 2007 and 2008, Shultz, Kissinger, Nunn, and I called for specific practical actions to enhance near-term world security, actions that could eventually lead to a world without nuclear weapons; and since then remarkably broad international support has arisen for the ideas outlined in those op-eds, including: letters, editorials, the formation of prominent advocacy groups, President Obama's Prague speech, and the unanimous UN Security Council resolution calling for a move toward a world free of nuclear weapons.

But we must reflect on the old distinction between saying and doing. Although the leading nations of the world have said the right things, what have they done?

The answer is: they have done enough to justify hope.

Importantly, the year after President Obama's Prague speech, the United States and Russia signed the New START treaty requiring reductions on the deployed nuclear forces of both sides. The reductions themselves are only modest; the chief value of the treaty, one of absolutely crucial importance, has been to revitalize the dialogue between the US and Russia on nuclear issues and to establish comprehensive verification measures leading to greater transparency in our deployed nuclear forces.

But perhaps an even more important action following President Obama's Prague speech was the creation of biennial nuclear summits focused on achieving much better control over the fissile material widespread in the world. Since the main obstacle for a terror group seeking a nuclear bomb is the difficulty and complexity of making the fissile material, securing those materials tightly is the best way to stop that awful contingency from happening. And we must not forget that the arsenals of the United States and Russia, while still at an overkill level, are a fraction of what they were at the height of the Cold War.

These actions show that responsible governments can recognize the danger of nuclear weapons and undertake actions to lower the risks. But there is no wisdom in congratulating ourselves on accomplishments to date other than seeing them as welcome building blocks. We must be working broadly and seriously, with great urgency, to reduce the danger of nuclear weapons; the measures for doing so were outlined in the previous chapter.

All of these actions are complex and will take many years to implement fully. Some of my colleagues, particularly those in the Global Zero movement, believe that our emphasis on practical steps detracts from their goal of reducing nuclear weapons to zero through an international agreement—in a sense, a major sequel to the Nuclear Non-Proliferation Treaty. But my view, which has been informed by my long history engaged with the nuclear crisis, is that the steps are an indispensable prelude to making real progress in reducing nuclear dangers.

Indeed, I believe we have no hope of achievng a world without nuclear weapons without taking the initial steps. But I also believe that we will not muster the will to take these difficult steps without tying them to a vision. The problem is not how long it will take to implement the steps; rather, it is that governments of the world are not now moving to implementation.

This failure of governments arises in the first instance because they are not getting sufficient pressure from their constituents to act. To reiterate a fundamentally important point: people in the United States and around the world simply do not effectively understand the dangers they are facing from today's nuclear weapons arsenals. A considerable part of the general public apparently believes that nuclear dangers ended with the Cold War. Although (and thankfully) our school children are no longer being trained in "duck-and-cover" drills, the lack of awareness and concern of citizens about such a transcendental problem renders it very difficult for democratic governments to take costly and inconvenient actions. Obviously, after a nuclear attack the disregard by the public—that is, what might be left of the public—would immediately vanish; but how much better to mitigate the threat before an attack.

For the world to make real progress in reducing nuclear dangers, the United States must lead; and the US will not lead unless Americans understand the importance of doing so—that today nuclear weapons no longer provide for our security, as they did in the Cold War, but are endangering our security. It must be clear to the public and leaders that prevention of nuclear conflict serves an overriding common good and outweighs parochial concerns and politics as usual.

The key to taking constructive actions that can prevent nuclear weapons from ever being used again is education of the public. The Nuclear Threat Initiative is undertaking significant programs, described in the previous chapter, that will increase public awareness of nuclear dangers. I have dedicated my own efforts to increasing the awareness of our younger generation—the millennial generation and those who follow, now in their teens and twenties. That is a natural choice because I am at a university, surrounded by young people. But I want to reach a far greater audience than the students at one university—programs that are able to reach students at all universities, to reach students at high schools, and to reach young people not affiliated with a school. Dealing with the problem of nuclear dangers will take decades, and will ultimately need to be solved by today's youth, in America and around the globe. My generation dealt with the nuclear dangers of the Cold War; later generations must deal with the deadly nuclear legacy that we left behind.

During my journey, I have developed great faith in the human ability to respond to crises, even the most dire wartime contingencies, by coming together out of a common humanity to make sacrifices and commitments that further the greatest good. I have chronicled in these pages examples involving heads of state, diplomats, military leaders, legislators, scientists, technologists, corporate leaders, and ordinary citizens from all over the world. When people are heard, when they are engaged in thinking about the nuclear danger, when they collaborate in fashioning agreements in which all parties are considered fairly, great progress can be made. The nuclear age has raised the need for new modes of thinking, and people will realize this. Given a chance, people understand.

With that belief in mind, I have embarked on a project (www.wjperryproject.org) in which I have sought to practice my experienced convictions about people and the nuclear crisis on the largest scale I can attain. This book is the first step. While it has allowed me to crystallize my thoughts, this book alone will not reach the great number of people who need to hear my call to action. In particular, it will not reach as many of the younger generation as could be reached by the Internet to convey my message. Accordingly, I have produced online content open to all and accessible using mobile devices in hopes that it will reach young people all over the world.

I do understand from considerable experience just how hard the challenge I have laid out will be. I understand that my efforts to mitigate the nuclear dangers the world faces today may, in fact, be an impossible quest.

But the stakes are so high, the danger to humanity is so great, that instead of retreating into a comfortable retirement, I am dedicating the balance of my life to doing whatever I can to reduce the dangers. I do this because I believe that time is not on our side. And I do this because, having helped to create our Cold War nuclear forces, I understand what it will take to dismantle them, and I believe that I have a special responsibility to do so. Thus I continue my journey at the nuclear brink.

Whenever I am beset by discouragement; whenever the barriers seem insuperable; whenever I am disheartened by the apathy I see around me; whenever I despair that we will let nuclear weapons bring an end to our civilization; whenever I am ready to give up on this mission ... I return to the timeless words of William Faulkner, spoken at his Nobel acceptance speech in December 1950, just six months after North Korea invaded South Korea, at the perilous beginning of the Cold War:

> There are no longer problems of the spirit. There is only the question: When will I be blown up? ... I decline to accept the end of man. It is easy enough to say that man is immortal simply because he will endure: that when the last dingdong of doom has clanged and faded from the last worthless rock hanging tideless in the last red and dying evening, that even then there will still be one more sound: that of his puny inexhaustible voice, still talking. I refuse to accept this. I believe that man will not merely endure: he will prevail.

# Notes

Preface

1.  Coll, Steve. *Ghost Wars: The Secret History of the CIA, Afghanistan, and Bin Laden from the Soviet Invasion to September* 10, 2001. New York: Penguin, 2005. Pg. 10. Bergen, Peter L. *Holy War, Inc.: Inside the Secret World of Osama Bin Laden*. New York: Free Press, Simon and Schuster, 2001. Pg. 97.

Chapter 1

1.  Kennedy, John F. "Radio and Television Report to the American People on the Soviet Arms Buildup in Cuba, October 22, 1962." JFKWHA-142-001, 22 October 1962. Accessed 25 August 2014.

2.  Ibid. In JFK's 22 October 1962 report to the American people on the Soviet arms buildup in Cuba, he announced: "A strict quarantine on all offensive military equipment under shipment to Cuba is being initiated. All ships of any kind bound for Cuba from whatever nation or port will, if found to contain cargoes of offensive weapons, be turned back."

3.  Kessler, Glen. "An 'Eyeball to Eyeball' Moment That Never Happened." *New York Times*, 23 June 2014. Accessed 25 August 2014. After the Cuban Missile Crisis, some newspapers published articles about the triumph of Kennedy and the United States, citing Secretary of State Dean Rusk as saying: "We're eyeball to eyeball, and I think the other fellow just blinked."

Chapter 2

1.  Albert Einstein, telegram, 23 May 1946, quoted in "Atomic Education Urged by Einstein; Scientist in Plea for $200,000 to Promote New Type of Essential Thinking." *New York Times*, 24 May 1946.

2.  Senauth, Frank. *The Making of the Philippines*. Bloomington, IN: Author-House, 2012. Pg. 85.

Chapter 3

1. Powers, Thomas. *Intelligence Wars: American Secret History from Hitler to Al-qaeda.* New York: New York Review of Books, 2002. Pg. 320.

2. Eckhardt, Roger. "Stan Ulam, John von Neumann, and the Monte Carlo Method." *Los Alamos Science,* Special Issue (1987). Accessed 7 November 2013. The Monte Carlo method is a statistical sampling technique created by both Stan Ulam and John Von Neumann. The first idea of the technique occurred to Stan Ulam in 1946 as a way to predict the probability of a successful solitaire card game, and it was later developed by Ulam and John von Neumann as a way to predict the explosive behavior of fission weapons, in development at Los Alamos, by estimating neutron multiplication rates. In 1948, Stan Ulam reported to the Atomic Energy Commission about the application of this method for uses beyond fission weapons.

3. Snow, C. P. *Science and Government.* Cambridge: Harvard University Press, 1960. Pg. 47.

4. Pedlow, Gregory, and Donald Welzenbach. *The CIA and the U-2 Program, 1954–1974.* US Central Intelligence Agency, History Staff Center for the Study of Intelligence, 1998. Pgs. 100–104. Accessed 25 August 2014. The first operational use of a U-2 took place on Wednesday, 20 June 1956. On Wednesday, 4 July 1956, the first U-2 flight over the Soviet Union took place.

5. Taubman, Philip. *Secret Empire: Eisenhower, the CIA, and the Hidden Story of America's Space Espionage.* New York: Simon and Schuster, 2003.

6. US Central Intelligence Agency. "Report of DCI Ad Hoc Panel on Status of the Soviet ICBM Program." DCI Ad Hoc Panel to Director of Central Intelligence, 25 August 1959. Accessed 25 August 2014.

7. Preparatory Commission for the Comprehensive Nuclear-Test Ban Treaty Organization. "30 October 1961—The Tsar Bomba." Accessed 25 August 2014. The largest nuclear weapon ever constructed was set off over Novaya Zemlya Island in the Russian Arctic Sea on 30 October 1961. It had a yield of 50 megatons. Soviet engineers had reduced the actual yield of 100 megatons by around half to limit fallout. The official designation of the bomb was RDS-220 hydrogen bomb; however, the nickname Tsar Bomba was given to it by the West. The bomb was air-dropped with a fall-retardation parachute attached in order to increase the plane's chance of escape. The probability of survival for the pilot and his crew had been estimated at only 50 percent. The explosion's shock wave caused the plane to instantly lose 1 kilometer of altitude, but it landed safely.

8. ESL (Electromagnetic Systems Laboratory), Inc., was founded in January 1964 and incorporated in California. The founding directors were William J. Perry (chief executive), James M. Harley, Clarence S. Jones, James F. O'Brien, and Alfred Halteman.

Chapter 4

1.   Stanford Graduate School of Business. "Franklin Pitch Johnson." Accessed 6 November 2013. Franklin P. "Pitch" Johnson launched Draper and Johnson Investment Company in 1962.

2.   Stanford University, Stanford Linear Acceleration Center. "A Brief Biography of Wolfgang K. H. Panofsky." Accessed 26 August 2014. Wolfgang K. H. Panofsky, known as "Pief," had a profound impact on the field of elementary particle physics as a researcher, machine builder, and an administrator of basic research. He served as a professor of physics at Stanford University from 1951 to 1963, as director of the Stanford High Energy Physics Laboratory from 1953 to 1961, and as director of the Stanford Linear Accelerator Center (SLAC) from 1961 to 1989. He served as director emeritus of SLAC from 1989 until September 2007, when he passed away in his home in Los Altos, California.

3.   Stanford University, Center for International Security and Cooperation. "Sidney D. Drell, MA, PhD." Accessed 26 August 2014. Sid Drell (Sidney D. Drell) is currently a senior fellow at the Hoover Institution and professor of theoretical physics (emeritus) at the SLAC National Accelerator Laboratory, Stanford University. He cofounded the Center for International Security and Cooperation, and jointly directed it from 1983 to 1989. He is one of the original members of JASON, a group of academic scientists who consult for the government on issues of national importance, as well as a member of the governing board of the Los Alamos National Laboratory.

Chapter 5

1.   From a conversation between Gene Fubini and Bill Perry at the Pentagon, March 1977; paraphrased by Perry.

2.   Center for Strategic and International Studies. "Harold Brown." Accessed 26 August 2014. Harold Brown was nominated by President Jimmy Carter to be secretary of defense on 20 January 1977. He was confirmed by the US Senate and took the oath of office on the same day, 21 January, and served as secretary of defense until 20 January 1981.

3.   Pace, Eric. "Eugene Fubini, 84; Helped Jam Nazi Radar." *New York Times*, 6 August 1997. Accessed 26 August 2014. Eugene Fubini (Gene Fubini) was a physicist and electronics engineer and served as an assistant secretary of defense in the Kennedy and Johnson administrations. Fubini was also a technical observer and scientific consultant to the American army and navy in the European theater in 1943 and 1944, where he helped set up operations for locating and jamming Axis radar. In 1961, he joined the Office of Defense Research and Engineering at the Pentagon. In 1963, President Kennedy selected him for the additional position of

assistant defense secretary with responsibilities encompassing military research and development programs.

4. Stanford Engineering. "Paul Kaminski (PhD '71 AA)." November 2007. Accessed 26 August 2014. Paul Kaminski met Perry while he was attending the Industrial College of the Armed Forces, as an Air Force officer, from 1976 to 1977. Perry invited Kaminski to work for him as his special assistant. This is where Kaminski was first exposed to the stealth program. Kaminski went on to become the undersecretary of defense for acquisition and technology from 3 October 1994 to 16 May 1997. He was responsible for all Department of Defense research, development, and acquisition programs.

5. Nuclear Threat Initiative. "Sam Nunn." Accessed 26 August 2014. Sam Nunn served as a US senator from Georgia for twenty-four years, from 1972 to 1996. During his time in the US Senate, he served as chairman of the Senate Armed Services Committee and the Permanent Subcommittee on Investigations. He also served on the Intelligence and Small Business committees. In 2001, he co-founded the Nuclear Threat Initiative, a nonprofit and nonpartisan organization to strengthen global security, with Ted Turner.

## Chapter 6

1. *The Atlantic.* "World War II: Operation Barbarossa." July 24, 2011. Accessed 26 August 2014. Operation Barbarossa was a massive invasion of the Soviet Union by Nazi Germany and its Axis allies on 22 June 1941.

2. US Army. *Army Ammunition Data Sheets: Artillery Ammunition.* Washington, DC: GPO, April 1973. Pg. 2. The Copperhead is a separate loading, laser-guided, high-explosive, cannon launched projectile designed for use against tanks, armored vehicles, and other moving or stationary hardened targets.

3. Raytheon. "AGM-65 Maverick Missile." Accessed 26 August 2014. The AGM-65 Maverick is a precision-attack missile launched from helicopters and fighter, attack, and multiplace patrol aircraft. The guidance of the missile provides attack capability against both fixed targets and high-speed moving targets. With accuracy to within 1 meter, the missile is used for close air support.

4. Boeing. "AMG-114 HELLFIRE Missile." Accessed 26 August 2014. The hell-fire missile (initially named the Helicopter Launched, Fire, and Forget Missile) is a short-range, laser- or radar-guided air-to-ground missile system designed to defeat tanks and other targets while minimizing the exposure of the launch vehicle from enemy fire. The missile was designed in the 1970s and advanced development began in 1976.

5. Boeing. "AGM-86B/C Air-Launched Cruise Missile." Accessed 26 August 2014. The AGM-86B/C ALCM (Air-Launched Cruise Missile) is a long-range, subsonic, self-guided missile carried by a B-52 bomber at high and low altitudes. With

a nuclear warhead it is designated ALCM, while with a conventional warhead it is designated CALCM. This program began in June 1974 and uses GPS for accurate inertial navigation.

6.   Schwartz, Stephen. *Atomic Audit: The Costs and Consequences of U.S. Nuclear Weapons since* 1940. The Brookings Institute, 1998. Pg. 18. The Tomahawk (BGM-109) is a cruise missile launched from a ship or submarine, using a complex navigation system beginning with an inertial-guidance system over the sea, transitioning to a more precise guidance method, TERCOM, over the missile's land trajectory, then finishing with a third guidance system, known as DSMAC (Digital Scene Matching Area Correlator), which takes the warhead to its target.

7.   US Air Force. "E-3 Sentry (AWACS)." 1 November 2003. Accessed 26 August 2014. The Airborne Warning and Control System, or AWACS, provides situational awareness of friendly, neutral, and hostile activity, command and control of an area of responsibility, battle management of theater forces, all-altitude and all-weather surveillance of the battle space, and early warning of enemy actions during joint, allied, and coalition operations. Engineering, testing, and evaluation began on the first E-3 Sentry in October 1975.

8.   Northrop Grumman. "E-8C Joint STARS." Accessed 26 August 2014. The Joint Surveillance Target Attack Radar System (Joint STARS) is an airborne battle management and command and control (C2) platform that conducts ground surveillance, enabling commanders to develop an understanding of the enemy situation and to support attack operations and targeting. Joint STARS evolved from army and air force programs to develop, detect, locate, and attack enemy armor at ranges beyond the forward area of troops. In 1982, the programs were merged and the air force became the lead agent. The contract was awarded to Northrop Grumman in September 1985 for two E-8C development systems. These aircraft deployed in 1992 to participate in Desert Storm, even though they were still in development.

9.   Federation of American Scientists. "Guardrail Common Sensors." Accessed 28 August 2014. Guardrail was essentially a signal intelligence collection/location system meant for integration into an airborne platform. Initial development began in the early 1970s and survived to a fifth iteration (Guardrail V) that lasted until the 1990s.

10.   Federal Aviation Administration. "Global Positioning Systems." Accessed 28 August 2014. The Global Positioning System was initiated in 1973 and began with the development of a network of twenty-four satellites orbiting the earth at approximately 11,000 miles to provide navigation information to a variety of users. The satellite constellation is operated and maintained by the Department of Defense.

11.   Fallows, James. *National Defense.* New York: Random House, 1981.

12. Perry, William J. "Fallows' Fallacies: A Review Essay." *International Security* 6:4 (Spring 1982). Pgs. 174–82.

13. Marquette University. The Les Aspin Center for Government. "The Honorable Les Aspin." Accessed 28 August 2014. Les Aspin was elected to the US House of Representatives eleven times from Wisconsin's 1st Congressional District beginning in 1970. He served as secretary of defense from 1993 to 1994 in the Clinton administration.

## Chapter 7

1. Garland, Cecil. "The MX Debate." CBS, 1 May 1980.

2. Academy of Achievement. "Paul H. Nitze." Accessed 28 August 2014. Paul Nitze was instrumental in developing US Cold War strategy, serving in several government positions from the beginning of 1940 and rising to deputy secretary of defense in 1963. After his tenure as deputy secretary, he continued to serve in government until 1989. He was a member of the US delegation to the Strategic Armament Limitation Talks (SALT I)(1969–73). Later, fearing Soviet rearmament, he opposed the ratification of SALT II (1979). Paul Nitze passed away 19 October 2004.

## Chapter 8

1. Nuclear Threat Initiative. "Strategic Arms Limitation Talks (SALT I)." Accessed 29 August 2014. SALT I, or the Strategic Arms Limitations Talks 1, refers to the negotiations between the United States and the Soviet Union that began on 17 November 1969 to limit both antiballistic missile (ABM) defensive systems and strategic nuclear offensive systems. What resulted from these talks were two things. One was an Interim Agreement on certain measures limiting strategic offensive arms. The second was the ABM Treaty on the limitation of strategic defensive systems. It was the first agreement between the United States and the USSR that placed limits and restraints on their nuclear weapons systems. The two documents were signed on 26 May 1972 and entered into force on 3 October 1972.

## Chapter 9

1. Katz, Richard, and Judith Wyer. "Carter's Foreign Policy Debacle." *Executive Intelligence Review* 7:2 (1980). Accessed 22 January 2014. In 1980, the Chinese defense minister visited the United States and got an agreement from Secretary Brown and President Carter that the US would help China modernize its conventional military forces—Carter had decided to play the "China Card" against the Soviet Union.

2. *From Mao to Mozart.* Directed by Murray Lerner. United States: Harmony Film, 1981.

3. British Broadcasting Corporation. "1976: China's Gang of Four Arrested."

Accessed 22 January 2014. The Gang of Four was a group of four Chinese adults who were active proponents of the Cultural Revolution, consisting of Jian Qing, as well as Wang Hongwen, Yao Wenyuan, and Zhang Chunqiao.

## Chapter 10

1. Public Broadcasting Service. "Reagan: National Security and SDI." Accessed 4 February 2014. On 23 March 1983, President Reagan announced his vision of a world safe from nuclear threat. His Strategic Defense Initiative (SDI) was later dubbed "Star Wars" by the press.

2. Perry, William J. "An Expensive Technological Risk." *Washington Post*. Editorial, 27 March 1983.

3. Perry, William J. "A Critical Look at Star Wars." *SIPIscope*. Scientists' Institute for Public Information 13:1 (January–February 1985). Pgs. 10–14.

4. Institute of Contemporary Development, Russia. "Andrei Kokoshin Management Board Member." Accessed 19 November 2013. Andrei Kokoshin served as Russian deputy minister of defense from 1992 to 1997, state military inspector, secretary of defense council, and secretary of the security council from 1997 to 1998, and vice president of the Russian Academy of Sciences from 1998 to 1999.

5. US Department of Defense. "Ashton B. Carter." Accessed 13 February 2015. Ashton B. Carter was confirmed as secretary of defense on 12 February 2015. He served as deputy secretary of defense from October 2011 to December 2013, and as undersecretary of defense for acquisition, technology, and logistics from April 2009 to October 2011. Prior to his most recent service in the Defense Department, Carter was chair of the International and Global Affairs faculty at Harvard University's John F. Kennedy School of Government and codirector of the Preventive Defense Project with William J. Perry. Carter worked previously in the Defense Department while Perry was secretary of defense, collaborating on dismantling nuclear weapons through implementation of the Nunn-Lugar Cooperative Threat Reduction Program.

6. Arms Control Association. "The Intermediate-Range Nuclear Force (INF) Treaty at a Glance." February 2008. Accessed 7 February 2014. The 1987 Intermediate-Range Nuclear Forces (INF) Treaty required the United States and the Soviet Union to eliminate and permanently forswear all of their nuclear and conventional ground-launched ballistic and cruise missiles with ranges of 500 to 5,500 kilometers. As a result, the US and the Soviet Union destroyed a total of 2,692 short-, medium-, and intermediate-range missiles by the treaty's implementation deadline of 1 June 1991.

7. Nuclear Threat Initiative. "Treaty between the United States of America and the Union of Soviet Socialist Republics on Strategic Offensive Reductions (START I)." Accessed 7 February 2014. The US-Soviet Strategic Arms Reduction Treaty, known as START I, was signed on 31 July 1991 by US president George H. W. Bush

2at top

and Soviet president Mikhail Gorbachev. START I was the first treaty to provide for deep reductions of the US and Soviet/Russian strategic nuclear weapons. Strategic weapons, as defined by NTI, are high-yield nuclear weapons placed on long-range delivery systems, such as a land-based intercontinental ballistic missile (ICBM), a submarine-launched ballistic missile (SLBM), or a strategic bomber. START I established an aggregate limit of 1,600 delivery vehicles and 6,000 warheads for each party. Within that limit, the treaty established three sublimits: 4,900 warheads for ICBMs (land-based intercontinental ballistic missiles) and SLBMs (subma-rine-launched ballistic missiles), 154 heavy ICBMs, 1,540 warheads for these heavy ICBMs, and 1,100 warheads for mobile ICBMs.

    8.  Nuclear Threat Initiative. "Treaty between the United States of America and the Union of Soviet Socialist Republics on Strategic Offensive Reductions (START II)." Accessed 7 February 2014. The START II treaty was signed by US president George H. W. Bush and Russian president Boris Yeltsin on 3 January, just before the end of President Bush's time in office. Phase II required the elimination of all heavy ICBMs and all ICBMs on multiple independently targetable re-entry vehicles (MIRVs) (although some of the latter were to be downloaded to one warhead). The MIRV ban did not apply to SLBMs.

Chapter 11

    1.  President's Blue Ribbon Commission on Defense Management. "A Quest for Excellence: Final Report to the President." June 1986. Accessed 29 August 2014. The President's Blue Ribbon Commission on Defense (1986), also known as "The Packard Commission," was charged by President Ronald Reagan on 15 July 1985 to conduct a defense management study of important dimension, including: the budget process, the procurement system, legislative oversight, and the organizational and operational arrangements, both formal and informal, among the office of the secretary of defense, the organization of the Joint Chiefs of Staff, the Unified and Specified Command Systems, the military departments, and Congress.

Chapter 12

    1.  Live recording of Senate confirmation hearing, C-Span, 3 February 1994.

    2.  EBSCO Information Services. "Fact Sheet: Gore-Chernomyrdin Commission." Accessed 16 December 2013. The first Gore-Chernomyrdin Commission, which Vice President Gore had established with Russian prime minister Cherno-myrdin to facilitate cooperation between the two countries, occurred 1–2 September 1993 in Washington, DC, while the second meeting occurred in Moscow, 15–16 December 1993.

    3.  Halberstam, David. *War in a Time of Peace: Bush, Clinton, and the Generals.* New York: Scribner, 2002. Pgs. 265–66. The Battle of Mogadishu resulted in the

death of 18 US soldiers, as well as 84 wounded. At least 500 Somalis were killed, with more than 700 wounded.

4.   Carpenter, Ted Galen. *Beyond NATO: Staying out of Europe's Wars.* Washington, DC: Cato Institute, 1994. Pg. 86. The Trilateral Statement was signed by Clinton, Yeltsin, and then Ukrainian president Leonid Kravchuk in Moscow in January 1994. This agreement required Kiev to eliminate its arsenal in stages over seven years.

5.   Nuclear Threat Initiative. "Ukraine." Accessed 29 August 2014. Upon independence in 1991, Ukraine inherited the world's third largest nuclear arsenal, consisting of approximately 1,900 strategic nuclear warheads and 2,500 tactical nuclear weapons. The arsenal also included 130 SS-19 and 46 SS-4 intercontinental ballistic missiles, and 25 Tu-95 and 19 Tu-160 strategic bombers with air-launched cruise missiles.

6.   Public Broadcasting Service. "Comments on the Nunn-Lugar Program." Accessed 16 December 2013. The Nunn-Lugar program uses funds from the US defense budget every year to help the republics of the former Soviet Union eliminate and safeguard nuclear weapons and other weapons of mass destruction.

7.   "Budapest Memorandums on Security Assurances, 1994." 5 December 1994. Accessed 31 August 2014.

8.   Devroy, Ann. "Clinton Nominates Aspin's Deputy as Pentagon Chief." *Washington Post,* 25 January 1994. Accessed 5 January 2014. President Clinton officially nominated William J. Perry as secretary of defense on Monday, 24 January 1994.

9.   Perry, William J. "Defense Secretary Nomination." C-SPAN. 13:23. 24 January 1994. Accessed 29 August 2014.

10.   "Unanimous Senate Confirms Perry as Defense Secretary." *Washington Post,* 4 February 1994. Accessed 6 January 2014. William Perry was confirmed in the US Senate on 3 February 1994, by a unanimous vote of 97 to 0.

## Chapter 13

1.   Nunn, Sam. Interview with Jamie McIntyre. CNN, Sevmash Shipyard, Severodvinsk, Russia, 18 October 1996.

2.   Bernstein, Paul, and Jason Wood. "The Origins of Nunn-Lugar and Cooperative Threat Reduction." *Case Study Series* 3. Washington, DC: National Defense University Press, April 2010. Accessed 14 January 2013. Under the Nunn-Lugar program, representatives from the United States made four visits to Pervomaysk, Ukraine, between 1994 and 1996 to dismantle powerful rockets. On the first visit, the warheads were removed from the missiles. On the second visit, the missiles were removed from the silo and destroyed. On the third visit, the silo was destroyed and the site restored. On the fourth visit, US secretary of defense Bill Perry, Russian minister of defense Pavel Grachev, and Ukrainian minister of defense Valery Shma-

rov planted sunflowers atop the place where a missile silo holding a missile carrying ten warheads, targeted at the United States, had once been. Instead they planted sunflowers, a cash crop in that region.

3. Sitovskiy Family. Sitovskiy Family to William J. Perry (translation).

4. Graham, Bradley. "US, Russia Reach Accord on Europe Treaty." *Washington Post*, 29 October 1995. Accessed 4 September 2014.

5. United States Enrichment Corporation. "Megatons to Megawatts Program 95 Percent Complete." 24 June 2013. Accessed 17 February 2014. As of mid-2013, the low enriched uranium created by the down blending of Russian highly enriched uranium (HEU) to low enriched uranium (LEU) for use as commercial reactor fuel could generate electricity that would meet the demand for a city the size of Boston for approximately 730 years. In the past years, up to 10 percent of the electricity generated in the United States came from nuclear power plants using this fuel. This information covers all of the uranium taken from former Soviet nuclear weapons, not just the nuclear weapons from Pervomaysk.

6. Rosenberg, Steve. "WWII Arctic Convoy Veterans Recall 'Dangerous Journey.'" British Broadcasting Company, 30 August 2011. Accessed 18 February 2014. After the Soviet Union had been invaded by Nazi Germany in World War II, convoys of ships steered from the UK through the icy waters of the Arctic Ocean to bring tanks, fighter planes, fuel, ammunition, raw materials, food, and other emergency supplies from Western Allies to the Soviets in order to help the Red Army fight back. Winston Churchill once called this route "the worst journey in the world." The Germans would attack the convoys from below with U-boats and from above with aircraft. Bad weather was also the enemy, with thick fog, park ice, and raging storms.

7. Nunn, Sam. Interview with Jamie McIntyre. CNN, Sevmash Shipyard, Severodvinsk, Russia, 18 October 1996.

8. Hoffman, David. "The Bold Plan to Grab Soviet Uranium." *The Age* 23 (September 2009). Accessed 25 February 2014. Project Sapphire is the code name for a mission to secure a portion of approximately 1,322 pounds of highly enriched uranium (enough to make twenty-four nuclear bombs) that was left behind in Kazakhstan after the break up of the Soviet Union.

9. Shields, John, and William Potter, eds. *Dismantling the Cold War: US and NIS Perspectives on the Nunn-Lugar Cooperative Threat Reduction Program*. Cambridge: MIT Press, 1997. Pgs. 345–62: "Having reached his conclusion, President Nazarbaev authorized the communication to the United States of information about the existence of weapons-grade nuclear material at Ulba. This information was passed to US Ambassador to Kazakhstan William Courtney in August 1993. Ambassador Courtney's deliberations with senior Kazakhstani officials in October 1993 set in motion US-Kazakhstani collaboration to remove the HEU . . . . [T]he

United States was unable to get firsthand confirmation of the Ulba situation until February 1994 . . . [when] Elwood Gift, a nuclear engineer from the Department of Energy's Oak Ridge Y-12 Plant . . . revealed assays of U-235 of approximately 90 percent . . . . Following a meeting in early March among the three senior US nonproliferation officials—Robert Gallucci from the Department of State, Ashton Carter from the Department of Defense, and Dan Ponemena from the National Security Council (NSC)—a decision was made to have DoD take the lead in coordinating US efforts to secure the Ulba fissile material."

## Chapter 14

1.  "US Military Leader's War Outbursts." *Rodong Sinmum,* 5 April 1994. Translated by Dave Straub.

2.  Ibid.

3.  Cosgrove, Peter. "Retired Army Gen. John Shalikashvili Dies." *USA Today,* 23 July 2011. Accessed 4 September 2014. General John Shalikashvili was the first foreign-born chairman of the Joint Chiefs of Staff. He served as chairman from 1993 to 1997.

4.  Kempster, Norman. "US to Urge Sanctions for N. Korea: Strategy: National security advisers meet after Pyongyang official storms out of nuclear arms talk with Seoul. Clinton administration also will pursue joint military maneuvers with S. Korea." *Los Angeles Times,* 20 March 1994. Accessed 28 March 2014. When threatened with sanctions, a North Korean delegate, Park Young Su, threatened to turn Seoul into a "sea of flames" as he stormed out of talks on the denuclearization of the Korean Peninsula.

5.  Scowcroft, Brent, and Arnold Kanter. "Korea: Time for Action." *Washington Post,* 15 June 1994. A25. In his 1994 op-ed "Korea: Time for Action," Scowcroft wrote: "It either must permit continuous, unfettered IAEA monitoring to confirm that no further reprocessing is taking place, or we will remove its capacity to reprocess. The potential military action, if required, is intentionally quite limited and consciously designed to minimize the risks of unintentional damage. That said, the policy's stated willingness to use military force if necessary should send Pyongyang an unmistakable signal of the US determination to resolve past North Korean nuclear transgressions as well as to preclude future nuclear threats."

## Chapter 15

1.  Collins, Cheryl. "Vladimir Zhirinovsky." *Encyclopaedia Britannica,* 26 May 2014. Accessed 4 September 2014. Vladimir Zhirinovsky is a Russian politician and leader of the far-right Liberal Democratic Party of Russia, which he founded in 1989. In December 1993 Zhirinovsky's LDPR shocked the West when it won 22.8 percent of the vote in the Russian parliamentary elections. His party roster was disquali-

fied in the 1999 parliamentary elections because two of its top three candidates were charged with money laundering. He then created another roster, and was able to win seventeen seats in the Duma. He was elected speaker of the Duma in 2000 and 2004.

2. Perry, William J. "Support START II's Nuclear Reductions." Speech, Moscow, Russia, 17 October 1996. Department of Defense. Accessed 4 September 2014.

3. Dobbs, Michael. "Senate Overwhelmingly Ratifies 1993 Arms Treaty with Russia." *Washington Post*, 27 January 1996. Accessed 21 March 2014. The US Senate ratified the Start II treaty on the night of 26 January 1996 by a vote of 84–7 .

4. Pikayev, Alexander. "Working Papers: The Rise and Fall of START II, The Russian View." Carnegie Endowment for International Peace. No. 6, September 1999. Accessed 25 September 2014. After Perry's presentation, representatives of the ultranationalistic Liberal Democratic Party (including Vladimir Zhirinovsky) responded in an unusually hostile manner.

5. Keeny, Spurgeon, Jr. "Damage Assessment: The Senate Rejection of the CTBT." *Arms Control Today* 29:6 (1999). Pgs. 9–14. Accessed 21 March 2014. On 23 September 1992, the United States conducted its 1,030th and final nuclear weapon test explosion.

6. Ottaway, David. "War Games in Poland Proposed." *Washington Post*, 8 January 1994. Accessed 21 March 2014. In 1995, the president established an annual stockpile assessment and reporting requirement to help ensure that the nation's nuclear weapons remained safe and reliable without underground nuclear testing. Subsequently, the Congress enacted into law the requirement for an annual stockpile assessment process in section 3141 of the National Defense Authorization Act for fiscal year 2003. This section requires that the secretaries of energy and defense submit a package of reports on the results of their annual assessment to the president by 1 March of each year.

## Chapter 16

1. Kozaryn, Linda. "Joe Kruzel, DoD's Peacemaker." *American Forces Press Service*, 24 January 1995. Accessed 3 March 2014. One of Joe Kruzel's first undertaking as deputy assistant secretary of defense for European and NATO policy was the creation of Partnership for Peace, a program designed to bring the former Warsaw Pact nations closer to NATO. He had previously served as special assistant to Defense Secretary Harold Brown and as legislative assistant for defense and foreign policy for Senator Edward Kennedy. Kruzel was killed outside Sarajevo in August 1995, when a rain-soaked dirt road collapsed beneath the armored personnel carrier in which he and two other US negotiators were traveling to Sarajevo, sending the vehicle rolling down a 500-meter slope.

2. The Marshall Center. "About Marshall Center." Accessed 13 January 2014. The Marshall Center, officially dedicated in Garmisch-Partenkirchen, Germany, on

5 June 1993, is a renowned international security and defense studies institute that promotes dialogue and understanding among the nations of North America, Europe, and Eurasia.

3. Asia-Pacific Center for Security Studies. "History & Seal of the APCSS." Accessed 3 March 2014. The Asia-Pacific Center for Security Studies, patterned after the George C. Marshall European Center for Security Studies, officially opened on 4 September 1995 with a ribbon-cutting ceremony attended by the Honorable William J. Perry and General John M. Shalikashvili.

4. William J. Perry Center for Hemispheric Defense Studies. "About William J. Perry Center for Hemispheric Defense Studies." Accessed 4 September 2014. Center for Hemispheric Defense Studies (CHDS) was proposed by Perry during the second Defense Ministerial held at Bariloche, Argentina, in 1996 and was activated on 17 September 1997. It was renamed the William J. Perry Center for Hemispheric Defense Studies in 2013.

5. North Atlantic Treaty Organization. "Peace Support Operations in Bosnia and Herzegovina." 5 June 2012. Accessed 4 September 2014. NATO conducted its first major crisis response operation in Bosnia and Herzegovina, with the deployment of the NATO-led Implementation Force (IFOR) in December 1995 and the NATO-led Stabilization Force (SFOR) a year later. A total of thirty-six allied and partner countries contributed troops to the missions.

6. Churchill, Winston. "Give Us the Tools." Speech, London, 9 February 1941, paraphrased in Thatcher, Margaret. "Speech to the Aspen Institute." Aspen, 4 August 1995. Accessed 4 September 2014. The quotation used by Margaret Thatcher in her speech was "Give us the tools and we'll finish the job." The actual quotation from the Winston Churchill speech is: "Give us the tools, and we will finish the job."

7. Perry, William J. Day Notes. The London conference ended with an ultimatum to Bosnia that was essentially a US-British-French accord endorsed by the attendees of the conference, which included foreign ministers, defense ministers, and chiefs of defense staffs from sixteen countries, including Russia, members of the Contact Group, countries with troops on the ground, NATO, EU, and UN. In a memorandum to the president after the London conference, Perry explained the international community ultimatum: if Gorazde is attacked, or if an attack seems imminent, an air campaign will begin that inflicts enough pain to make the Serbs cease the action that provoked the attack.

8. Clinton, Bill. "Dayton Accords." *Encyclopaedia Britannica.* Accessed 4 September 2014. The Dayton Accords were a peace agreement reached on 21 November 1995 by the presidents of Bosnia, Croatia, and Serbia, ending the war in Bosnia and outlining a General Framework Agreement for Peace in Bosnia and Herzegovina.

9. Holbooke, Richard. *To End a War.* New York: Random House, 1998.

10.  Patton, George. Speech, Los Angeles, 1945, quoted in Case, Linda. *Bold Beliefs in Camouflage: A–Z Briefings.* Neche, ND: Friesen Press, 2012. Pg. 187. This quotation has been used by many great people, including General George Patton in a speech shortly after World War II, and has been attributed to a Chinese proverb by Sun Tzu, Indian proverb by Vijaya Lakshmi Pandit, and the Romans.

11.  The George C. Marshall Foundation. "The Marshall Plan." Accessed 4 September 2014. The Marshall Plan (officially known as the European Recovery Program), shared with the world in a speech on 5 June 1947, was intended to rebuild the economies and spirits of Western Europe, primarily. Sixteen nations, including Germany, became part of the program and shaped the assistance they required, state by state, with administrative and technical assistance provided through the Economic Cooperation Administration of the United States.

Chapter 17

1.  *National Security Issues in Science, Law and Technology*, ed. T. A. Johnson. Boca Raton: CRC Press, 2007.

2.  United States Institute of Peace. "Truth Commission: Haiti." Accessed 4 September 2014. Haiti's president, Jean Bertrand Aristide, was overthrown in a military coup in September 1991. The military's leader, General Raoul Cedras, led an oppressive regime marked by numerous human rights violations. President Aristide was set to return to power in October 1993, but because of military resistance, he was not reinstated until July 1994, with the backing of the United Nations and twenty thousand US troops.

3.  Girard, Philippe. *Peacekeeping, Politics, and the 1994 US Intervention in Haiti. Journal of Conflict Studies* 24:1 (2004); and Ballard, John. *Upholding Democracy: The United States Military Campaign in Haiti, 1994–1997.* Westport, CT: Praeger, 1998. Pgs. 61–84. There were initially three separate plans prepared for intervention in Haiti. OPLAN 2370, asking Joint Task Force 180, the 82nd Airborne Division, to fight its way into Haiti; OPLAN 2380, planning to employ Joint Task Force 190, the 10th Mountain Division, as a purely peacekeeping force; and OPLAN 2375, which incorporated elements of both plans. On 18 September 1994 planes were loaded with paratroopers of the 82nd Airborne Division and departed Pope Air Force Base near Fort Bragg, North Carolina, while an invading fleet, including two aircraft carriers, steamed toward Haiti. However, a negotiation team sent by President Clinton and headed by former president Jimmy Carter was able to sign a deal with the junta-nominated president, Emile Jonassaint, just hours before the invasion forces were set to arrive, and the operation was called off. The Carter-Jonassaint agreement offered political amnesty in exchange for a promise that Jean-Bertrand Aristide, the Haitian president, would be allowed to return. In all, the military invasion plan consisted of more than twenty thousand troops, primarily army.

4.  US Congress. House of Representatives. *H.R.* 4310, *National Defense Authorization Act for Fiscal Year* 2013. 112th Cong., 2nd Sess., 2012. H. Act. H.R. 4310. The Center for Hemispheric Defense Studies was redesignated the William J. Perry Center for Hemispheric Defense Studies in (Sec. 2854) of the National Defense Authorization Act for Fiscal Year 2013.

Chapter 18

1.  Kozaryn, Linda D. "Secretary and Top NCOs Keep DoD's Focus on Quality of Life." *American Forces Press Service*, 26 July 1995. Accessed 14 January 2014. "Since he started visiting military bases with the services' top NCOs about three years ago, Defense Secretary William J. Perry has put DoD's focus on improving quality of life, and that's where he intends to keep it."

2.  US Office of the Assistant Secretary of the Army, Installations, Energy and Environment. *Privatizing Military Family Housing: A History of the U.S. Army's Residential Communities Initiative*, 1995–2010, by Matthew Godfrey and Paul Sadin. Washington, DC: GPO, 2012. Accessed 15 September 2014.

Chapter 19

1.  Kozaryn, Linda. "President, Armed Forces Bid Perry Farewell." *American Forces Press Service*, 17 January 1997. Accessed 14 January 2014. "It was said of Omar Bradley that he was the GI's general," said Army General John M. Shalikashvili. "Well, surely Bill Perry has been the GI's secretary of defense."

2.  The Freeman Spogli Institute for International Studies at Stanford University. "Preventive Defense Project." Accessed 21 January 2014. The Preventive Defense Project (PDP) was founded in 1997 by William J. Perry and Ashton B. Carter as a joint venture operated out of their respective universities, Stanford and Harvard. PDP currently operates out of Stanford.

3.  Carter, Ashton, and Perry, William J. *Preventive Defense: A New Security Strategy for America*. Washington, DC: Brookings Institute Press, 1999.

Chapter 20

1.  Friedman, Thomas L. "World Affairs; Now a Word from X." *New York Times*, 2 May 1998. Accessed 22 July 2015. The quote is from Friedman's interview with George Kennan, U.S. ambassador to Moscow in 1952, whose anonymous article in *Foreign Affairs*, signed "X," defined America's Cold War containment for forty years.

2.  Stanford University, Center for International Security and Cooperation. "Siegfried S. Hecker, PhD." Accessed 31 August 2014. Siegfried S. Hecker is a professor (research) in the Department of Management Science and Engineering and a senior fellow at the Freeman Spogli Institute for International Studies (FSI). He was codirector of CISAC from 2007 to 2012. From 1986 to 1997, Hecker served as the fifth

director of the Los Alamos National Laboratory. Hecker is an internationally recognized expert in plutonium science, global threat reduction, and nuclear security.

3. "Russia Can Turn US to Radioactive Ash-Kremlin-Backed Journalist." *Reuters*, 16 March 2014. Accessed 19 November 2014. Dmitry Kiselyov, speaking on state-backed TV, in Moscow on 16 March 2014. In 2013, Kiselyov was appointed by Vladimir Putin as head of a new state news agency to portray Russia favorably.

## Chapter 21

1. Findings (paraphrased by Perry) from a US-Pakistan Dialogue: Regional Security Working Group, chaired by William J. Perry and George P. Shultz, held at Stanford University, 23–24 August 2012.

## Chapter 22

1. US Department of State, Office of the North Korea Policy Coordinator. *Review of United States Policy towards North Korea: Findings and Recommendations*, by William J. Perry, 12 October 1999. Accessed 28 March 2014.

2. US Department of State. "Madeleine Korbel Albright." Accessed 31 March 2014. Madeleine Albright served as the US permanent representative to the United Nations from 1993 to 1996. She was nominated by President Clinton as secretary of state on 5 December 1996. She was the first female secretary of state and the highest ranking woman in the history of the US government.

3. "US Military Leader's War Outbursts." *Rodong Sinmum,* 5 April 1994. Translated by Dave Straub.

4. "Perry and Oldest Grandson Heartily Cheer Soccer Match." *Chosun Ilbo*, 28 March 1999.

5. Academy of Achievement. "Jeong Kim." Accessed 1 April 2014. In 1992, Jeong Kim started Yurie Systems, Inc., a company specializing in advanced data transmission. Six years later, he reached an agreement to sell Yurie Systems to Lucent Technologies for more than $1 billion. He then went to work for Lucent, running several divisions at once. He later became president of Bell Labs.

6. Academy of Achievement. "General Colin L. Powell." Accessed 1 April 2014. Following a distinguished military career in which he served as both national security adviser and chairman of the Joint Chiefs of Staff, Colin Powell became the secretary of state in 2001. He stepped down in 2004.

7. Mufson, Steven. "Bush to Pick up Clinton Talks." *Washington Post*, 7 March 2001.

8. White House, Office of the Press Secretary. "Joint US-Japan-Rok Trilateral Statement." 26 October 2001. Accessed 3 April 2014.

9. The National Defense Commission (DPRK), quoted in Hyung-Jin Kim, "North Korea Plans Nuclear Test, Says Its Rockets Are Designed to Hit U.S." *San Jose Mercury News*, 24 January 2013. Accessed 3 April 2014.

Chapter 23

1.   Ricks, Thomas. *Fiasco: The American Military Adventure in Iraq.* London: Penguin Press, 2006. Ch. 1.

2.   US Department of Defense. "Dr. Robert M. Gates, 22nd Secretary of Defense." Accessed 25 February 2014. Dr. Robert M. Gates served as the 22nd secretary of defense and is the only defense secretary to be asked to remain in that office by a newly elected President. Gates served from 2006 to 2011.

Chapter 24

1.   Obama, Barack. "Remarks by President Barack Obama." Speech, Prague, Czech Republic, 5 April 2009. The White House: Office of the Press Secretary. Accessed 31 August 2014.

2.   Brookings Institute. "James E. Goodby." Accessed 7 April 2014. James E. Goodby was selected for the US Foreign Service in 1952. He rose to the rank of career minister in the Senior Foreign Service and was given five presidential appointments to ambassadorial rank. In his career, Goodby was involved as a negotiator or as a policy adviser in the creation of the International Atomic Energy Agency, the negotiation of the limited nuclear test ban treaty, START, the Conference on Disarmament in Europe, and cooperative threat reduction (the Nunn-Lugar program).

3.   Stanford University, Hoover Institute. "Reykjavik Revisited: Steps toward a World Free of Nuclear Weapons." October 2007. Accessed 7 April 2014. The conference, "Reykjavik Revisited," took place at the Hoover Institute at Stanford from 11–12 October 2006.

4.   Schudel, Matt. "Max Kampelman, Top Nuclear Adviser during Cold War, Dies at 92." *Washington Post*, 26 January 2013. Accessed 7 April 2014. Max M. Kampelman was a longtime lawyer and political advisor who eventually became a top Cold War diplomat. He began his career working for Senator Hubert Humphrey (D-Minn.), who eventually was vice president under Lyndon Johnson. He later was a key diplomat for the Reagan administration. During the 1980s, Kampelman was responsible for leading two prolonged series of international negotiations: the Madrid Conference on Security and Cooperation from 1981 to 1983, and the discussions between the United States and the Soviet Union regarding the limiting of nuclear arms before the signing of the first START treaty in 1991.

5.   Shultz, George P., William J. Perry, Henry Kissinger, and Sam Nunn. "A World Free of Nuclear Weapons." *Wall Street Journal,* 4 January 2007. Accessed 31 August 2014.

6.   Shultz, George P., William J. Perry, Henry Kissinger, and Sam Nunn. "Toward a Nuclear-Free World." *Wall Street Journal,* 15 January 2008. Accessed 31 August 2014.

7. *Last Best Chance.* Directed by Ben Goddard. Berkeley: Bread and Butter Productions, 2005.

8. *Nuclear Tipping Point.* Directed by Ben Goddard. Nuclear Security Project, 2010.

9. Nuclear Threat Initiative. "Nuclear Tipping Point Premiere." Accessed 8 April 2014. *Nuclear Tipping Point* premiered at Universal Studios in Los Angeles on 27 January 2010.

10. Taubman, Philip. *The Partnership: Five Cold Warriors and Their Quest to Ban the Bomb.* New York: Harper, 2012.

11. Obama, Barack. "Remarks by President Barack Obama." Speech, Prague, Czech Republic, 5 April 2009. The White House: Office of the Press Secretary. Accessed 31 August 2014.

12. Kessler, Glenn, and Mary Beth Sheridan. "Security Council Adopts Nuclear Weapons Resolution." *New York Times,* 24 September 2009. Accessed 7 April 2014. The UN Security Council unanimously adopted the US-drafted nuclear weapons resolution on 24 September 2009. This resolution affirmed many of the steps that President Obama deemed essential for working toward a "world without nuclear weapons."

13. International Commission on Nuclear Non-proliferation and Disarmament. "About the Commission." Accessed 8 April 2014. The International Commission on Nuclear Non-proliferation and Disarmament is a joint initiative of the Australian and Japanese governments. Australian prime minister Kevin Rudd proposed the commission on 9 June 2008 in Kyoto. On 9 July, Prime Minister Rudd and Japanese prime minister Yasuo Fukuda agreed to establish the commission.

14. Shultz, George P., William J. Perry, Henry Kissinger, and Sam Nunn. "Next Steps in Reducing Nuclear Risks: The Pace of Nonproliferation Work Today Doesn't Match the Urgency of the Threat." *Wall Street Journal,* 6 March 2013. Accessed 19 November 2014.

15. Sagan, Scott. *The Limits of Safety: Organizations, Accidents, and Nuclear Weapons.* NJ: Princeton University Press, 1993.

16. Schlosser, Eric. *Command and Control: Nuclear Weapons, the Damascus Accident, and the Illusion of Safety.* New York: Penguin Press, 2013.

## Chapter 25

1. Faulkner, William. Speech, Stockholm, Sweden, 10 December 1950. Nobelprize.org. Accessed 31 August 2014.

2. Kennedy, John F. Speech, American University, Washington, DC, 10 June 1963. In a commencement address, Kennedy called on the Soviet Union to work with the United States on a nuclear test ban treaty. American.edu. Accessed 21 October 2013.

# Index

with Clinton, 123, 124; NATO meetings, 89, 120, 121; nomination and confirmation, 87–89, 207n10; press conferences, 88–89, 90; staff, 142, 143, 144–45; swearing in ceremony, 90; taking care of troops, 90, 135–40, 143; travels, 89–90, 91–99, 105, 111–12, 123–25, 132–33. *See also* Nunn-Lugar program

DeLauer, Dick, 42
DeLeon, Rudy, 77, 78
Democratic Party, 87
Democratic People's Republic of Korea (DPRK), *see* North Korea
Desert Storm: Joint STARS use, 40; lessons learned, 43, 135; smart weapons, 43; stealth aircraft, 38, 41, 42
Détente, 73
Deterrence: Carter administration policies, 50–51; economic ties and, 154, 159; global perspective, 159; in India-Pakistan relations, 158–59; NATO plans, 115; of North Korea, 163; political imperative, 46; size of nuclear forces, 46; tactical nuclear weapons, 115; uncertainties about Soviet capabilities, 12. *See also* Offset strategy
Deutch, John, 82, 141
DiaoYu (Senkaku) islands, 155
Digital technology, *see* Computers; Integrated circuits; Technology
Dinneen, Gerald (Gerry), 29, 59
Diplomacy: Camp David Accords, 61–62; coercive, 107, 132–33, 163; collaborative, 162; Haitian crisis, 131–33; North Korea crisis, 106–9; nuclear threat reduction, 62, 190; Perry's experiences, 56, 57–62, 68–71,

72, 139; Perry's style, 62, 139; treaty negotiations, 157. *See also* Track 2 diplomacy
Director of defense research and engineering (DDR&E), 28, 30
Disarmament, *see* Nuclear disarmament
DoD (Department of Defense), *see* Defense Department
Douglas, John, 83
DPRK (Democratic People's Republic of Korea), *see* North Korea
Draper and Johnson, 23
DRC, *see* Defense Reform Caucus
Drell, Sidney D., 27, 180, 181, 183, 201n3 (ch 4)
Duckett, Carl, 16
Duffy, Gloria, 79–80
Dulles, Allen, 16
Duma, Russian, 111–12, 187, 209–10n1
Duncan, Charles, 29, 31

Earth Resources Technology Satellite (ERTS), 26
Eastern Europe: Ballistic Missile Defense system, 148–49; NATO enlargement, 116, 117, 127–29, 148, 152; Partnership for Peace, 116–17, 118, 121, 125–28
Egypt: Camp David Accords, 61–62; Perry's visits, 62; US military aid, 62
Einstein, Albert, 8, 68, 186
Eisenhower, Dwight D., 34
Electromagnetic Systems Laboratory, *see* ESL, Inc.
Energy Department: Los Alamos National Laboratory, 149; nuclear stockpile assessments, 113, 114, 210n6; Oak Ridge National Laboratory, 101, 208–9n9

program, 56; tactical, 34–35, 115, 158, 187, 188–89; Taiwanese program, 56; tests, 150–51. *See also* Arms control; Soviet nuclear weapons program

Nuclear weapons, US: current number, 46, 194; in Europe, 188; missiles dismantled under Nunn-Lugar, 95–96; modernization, 190; as offset to Soviet conventional forces, 34–35; reducing, 188–89; stockpile assessments, 113, 114, 210n6; tactical, 34–35, 115, 188–89; testing moratorium, 113, 151, 210n5; Triad, 46–47, 50; upgrading, 45–50. *See also* Intercontinental ballistic missiles

Nunn, Sam: confirmation hearings, 30, 89; Defense Distinguished Civilian Service Medal, 102; in Eastern Europe, 73; Haiti negotiations, 131–32; loose nukes problem, 75–76, 77, 101–2; nuclear disarmament op-eds, 181–83, 188, 194; nuclear disarmament support, 185–86; Nuclear Threat Initiative, 183, 184, 202n5 (ch 5); political career, 202n5 (ch 5); as possible defense secretary, 141; relationship with Perry, 30; in Russia, 98–99; as senator, 37, 38, 79, 183; support of offset strategy, 37, 38, 42

Nunn-Lugar program: achievements, 101–2, 194; blowing up missile silos, 94, 96; chemical demilitarization, 99–100; Cooperative Threat Reduction program, 96–100; employment program, 100; funding, 78–79, 99, 207n6; implementation, 77–81, 85, 91–101, 111; legislation, 75–76, 101–2; meetings with Russians, 79–80; Megatons to Megawatts

project, 85, 96, 208n5; Project Sapphire, 100–101, 208–9nn8–9; Russian bombers and submarines dismantled, 96–99; securing fissile material, 100–101, 208–9nn8–9; Ukrainian weapons dismantled, 91–95, 96, 145, 207–8n2; US missiles dismantled, 95–96

Oak Ridge National Laboratory, 101, 208–9n9

Obama, Barack: nuclear disarmament support, 185, 186, 194, 216n12; Prague speech, 185, 194

Obama administration: Defense Department, 149; negotiations with Iran, 156–57; New START treaty, 46, 149, 150, 152, 186–87, 188–89, 194; Nuclear Posture Review, 186; relations with Russia, 149–50

O'Brien, James F., 200n8

Obuchi, Keizo, 162, 163

Office of Management and Budget (OMB), 40, 41

Office of the Secretary of Defense (OSD), 142

Offset strategy: acquisitions process, 36–37, 82; components, 38; critics, 42–43; of Eisenhower, 34; new weapons technology, 35–39, 41; smart sensors, 38, 39–41, 47–48; success, 43–44, 81; tactical nuclear weapons, 34–35, 115

Okinawa, 7–8

Olympic Games: Moscow, 55; Sochi, 151; Sydney, 165

OMB, *see* Office of Management and Budget

Operation Desert Storm, *see* Desert Storm